C000318830

Classic Dinners

Everyday Cookbook

STAR
FIRE

This is a Star Fire book
First published in 2006

06 08 10 09 07

1 3 5 7 9 10 8 6 4 2

Star Fire is part of
The Foundry Creative Media Company Limited
Crabtree Hall, Crabtree Lane, Fulham, London, SW6 6TY

Visit our website: www.star-fire.co.uk

Copyright © The Foundry 2006

All rights reserved. No part of this publication may be reproduced, stored in a retrieval system
or transmitted, in any form or by any means, electronic, mechanical, photocopying, recording
or otherwise, without the prior permission of the copyright holder.

ISBN-10: 1-84451-532-X ISBN-13: 978-1-84451-532-5
Special Edition: ISBN-10: 1-84451-575-3 ISBN-13: 978-1-84451-575-2

The CIP record for this book is available from the British Library.

Printed in China

ACKNOWLEDGEMENTS

Publisher and Creative Director: Nick Wells
Editorial Planning: Rosanna Singler
Design and Production: Chris Herbert, Mike Spender, Colin Rudderham and Claire Walker

Authors: Catherine Atkinson, Juliet Barker, Gina Steer, Vicki Smallwood,
Carol Tennant, Mari Mererid Williams, Elizabeth Wolf-Cohen and Simone Wright
Editorial: Sara Goulding and Sara Robson
Photography: Colin Bowling, Paul Forrester and Stephen Brayne
Home Economists and Stylists: Jacqueline Bellefontaine,
Mandy Phipps, Vicki Smallwood and Penny Stephens

All props supplied by Barbara Stewart at Surfaces

NOTE
Recipes using uncooked eggs should be avoided by infants,
the elderly, pregnant women and anyone suffering from an illness.

Contents

Vegetables & Salads

Desserts

Hygiene in the Kitchen

It is important to remember that many foods can carry some form of bacteria. In most cases, the worst it will lead to is a bout of food poisoning or gastroenteritis, although for certain people this can be serious. The risk can be reduced or eliminated, however, by good hygiene and proper cooking.

Do not buy food that is past its sell-by date and do not consume food that is past its use-by date. When buying food, use the eyes and nose. If the food looks tired, limp or a bad colour or it has a rank, acrid or simply bad smell, do not buy or eat it under any circumstances.

Take special care when preparing raw meat and fish. A separate chopping board should be used for each, and the knife, board and your hands should be thoroughly washed before handling or preparing any other food.

Regularly clean, defrost and clear out the refrigerator or freezer – it is worth checking the packaging to see exactly how long each product is safe to freeze. Avoid handling food if suffering from an upset stomach as bacteria can be passed on through food preparation.

Dish cloths and tea towels must be washed and changed regularly. Ideally use disposable cloths which should be replaced on a daily basis. More durable cloths should be left to soak in bleach, then washed in the washing machine at a high temperature.

Keep your hands, cooking utensils and food preparation surfaces clean and do not allow pets to climb on to any work surfaces.

Buying

Avoid bulk buying where possible, especially fresh produce such as meat, poultry, fish, fruit and vegetables. Fresh foods lose their nutritional value rapidly, so buying a little at a time minimises loss of nutrients. It also means your fridge will not be so full, which reduces the effectiveness of the refrigeration process.

When buying prepackaged goods such as cans or pots of cream and yogurts, check that the packaging is intact and not damaged or pierced at

all. Cans should not be dented, pierced or rusty. Check the sell-by dates even for cans and packets of dry ingredients such as flour and rice. Store fresh foods in the refrigerator as soon as possible – not in the car or the office.

When buying frozen foods, ensure that they are not heavily iced on the outside and that the contents feel completely frozen. Ensure that the frozen foods have been stored in the cabinet at the correct storage level and the temperature is below -18°C/-0.4°F. Pack in cool bags to transport home and place in the freezer as soon as possible after purchase.

Preparation

Make sure that all work surfaces and utensils are clean and dry. Hygiene should be given priority at all times. Separate chopping boards should be used for raw and cooked

meats, fish and vegetables. Currently, a variety of good quality plastic boards come in various designs and colours. This makes differentiating easier and the plastic has the added hygienic advantage of being washable at high temperatures in the dishwasher. If using the board for fish, first wash in cold water, then in hot to prevent odour. Also remember that knives and utensils should always be thoroughly cleaned after use.

When cooking, be particularly careful to keep cooked and raw food separate to avoid any contamination. It is worth washing all fruits and vegetables regardless of whether they are going to be eaten raw or lightly cooked. This rule should apply even to prewashed herbs and salads.

Do not reheat food more than once. If using a microwave, always check that the food is piping hot all the way through – in theory, the food should reach 70°C/158°F and needs to be cooked at that temperature for at least three minutes to ensure that all bacteria are killed.

All poultry must be thoroughly thawed before using, including chicken and poussin. Remove the food to be thawed from the freezer and place in a shallow dish to contain the juices. Leave the food in the refrigerator until it is completely thawed. A 1.4 kg/3 lb whole chicken will take about 26–30 hours to thaw. To speed up the process, immerse the chicken in cold water, making sure that the water is changed regularly. When the joints can move freely and no ice crystals remain in the cavity, the bird is completely thawed.

Once thawed, remove the wrapper and pat the chicken dry. Place the chicken in a shallow dish, cover lightly and store as close to the base of the refrigerator as possible. The chicken should be cooked as soon as possible. Some foods can be cooked from frozen including many prepacked foods such as soups, sauces, casseroles and breads. Where applicable follow the manufacturers' instructions.

Vegetables and fruits can also be cooked from frozen, but meats and fish should be thawed first. The only time food can be refrozen is when the food has been thoroughly thawed then cooked. Once the food has cooled then it can be frozen again, but it should only be stored for one month.

All poultry and game (except for duck) must be cooked thoroughly. When cooked, the juices will run clear on the thickest part of the bird – the best area to try is usually the thigh. Other meats, like minced meat and pork should be cooked right the way through. Fish should turn opaque, be firm in texture and break easily into large flakes.

When cooking leftovers, make sure they are reheated until piping hot and that any sauce or soup reaches boiling point first.

Storing, Refrigerating and Freezing

Meat, poultry, fish, seafood and dairy products should all be refrigerated. The temperature of the refrigerator should be between 1–5°C/34–41°F while the freezer temperature should not rise above -18°C/-0.4°F.

To ensure the optimum refrigerator and freezer temperature, avoid leaving the door open for long periods of time. Try not to overstock the refrigerator as this reduces the airflow inside and therefore the effectiveness in cooling the food within.

When refrigerating cooked food, allow it to cool down quickly and completely before refrigerating. Hot food will raise the temperature of the refrigerator and possibly affect or spoil other food stored in it.

Food within the refrigerator and freezer should always be covered. Raw and cooked food should be stored in separate parts of the refrigerator. Cooked food should be kept on the top shelves of the refrigerator, while raw meat, poultry and fish should be placed on bottom shelves to avoid

drips and cross-contamination. It is recommended that eggs should be refrigerated in order to maintain their freshness and shelf life.

Take care that frozen foods are not stored in the freezer for too long. Blanched vegetables can be stored for one month; beef, lamb, poultry and pork for six months and unblanched vegetables and fruits in syrup for a year. Oily fish and sausages should be stored for three months. Dairy products can last four to six months, while cakes and pastries can be kept in the freezer for three to six months.

High Risk Foods

Certain foods may carry risks to people who are considered vulnerable such as the elderly, the ill, pregnant women, babies, young infants and those suffering from a recurring illness.

It is advisable to avoid those foods listed below which belong to a higher-risk category.

There is a slight chance that some eggs carry the bacteria salmonella. Cook the eggs until both the yolk and the white are firm to eliminate this risk. Pay particular attention to dishes and products incorporating lightly cooked or raw eggs which should be eliminated from the diet. Hollandaise sauce, mayonnaise, mousses, soufflés and meringues all use raw or lightly cooked eggs, as do custard-based dishes, ice creams and sorbets. These are all considered high-risk foods to the vulnerable groups mentioned above.

Certain meats and poultry also carry the potential risk of salmonella and so should be cooked thoroughly

until the juices run clear and there is no pinkness left. Unpasteurised products such as milk, cheese (especially soft cheese), pâté, meat (both raw and cooked) all have the potential risk of listeria and should be avoided.

When buying seafood, buy from a reputable source which has a high turnover to ensure freshness. Fish should have bright clear eyes, shiny skin and bright pink or red gills. The fish should feel stiff to the touch, with a slight smell of sea air and iodine. The flesh of fish steaks and fillets should be translucent with no signs of discolouration. Molluscs such as scallops, clams and mussels are sold fresh and are still alive. Avoid any that are open or do not close when tapped lightly. In the same way, univalves such as cockles or winkles should withdraw back into their shells when lightly prodded. When choosing cephalopods such as squid and octopus they should have a firm flesh and pleasant sea smell.

As with all fish, whether it is shellfish or seafish, care is required when freezing it. It is imperative to check whether the fish has been frozen before. If it has been frozen, then it should not be frozen again under any circumstances.

Pasta Techniques and Tips

Steps to Cooking Perfect Pasta

Follow a few simple rules to ensure that your pasta is cooked to perfection every time:

1 Choose a big saucepan – there needs to be plenty of room for the pasta to move around during cooking so that it does not stick together. The most convenient type of saucepan has a built-in perforated inner pan, so that the pasta can be lifted out of the water and drained as soon as it is cooked.

2 Cook the pasta in a large quantity of fast-boiling, well-salted water; ideally about 4 litres/7 pints of water and 1¹/₂–2 tablespoons of salt for every 350 g/12 oz–450 g/1 lb of pasta. Some cooks say that the addition of 1–2 teaspoons of olive or sunflower oil not only helps to stop the water boiling over but also helps to prevent the pasta from sticking. However, other cooks believe that as long as the saucepan is large enough and the water is on a full-rolling boil, the pasta will not stick together nor will the water boil over.

3 Tip in the pasta all at once, give it a stir and cover with a lid. Quickly bring back to a rolling boil then remove the lid – do not cover with a lid during cooking. Once it is boiling, turn down the heat to medium-high and cook the pasta for the required time. It should be 'al dente' which literally translates as 'to the tooth' and means that the pasta should be tender, but still firm to the bite. Test frequently towards the end of cooking time; the only way to do this is to take out a piece and try it. Stir the pasta occasionally during cooking with a wooden spoon or fork to make sure that it does not stick to the pan.

4 As soon as the pasta is ready, drain in a colander (or by lifting the draining

pan up and out of the water if you have a pasta pot with an inner drainer). Give it a shake, so that any trapped water can drain out. At this stage you can toss the pasta in a little oil or butter if you are not mixing it with a sauce. Reserve a little of the cooking water to stir into the pasta, this not only helps to thin the sauce if necessary, but also helps prevent the cooked pasta sticking together as it cools.

Some pastas need a little more care when cooking than others. Never stir stuffed pastas vigorously, or they may split open and the filling will be lost in the cooking water. When cooking long, dried pasta such as spaghetti, you will need to coil the pasta into the water as it starts to soften. Hold one end of the strands of spaghetti and push the other to the bottom of the pan, coiling them round, and using a wooden spoon or fork, when the boiling water gets too close to your hand.

An alternative cooking method is to add the pasta to boiling salted water as before, then boil rapidly for 2 minutes. Cover the pan with a tight-fitting lid and turn off the heat. Leave to stand for the full cooking time, then drain and serve in the usual way. Pasta may also be cooked successfully in a microwave, although it does not cook any faster than on the hob. Put the pasta in a large bowl, add salt, then pour over enough boiling water to cover the pasta by at least 2.5 cm/1 inch. Microwave on high (100% power) for the times given below. Allow the pasta to stand for 2–3 minutes before draining.

Pasta Cooking Times

Start timing from the moment that the pasta returns to the boil; not from when it was added. Use a kitchen timer if possible, as even a few seconds too long may spoil the pasta.

Fresh 2–3 minutes for thin noodles (although very fine pastas may be

ready within seconds of the pasta boiling), thick noodles and shapes 3–4 minutes and filled pastas 5–7 minutes.

Dried 8–12 minutes; filled pastas can take up to 20 minutes to cook, however, you should always check the packet instructions, as some pastas labelled 'quick cook' only take about 4 minutes.

Serving Quantities

As an approximate guide, allow 75–125 g (3–4 oz) uncooked pasta per person. Obviously the amount will depend on whether the pasta is being served for a light or main meal and the type of sauce that it is being served with.

Matching Pasta Types and Sauces

It is entirely up to you which pasta you serve with which sauce but in general, heavier sauces with large chunks of meat or vegetables go less with pastas that will trap the sauce and meat in curls and hollows, such as penne, shells, riagatoni or spirals. On the other hand, soft fluid sauces suit long pastas such as linguine, pappardelle, or tagliatelle.

Classic Sauces
Alla Carbonara Pasta with ham, eggs and cream – the heat of the pasta cooks the eggs to thicken the sauce.

Alla Napoletana Made from fresh tomatoes, but with olive oil, garlic and onions.

All'arrabiata A hot sauce with red chillies, tomatoes and chopped bacon.

All'aglio e Olio Pasta with olive oil and finely chopped garlic.

Alla Marinara A fresh tomato and basil sauce, sometimes with wine (not seafood).

Con Ragu Meat sauce from Bologna (known as bolognaise sauce in English), often made with half minced pork and half minced beef. This is traditionally served with tagliatelle and not spaghetti.

Serving Pasta

In Italy, pasta is usually dressed with the sauce before serving to combine the flavours, but you can top the pasta with the sauce if you prefer, in which case, toss it in a little olive oil or butter to give it an attractive sheen. Cook the sauce and pasta so that they will both be ready at the same time; most sauces can be left to stand for a few minutes and reheated when the pasta is ready. If the pasta is ready before the sauce, drain it, and return to the pan with a tight-fitting lid – it should be fine for a few minutes. Always serve in warmed serving bowls or plates, as pasta loses heat very quickly.

Serving Wines with Pasta

If possible, choose a wine that comes from the same region as the dish you are serving. If there is wine in the sauce, you will be able to serve the rest of the bottle with your meal, so make sure you choose one that you enjoy drinking. Otherwise, pick a wine that matches the strongest-flavoured ingredient in the sauce. Rich, meaty sauces or highly spiced ones with lots of garlic need a robust, full-bodied wine to go with them. Of course, there is no reason why you should stick to Italian wines and if you are serving an oriental pasta dish you may opt for lager or other drinks. Below are ten well-known types of Italian wine.

White Wines

Chardonnay This wine is produced in many parts of the world and is wonderful served with fish dishes. The Italian chardonnay has a faint lemony flavour.

Frascati This wine is made near Rome and is one of the most popular Italian wines. It is crisp and fruity and has quite a lot of body. It goes well with most foods.

Orvieto This wine is named after the town of the same name, just north of Rome. It is dry and soft with a slightly nutty and fruity flavour and is good for summer drinking and serving with fish and white meats.

Soave This wine is one of Italy's most famous wines. The best ones have a distinct hint of almonds and are dry and crisp. It goes well with shellfish, chicken and light vegetable pasta sauces.

Verdiccho This wine comes in a carved amphora bottle and in Italy is known as La Lollobrigida. A crisp, clean and dry white wine with a slightly metallic edge, it is best when served with fish and seafood.

Red Wines

Barbaresco This wine is full-bodied with an intense flavour and a high tannin content. It teams well with rich pasta dishes, especially beef.

Bardolino This is light and fruity with an almost cherry and slightly bitter almond taste; perfect for duck and game.

Barolo This is one of Italy's finest wines and is a full-bodied red. Serve with rich meaty dishes, game or spicy sausage pasta sauces.

Chianti This wine is best drunk when young and may be served slightly chilled. It is often regarded as the classic accompaniment to pasta.

Pasta Equipment

When making and cooking pasta, a bare minimum of equipment is needed; some would say that a rolling pin, a large pan and a colander would suffice, however, there are many gadgets that make the process a lot easier.

When Making

Rolling pin Try to use one that is quite slender and choose a conventional wooden one without handles. In Italy pasta rolling pins are very long, for rolling out large quantities of pasta at a time, and slightly thicker in the middle with tapering ends.

Pasta machine A traditional, hand-cranked pasta machine has adjusting rollers and usually cutters for making tagliatelle and finer tagliarini. More complicated ones come with a selection of cutters.

Pasta wheel This is useful for cutting noodles such as tagliatelle and pappardelle if you do not have a pasta machine and also for stuffed shapes such as ravioli. This is an inexpensive piece of equipment and less likely to drag or tear the pasta than a knife.

Ravioli cutter Specially designed, fluted-edged cutters can be bought for cutting pasta. A fluted or plain biscuit cutter works just as well.

When Cooking and Serving

Long-handled pasta fork This is useful for stirring the pasta to keep the pieces separate during cooking. You can also get wooden pasta hooks which will lift out the strands of pasta so that you can check whether or not it is cooked.

Parmesan graters These range from simple hand graters to electrical gadgets. If sharp, the fine side of a box grater works equally well.

Parmesan knife This is used to shave Parmesan off a block. A vegetable peeler may be used as an alternative.

Pasta cooking pot Officially this should be tall with straight sides and handles and should have an inner basket. When buying, choose one that is not too heavy, and will be easy to manage when full.

Pasta measurer This is a wooden gadget with several holes for measuring spaghetti. Each hole takes a different amount of pasta for a given number of people.

Cooking Techniques for Potatoes

Generally, new potato varieties have a firm and waxy texture that do not break up during cooking, so are ideal for boiling, steaming and salads. Main crop potatoes, on the other hand, have a more floury texture and lend themselves to mashing and roasting – both types are suitable for chips. When cooking potatoes, it is important to make sure the potatoes that you are using are the correct type for the dish being prepared. Whichever way you choose to serve potatoes, allow 175–225 g/6–8 oz per person.

Boiling Potatoes
New Potatoes

Most of the new potatoes available nowadays are fairly clean – especially those sold in supermarkets – and simply need a light scrub before cooking in their skins. If the potatoes are very dirty, use a small scrubbing brush or scourer to remove both the skins and dirt. Add them to a pan of cold, salted water and bring to the boil. Cover the pan with a lid and simmer for 12–15 minutes or until tender. Add a couple of sprigs of fresh herbs to the pan if you like – fresh mint is traditionally used to flavour potatoes. Drain the potatoes thoroughly and

serve hot, tossed in a little melted butter or, for a change, a tablespoon of pesto. The skins of first early new potatoes will peel away easily, but second earlies should be served in their skins or peeled when cooked – hold the hot potatoes with a fork to make this easier. Very firm new potatoes can be added to boiling water, simmered for 8 minutes, and then left to stand in the hot water for a further 10 minutes until cooked through.

Old Potatoes

Choose a main crop potato suitable for boiling, then thinly peel and cut into even-sized pieces. Add to a saucepan of cold, salted water and bring to the boil. Cover the pan with a lid and simmer for 20 minutes or until tender.

Alternatively, you can cook the potatoes in their skins and peel them after cooking. It is particularly important to cook floury potatoes gently or the outsides may start to fall apart before they are tender in the centre. Drain the potatoes in a colander, then return them to the pan to dry out over a very low heat for 1–2 minutes. If you are planning to serve the potatoes mashed, roughly mash them and add a knob of butter and

2 tablespoons of milk per person. Mash until smooth, either with a hand masher, mouli grater or a potato ricer. Season to taste with salt, freshly ground black pepper and a little freshly grated nutmeg if liked, then beat for a few seconds with a wooden spoon until fluffy. As an alternative to butter, use a good quality olive oil or crème fraîche. Finely chopped red and green chillies, crispy-cooked crumbled bacon, fresh herbs or grated Parmesan cheese can also be stirred in for additional flavour.

Steaming Potatoes

All potatoes are suitable for steaming. Floury potatoes, however, are ideal for this method of cooking as they fall apart easily.

New and small potatoes can be steamed whole, but larger ones should be cut into even-sized pieces. Place the potatoes in a steamer, colander or sieve over boiling water and cover. Steam for 10 minutes if the potatoes are very small or if they are cut into large chunks cook for 20–25 minutes.

Frying Potatoes
Chipped Potatoes

To make chips, wash, peel and cut the potatoes into 1.5 cm/½ inch slices. Cut the slices into long strips also about 1.5 cm/½ inch wide. Place the strips in a bowl of cold water and leave for 20 minutes, then drain and dry well on kitchen paper – moisture will make the fat spit. Pour some oil into a deep, heavy based saucepan or deep-fat fryer, making sure that the oil does not go any further than halfway up the sides of the pan. Heat the oil to 190°C/375°F, or until a chip dropped into the fat rises to the surface straight away and is surrounded by bubbles. Put the chips into a wire basket and lower into the oil and cook for 7–8 minutes or until golden. Remove and increase the heat of the oil to 200°C/400°F. Lower the chips into the oil again and cook for 2–3 minutes, or until they are crisp and golden brown. Drain on kitchen paper before serving.

Slightly finer chips are properly known as *pommes frites*, even finer ones as *pommes allumettes* and the finest of all as *pommes pailles* (straw chips). Paper-thin slices of peeled potatoes, cut with a sharp knife or using a mandoline or food processor, can be deep-fried a few at a time to make crisps or game chips.

Healthy Chips

To make lower-fat chips, preheat the oven to 200°C/400°F/Gas Mark 6 and place a non-stick baking tray in the oven to heat up. Cut the potatoes into chips as above or into chunky wedges, if preferred. Put the chips or wedges in a pan of cold water and quickly bring to the boil. Simmer for 2 minutes, then drain in a colander. Leave for a few minutes to dry, then drizzle over 1½–2 tablespoons of olive or sunflower oil and toss to coat. Tip on to the heated baking tray and cook in the preheated oven for 20–25 minutes, turning occasionally until golden brown and crisp.

Sauteed Potatoes

Cut peeled potatoes into rounds about 0.5 cm/¼ inch thick and pat dry. Heat 25 g/1 oz unsalted butter and 2 tablespoons of oil in a large, heavy based frying pan until hot. Add the potatoes in a single layer and cook for 4–5 minutes until the undersides are golden. Turn with a large fish slice and cook the other side until golden and tender. Drain on kitchen paper and sprinkle with a little salt before serving.

Baking Potatoes

Allow a 300–350 g/11–12 oz potato per person and choose a variety such as Maris Piper, Cara or King Edward. Wash and dry the potatoes, prick the skins lightly, then rub each one with a little oil and sprinkle with salt. Bake at 200°C/400°F/Gas Mark 6 for 1–1½ hours or until the skins are

crisp and the centres are very soft. To speed up the cooking time, thread on to metal skewers as this conducts heat to the middle of the potatoes.

Roasting Potatoes

For crisp and brown outsides and fluffy centres choose potatoes suitable for baking. Thinly peel the potatoes and cut into even-sized pieces. Drop them into a pan of boiling, salted water and simmer for 5 minutes. Turn off the heat and leave for a further 3–4 minutes. Drain well and return the potatoes to the pan over a low heat for a minute to dry them and to roughen the edges. Carefully transfer them to a roasting tin containing hot oil or dripping. Baste well, then bake at 220°C/425°F/Gas Mark 7 for 20 minutes. Turn them and cook for a further 20–30 minutes, turning and basting at least one more time. Serve as soon as the potatoes are ready.

Potato Croquettes

Mash dry, boiled potatoes with just a little butter or olive oil, then stir in 1 egg yolk mixed with 1–2 tablespoons of milk or crème fraîche to make a firm mixture. Shape the mashed potatoes into small cylinders about 5 cm/2 inches long, rolling them in flour. Dip in beaten egg and then in fresh, white breadcrumbs. Chill the croquettes in the refrigerator for 30 minutes. Place a little unsalted butter and oil in a heavy-based frying pan and slowly heat until the butter has melted. Shallow fry the croquettes, turning occasionally until they are golden brown and crisp.

Rosti

Parboil peeled, waxy potatoes in boiling, salted water for 8 minutes, then drain and leave to cool before coarsely grating into a bowl. Season well with salt and freshly ground black pepper and freshly chopped herbs if liked. Heat a mixture of unsalted butter and oil in a heavy based frying pan until bubbling. Add tablespoonfuls

of the grated potato into the pan and flatten with the back of a fish slice. Cook over a medium heat for about 7 minutes or until crisp and golden. Turn and cook the other side, then serve while still hot.

Cooking Potatoes in a Clay Pot

Terracotta potato pots can cook up to 450 g/1 lb of whole potatoes at a time. Soak the clay pot for at least 20 minutes before use, then add even-sized, preferably smallish potatoes. Drizzle over a little olive oil and season generously with salt and freshly ground black pepper. Cover the pot with the lid and put in a cold oven, setting the temperature to 200°C/400°F/Gas Mark 6. The potatoes will take about 45 minutes to cook.

Microwaved Potatoes

This method of cooking is suitable for boiling and baking potatoes, providing you do not want the skins to be crispy. To cook new potatoes, prick the skins with a skewer to prevent them from bursting, then place in a bowl with 3 tablespoons of boiling water. Cover with clingfilm which has been pierced two or three times and cook on high for 12–15 minutes, or until tender. Peeled chunks of potato can be cooked in the same way. To bake potatoes, place each potato on a circle of kitchen paper. Make several cuts in each to ensure that the skins do not burst. Transfer to the microwave plate and cook on high for 4–6 minutes per potato, allowing an extra 3–4 minutes for every additional potato. Turn the potatoes at least once during cooking. Leave to stand for 5 minutes before serving.

Health and Nutrition

Potatoes are high in complex carbohydrates, providing sustained energy. They are also an excellent source of vitamins B and C and minerals such as iron and potassium. They contain almost no fat and are high in dietary fibre.

Cooking Techniques for Rice

There are countless ways to cook rice and there are even more opinions about how to do so! Much, of course, depends on the variety and brand of rice being used, the dish being prepared and the desired results. Each variety of rice has its own characteristics. Some types of rice cook to light, separate grains; some to a rich, creamy consistency; and some to a consistency where the grains stick together. It is important, therefore, to ensure that the appropriate rice is used. Different types of rice have very different powers of absorption. Long-grain rice will absorb about three times its weight in water, whereas just 25 g/1 oz of plump and short-grained pudding rice can soak up a massive 300 ml/½ pint of liquid.

Cooking Long-grain Rice

By far the simplest method of cooking long-grain rice – whether white, brown or basmati – is to add it to plenty of boiling, salted water in a large saucepan, so that the rice grains can move freely and do not stick together. Allow about 50 g/2 oz of rice per person when cooking as an accompaniment. Rinse it under cold, running water until clear – this removes any starch still clinging to the grains – then tip into the rapidly boiling water. Stir once, then when the water comes back to the boil, turn down the heat a little and simmer uncovered, allowing 10–12 minutes for white rice and 30–40 minutes for brown (check the packet timings, as brands of rice vary). The easiest way to test if the rice is cooked is to bite a couple of grains – they should be tender but still firm. Drain the rice straight away, then return to the pan with a little butter and herbs if liked. Fluff the grains with a fork and serve. If you need to keep the rice warm, put it in a bowl and place over a pan of barely simmering water. Cover the top of the bowl with a clean tea towel until ready to serve.

Absorption Method

Cooking rice using the absorption method is also very simple and is favoured by many because no draining is involved and therefore no water is wasted. Also, by using this method, stock and other flavourful ingredients can be added and will be absorbed by the rice. Furthermore, valuable nutrients are retained that would otherwise be lost in the cooking water when drained. To cook rice this way, weigh out the quantity of rice you require, then measure it by volume in a measuring jug – you will need about 150 ml/¼ pint for two people. Briefly rinse the rice in a sieve under cold running water, then tip into a large heavy based saucepan. If liked, you can cook the rice in a little butter or oil for about 1 minute. Pour in two parts water to one part rice (or use stock if you prefer), season with salt and bring to the boil uncovered. Cover the pan with a tight-fitting lid, then simmer gently without lifting the lid, until the liquid is absorbed and the rice is tender. White rice will take 15 minutes to cook, whereas brown rice will take about 35 minutes. It is important to simmer over a very low heat or the liquid will cook away before the rice is ready. Do not be tempted to check the rice too often while it is cooking as you will let out steam and therefore moisture. If there is still a little liquid left when the rice is tender, remove the lid and cook for about a minute until evaporated. Remove from the heat and leave to stand with the lid on for 4–5 minutes. Do not rinse the rice when it is cooked, just fluff up with a fork before serving. This method is also good for cooking Jasmine and Valencia rice.

Oven-baked Method

The oven-baked method also works by absorption. It takes a little longer than cooking rice on the hob, but is ideal to add to the oven if you are roasting or simmering a casserole.

To make oven-baked rice for two people, gently fry a chopped onion in 1 tablespoon of olive oil in a 1.1 litre/ 2 pint flameproof casserole dish until soft and golden (leave the onion out if preferred). Add 75 g/3 oz long-grain rice and cook for 1 minute, then stir in 300 ml/½ pint of stock – you can also add a finely pared strip of lemon rind or a bay leaf at this stage. Cover with a lid or tinfoil and bake on the middle shelf of a preheated oven at

180°C/350°F/Gas Mark 4 for 40 minutes, or until the rice is tender and all the stock has been absorbed. Fluff up with a fork before serving.

Cooking in the Microwave

Rinse long-grain white or brown rice in cold running water, then place in a large heat-proof bowl. Add boiling water or stock to the bowl, allowing 300 ml/ ¹/₂ pint for 125 g/4 oz rice and 550 ml/ 18 fl oz for 225 g/8 oz rice. Add a pinch of salt and a knob of butter, if desired. Cover with clingfilm, making a few air holes to allow the steam to escape and microwave on high for 3 minutes. Stir, then re-cover and microwave on medium for 12 minutes for white rice and 25 minutes for brown. Leave to stand, covered, for 5 minutes before fluffing up with a fork and serving.

In a Pressure Cooker

Follow the quantities given for the absorption method and bring to the boil in the pressure cooker. Stir once, cover with the lid and bring to a high 6.8 kg/15 lb pressure. Lower the heat and cook for 5 minutes if white rice or cook for 8 minutes if brown rice.

In a Rice Cooker

Follow the quantities given for the absorption method. Put the rice, salt and boiling water or stock in the cooker, bring back to the boil and cover. When all the liquid has been absorbed the cooker will turn itself off automatically.

Wild Rice

This type of rice can be cooked by any of the methods used for long-grain rice, but the cooking time required is longer. It will take between 35–50 minutes to cook wild rice, depending on whether you like your rice slightly chewy or very tender. To speed up the cooking time by 5–10 minutes, soak the rice in cold water first for 30 minutes. This also increases the volume of the rice when it is cooked.

Red Rice

Cook this in the same way as brown rice as this type of rice has a very hard grain. It is best to cook the rice for about 40–60 minutes if you like your rice really tender – it will still keep its shape.

Risotto Rice

Most rices should not be stirred during cooking as it breaks up the grains and makes them soggy. Risotto rice is different as it can absorb nearly five times its weight in liquid and still retains its shape. A good risotto has a creamy texture, with a slight bite to the individual grains and is made by adding the cooking liquid gradually and stirring almost continuously during cooking.

For a classic risotto (known as *alla Milanese*) for four people, place 1 tablespoon of olive oil and a knob of butter in a large heavy based saucepan. Slowly heat the butter and oil until the butter has melted. Add 1 chopped onion to the pan and cook until tender. Add 150 ml/¹/₄ pint of dry white wine and boil rapidly until almost totally reduced. Stir in 300 g/11 oz risotto rice. Add 1 litre/1³/₄ pints boiling vegetable or chicken stock, a ladleful at a time – each ladleful should be completely absorbed by the rice before the next one is added. Continue adding the stock until the rice is tender. This will take 15–20 minutes, although it may not be necessary to add all of the stock to achieve the desired consistency. Serve the risotto straight away, sprinkled with grated Parmesan cheese. The basic risotto can be flavoured in many ways. Try adding a couple of bay leaves, a lemon grass stalk or a large pinch of saffron to the stock, or use more red or white wine and less stock.

Glutinous Rice

This rice is steamed (instead of being cooked in boiling water) until the grains are soft, tender and stick together in a mass. Cooking times vary slightly according to the brand, so check the packet instructions for specific directions.

Pudding Rice

For a simple rice pudding put 50 g/ 2 oz of pudding rice in a buttered 1.2 litre/2 pint ovenproof dish with sugar to taste. Pour over 600 ml/1 pint of near-boiling milk and bake in a preheated oven at 150°C/300°F/Gas Mark 2 for 30 minutes. Stir, then bake for a further 1–1¹/₄ hours until tender. Vary the flavour by infusing the milk with orange rind, adding nuts and dried fruit to the mixture or using 300 ml/¹/₂ pint coconut milk or single cream and 300 ml/¹/₂ pint of milk instead of milk alone.

Health and Nutrition

Rice has been the dietary staple of the East for centuries where it has provided a healthy, balanced diet and has added substance to the small quantities of meat used in Eastern cooking. It is low in fat and high in complex carbohydrates which are absorbed slowly, helping to maintain blood sugar levels. Rice is also a reasonable source of protein and provides most of the B vitamins and the minerals potassium and phosphorus. It is also a gluten-free cereal, making it suitable for coeliacs. Like other unrefined grains, brown rice is richer in nutrients and fibre than refined white rice.

Herbs and Spices

Herbs are easy to grow and a garden is not needed as they can easily thrive on a small patio, window box or even on a windowsill. It is worth the effort to plant a few herbs as they do not require much attention or nurturing. The reward will be a range of fresh herbs available whenever needed, and fresh flavours that cannot be beaten to add to any dish that is being prepared.

While fresh herbs should be picked or bought as close as possible to the time of use, freeze-dried and dried herbs and spices will usually keep for around six months.

The best idea is to buy little and often, and to store the herbs in airtight jars in a cool dark cupboard. Fresh herbs tend to have a milder flavour than dried and equate to around one level tablespoon of fresh to one level teaspoon of dried. As a result, quantities used in cooking should be altered accordingly. A variety of herbs and spices and their uses are listed below.

ALLSPICE
The dark allspice berries come whole or ground and have a flavour similar to that of cinnamon, cloves and nutmeg. Although not the same as mixed spices, allspice can be used with pickles, relishes, cakes and milk puddings or whole in meat and fish dishes.

ANISEED
Aniseed comes in whole seeds or ground. It has a strong aroma and flavour and should be used sparingly in baking and salad dressings.

BASIL
Best fresh but also available in dried form, basil can be used raw or cooked. It works well in many dishes but is particularly well suited to tomato-based dishes and sauces, salads and Mediterranean recipes.

BAY LEAVES
Bay leaves are available in fresh or dried form as well as ground. They make up part of a bouquet garni and are particularly delicious when added to meat and poultry dishes, soups, stews, vegetable dishes and stuffing. They also impart a spicy flavour to milk puddings and egg custards.

BOUQUET GARNI
Bouquet garni is a bouquet of fresh herbs tied with a piece of string or in a small piece of muslin. It is used to flavour casseroles, stews and stocks or sauces. The herbs that are normally used are parsley, thyme, and bay leaves.

CARAWAY SEEDS
Caraway seeds have a warm sweet taste and are often used in breads and cakes but are delicious with cabbage dishes and pickles as well.

CAYENNE
Cayenne is the powdered form of a red chilli pepper said to be native to Cayenne. It is similar in appearance to paprika and can be used sparingly to add a fiery kick to many dishes.

CARDAMOM
Cardamom has a distinctive sweet, rich taste and can be bought whole in the pod, in seed form or ground. This sweet aromatic spice is delicious in curries, rice, cakes and biscuits and is great served with rice pudding and fruit.

CHERVIL
Reminiscent of parsley and available either in fresh or dried form, chervil has a faintly sweet, spicy flavour and is particularly good in soups, cheese dishes, stews and with eggs.

CHILLI
Available whole, fresh, dried and in powdered form, red chillies tend to be sweeter in taste than their green counterparts. They are particularly associated with Spanish and Mexican-style cooking and curries, but are also delicious with pickles, dips, sauces and in pizza toppings.

CHIVES
Best used when fresh but also available in dried form, this member of the onion family is ideal for use when a delicate onion flavour is required. Chives are good with eggs, cheese, fish and vegetable dishes. They also work well as a garnish for soups, meat and vegetable dishes.

CINNAMON
Cinnamon comes in the form of reddish-brown sticks of bark from an evergreen tree and has a sweet, pungent aroma. Either whole or ground, cinnamon is delicious in cakes and milk puddings, particularly with apple, and is used in mulled wine and for preserving.

CLOVES
Mainly used whole although also available ground, cloves have a very warm, sweet pungent aroma and can be used to stud roast ham and pork, in mulled wine and punch and when pickling fruit. When ground, they can be used in making mincemeat and in Christmas puddings and biscuits.

CORIANDER
Coriander seeds have an orangey flavour and are available whole or ground. Coriander is particularly delicious (whether whole or roughly ground) in casseroles, curries and as a pickling spice. The leaves are used to flavour spicy aromatic dishes as well as a garnish.

CUMIN
Also available ground or as whole seeds, cumin has a strong, slightly bitter flavour. It is one of the main ingredients in curry powder and compliments many fish, meat and rice dishes.

DILL
Dill leaves are available fresh or dried and have a mild flavour, while the seeds are slightly bitter. Dill is particularly good with salmon, new potatoes and in sauces. The seeds are good in pickles and vegetable dishes.

FENNEL
Whole seeds or ground, fennel has a fragrant, sweet aniseed flavour and is sometimes known as the fish herb because it compliments fish dishes so well.

GINGER
Ginger comes in many forms but primarily as a fresh root and in dried ground form, which can be used in baking, curries, pickles, sauces and Chinese cooking.

LEMON GRASS
Available fresh and dried, with a subtle, aromatic, lemony flavour, lemon grass is essential to Thai cooking. It is also delicious when added to soups, poultry and fish dishes.

MACE
The outer husk of nutmeg has a milder nutmeg flavour and can be used in pickles, cheese dishes, stewed fruits, sauces and hot punch.

MARJORAM
Often dried, marjoram has a sweet slightly spicy flavour, which tastes fantastic when added to stuffing, meat or tomato-based dishes.

MINT
Available fresh or dried, mint has a strong, sweet aroma which is delicious in a sauce or jelly to serve with lamb. It is also great with fresh peas and new potatoes and is an essential ingredient in Pimms.

MUSTARD SEED
These yellow and brown seeds are available whole or ground and are often found in pickles, relishes, cheese dishes, dressings, curries and as an accompaniment to meat.

NUTMEG
The large whole seeds have a warm, sweet taste and compliment custards, milk puddings, cheese dishes, parsnips and creamy soups.

OREGANO
The strongly flavoured dried leaves of oregano are similar to marjoram and are used extensively in Italian and Greek cooking.

PAPRIKA
Paprika often comes in two varieties. One is quite sweet and mild and the other has a slight bite to it. Paprika is made from the fruit of the sweet pepper and is good in meat and poultry dishes as well as a garnish. The rule of buying herbs and spices little and often applies particularly to paprika as unfortunately it does not keep particularly well.

PARSLEY
The stems as well as the leaves of parsley can be used to compliment most savoury dishes as they contain the most flavour. They can also be used as a garnish.

PEPPER
This comes in white and black peppercorns and is best freshly ground. Both add flavour to most dishes, sauces and gravies. Black pepper has a more robust flavour, while white pepper is much more delicate.

POPPY SEEDS
These tiny, grey-black coloured seeds impart a sweet, nutty flavour when added to biscuits, vegetable dishes, dressings and cheese dishes.

ROSEMARY
Delicious fresh or dried, these small, needle-like leaves have a sweet aroma which is particularly good with lamb, stuffing and vegetable dishes. Also delicious when added to charcoal on the barbecue to give a piquant flavour to meat and corn on the cob.

SAFFRON
Deep orange in colour, saffron is traditionally used in paella, rice and cakes but is also delicious with poultry. Saffron is the most expensive of all spices.

SAGE
Fresh or dried sage leaves have a pungent, slightly bitter taste which is delicious with pork and poultry, sausages, stuffing and with stuffed pasta when tossed in a little butter and fresh sage.

SAVORY
This herb resembles thyme, but has a softer flavour that particularly compliments all types of fish and beans.

SESAME
Sesame seeds have a nutty taste, especially when toasted, and are delicious in baking, on salads, or with Far-Eastern cooking.

TARRAGON
The fresh or dried leaves of tarragon have a sweet aromatic taste which is particularly good with poultry, seafood, fish, creamy sauces and stuffing.

THYME
Available fresh or dried, thyme has a pungent flavour and is included in bouquet garni. It compliments many meat and poultry dishes and stuffing.

TURMERIC
Turmeric is obtained from the root of a lily from southeast Asia. This root is ground and has a brilliant yellow colour. It has a bitter, peppery flavour and is often combined for use in curry powder and mustard. Also delicious in pickles, relishes and dressings.

Potato & Fennel Soup

INGREDIENTS

Serves 4

25 g/1 oz butter
2 large onions, peeled
  and thinly sliced
2–3 garlic cloves, peeled and crushed
1 tsp salt
2 medium potatoes (about
  450 g/1 lb in weight), peeled
  and diced
1 fennel bulb, trimmed and
  finely chopped
$^{1}/_{2}$ tsp caraway seeds
1 litre/1$^{3}/_{4}$ pints vegetable stock
freshly ground black pepper
2 tbsp freshly chopped parsley
4 tbsp crème fraîche
roughly torn pieces of French stick,
  to serve

FOOD FACT

A fennel bulb is in fact the swollen stem of a plant known as Florence fennel. Originating in Italy, Florence fennel has a distinct aniseed flavour, which mellows and sweetens when cooked. Look out for well rounded bulbs with bright green fronds.

1 Melt the butter in a large heavy-based saucepan. Add the onions, with the garlic and half the salt, and cook over a medium heat, stirring occasionally, for 7–10 minutes, or until the onions are very soft and beginning to turn brown.

2 Add the potatoes, fennel bulb, caraway seeds and the remaining salt. Cook for about 5 minutes, then pour in the vegetable stock. Bring to the boil, partially cover and simmer for 15–20 minutes, or until the potatoes are tender. Stir in the chopped parsley and adjust the seasoning to taste.

3 For a smooth-textured soup, allow to cool slightly then pour into a food processor or blender and blend until smooth. Reheat the soup gently, then ladle into individual soup bowls. For a chunky soup, omit this blending stage and ladle straight from the saucepan into soup bowls.

4 Swirl a spoonful of crème fraîche into each bowl and serve immediately with roughly torn pieces of French stick.

Rocket & Potato Soup with Garlic Croûtons

INGREDIENTS

Serves 4

700 g/1½ lb baby new potatoes

1.1 litres/2 pints chicken or
   vegetable stock

50 g/2 oz rocket leaves

125 g/4 oz thick white
   sliced bread

50 g/2 oz unsalted butter

1 tsp groundnut oil

2–4 garlic cloves, peeled
   and chopped

125 g/4 oz stale ciabatta bread,
   with the crusts removed

4 tbsp olive oil

salt and freshly ground black pepper

2 tbsp Parmesan cheese,
   finely grated

1 Place the potatoes in a large saucepan, cover with the stock and simmer gently for 10 minutes. Add the rocket leaves and simmer for a further 5–10 minutes, or until the potatoes are soft and the rocket has wilted.

2 Meanwhile, make the croûtons. Cut the thick white sliced bread into small cubes and reserve. Heat the butter and groundnut oil in a small frying pan and cook the garlic for 1 minute, stirring well. Remove the garlic. Add the bread cubes to the butter and oil mixture in the frying pan and sauté, stirring continuously, until they are golden brown. Drain the croûtons on absorbent kitchen paper and reserve.

3 Cut the ciabatta bread into small dice and stir into the soup. Cover the saucepan and leave to stand for 10 minutes, or until the bread has absorbed a lot of the liquid.

4 Stir in the olive oil, season to taste with salt and pepper and serve at once with a few of the garlic croûtons scattered over the top and a little grated Parmesan cheese.

HELPFUL HINT

Rocket is now widely available in bags from most large supermarkets. If, however, you cannot get hold of it, replace it with an equal quantity of watercress or baby spinach leaves.

1

2

3

Carrot & Ginger Soup

INGREDIENTS

Serves 4

4 slices of bread, crusts removed
1 tsp yeast extract
2 tsp olive oil
1 onion, peeled and chopped
1 garlic clove, peeled and crushed
½ tsp ground ginger
450 g/1 lb carrots, peeled
  and chopped
1 litre/1¾ pint vegetable stock
2.5 cm/1 inch piece of
  root ginger, peeled and finely grated
salt and freshly ground
  black pepper
1 tbsp lemon juice

To garnish:
chives
lemon zest

1 Preheat the oven to 180°C/350°F/Gas Mark 4. Roughly chop the bread. Dissolve the yeast extract in 2 tablespoons of warm water and mix with the bread.

2 Spread the bread cubes over a lightly oiled baking tray and bake for 20 minutes, turning halfway through. Remove from the oven and reserve.

3 Heat the oil in a large saucepan. Gently cook the onion and garlic for 3–4 minutes.

4 Stir in the ground ginger and cook for 1 minute to release the flavour.

5 Add the chopped carrots, then stir in the stock and the fresh ginger. Simmer gently for 15 minutes.

6 Remove from the heat and allow to cool a little. Blend until smooth, then season to taste with salt and pepper. Stir in the lemon juice. Garnish with the chives and lemon zest and serve immediately.

2

4

6

Balsamic Strawberries with Mascarpone

INGREDIENTS

Serves 4–6

450 g/1 lb fresh strawberries
2–3 tbsp best-quality
  balsamic vinegar
freshly ground black pepper
fresh mint leaves, torn, plus
  extra to decorate (optional)
115–175 g/4–6 oz mascarpone cheese

1   Wipe the strawberries with a damp cloth, rather than rinsing them, so they do not become soggy. Using a paring knife, cut off the green stalks at the top and use the tip of the knife to remove the core.

2   Cut each strawberry in half lengthways, or into quarters if large. Transfer to a bowl.

3   Add the vinegar, allowing ½ tablespoon per person. Add several twists of ground black pepper, then gently stir together. Cover with clingfilm and chill for up to 4 hours.

4   Just before serving, stir in torn mint leaves to taste. Spoon the mascarpone cheese into individual bowls and spoon the berries on top. Decorate with a few mint leaves, if wished. Sprinkle with extra pepper to taste.

HELPFUL HINT

This is most enjoyable when it is made with the best-quality balsamic vinegar, one that has aged slowly and has turned thick and syrupy. Unfortunately, the genuine mixture is always expensive. Less expensive versions are artificially sweetened and coloured with caramel, or taste of harsh vinegar.

1

3

4

Fish Soup Provençale

INGREDIENTS

Serves 4–6

1 tbsp olive oil

2 onions, finely chopped

1 small leek, thinly sliced

1 small carrot, finely chopped

1 stalk celery, finely chopped

1 small fennel bulb, finely
  chopped (optional)

3 garlic cloves, finely chopped

225 ml/8 fl oz dry white wine

1.2 litres/2 pints water

400 g/14 oz can tomatoes in juice

1 bay leaf

pinch of fennel seeds

2 strips orange rind

¼ tsp saffron threads

350 g/12 oz skinless white
  fish fillets

salt and pepper

garlic croûtons, to serve

1 Heat the oil in a large saucepan over a medium heat. Add the onions and cook for about 5 minutes, stirring frequently, until softened. Add the leek, carrot, celery, fennel and garlic and continue cooking for 4–5 minutes until the leek is wilted.

2 Add the wine and let it bubble for a minute. Add the tomatoes, bay leaf, fennel seeds, orange rind, saffron and water. Bring just to the boil, reduce the heat, cover and cook gently, stirring occasionally, for 30 minutes.

3 Add the fish and cook for a further 20–30 minutes until it is very soft and flaky. Remove the bay leaf and orange rind if possible.

4 Allow the soup to cool slightly, then transfer to a blender or food processor and purée until smooth, working in batches if necessary. (If using a food processor, strain off the cooking liquid and reserve. Purée the soup solids with enough cooking liquid to moisten them, then combine with the remaining liquid.)

5 Return the soup to the saucepan. Taste and adjust the seasoning, if necessary, and simmer for 5–10 minutes until heated through. Ladle the soup into warm bowls and sprinkle with croûtons.

Pumpkin & Smoked Haddock Soup

INGREDIENTS

Serves 4–6

2 tbsp olive oil

1 medium onion, peeled and chopped

2 garlic cloves, peeled and chopped

3 celery stalks, trimmed and chopped

700 g/1½ lb pumpkin, peeled, deseeded and cut into chunks

450 g/1 lb potatoes, peeled and cut into chunks

750 ml/1¼ pints chicken stock, heated

125 ml/4 fl oz dry sherry

200 g/7 oz smoked haddock fillet

150 ml/¼ pint milk

freshly ground black pepper

2 tbsp freshly chopped parsley

1 Heat the oil in a large heavy-based saucepan and gently cook the onion, garlic, and celery for about 10 minutes. This will release the sweetness but not colour the vegetables. Add the pumpkin and potatoes to the saucepan and stir to coat the vegetables with the oil.

2 Gradually pour in the stock and bring to the boil. Cover, then reduce the heat and simmer for 25 minutes, stirring occasionally. Stir in the dry sherry, then remove the saucepan from the heat and leave to cool for 5–10 minutes.

3 Blend the mixture in a food processor or blender to form a chunky purée and return to the cleaned saucepan.

4 Meanwhile, place the fish in a shallow frying pan. Pour in the milk with 3 tablespoons of water and bring to almost boiling point. Reduce the heat, cover and simmer for 6 minutes, or until the fish is cooked and flakes easily. Remove from the heat and, using a slotted spoon remove the fish from the liquid, reserving both liquid and fish.

5 Discard the skin and any bones from the fish and flake into pieces. Stir the fish liquid into the soup, together with the flaked fish. Season with freshly ground black pepper, stir in the parsley and serve immediately.

TASTY TIP

Try to find undyed smoked haddock for this soup rather than the brightly coloured yellow type, as the texture and flavour is better.

1

4

5

Creamy Salmon with Dill in Filo Baskets

INGREDIENTS

Serves 4

1 bay leaf
6 black peppercorns
1 large sprig fresh parsley
175 g/6 oz salmon fillet
4 large sheets filo pastry
fine spray of oil
125 g/4 oz baby spinach leaves
8 tbsp low-fat fromage frais
2 tsp Dijon mustard
2 tbsp freshly chopped dill
salt and freshly ground
   black pepper

FOOD FACT

This is a highly nutritious dish combining calcium-rich salmon with vitamin- and mineral-rich spinach. The low-fat fromage frais in this recipe can be substituted with low-fat live yogurt if you want to aid digestion and give the immune system a real boost!

1 Preheat the oven to 200°C/400°F/Gas Mark 6. Place the bay leaf, peppercorns, parsley and salmon in a frying pan and add enough water to barely cover the fish.

2 Bring to the boil, reduce the heat and poach the fish for 5 minutes until it flakes easily. Remove it from the pan. Reserve.

3 Spray each sheet of filo pastry lightly with the oil. Scrunch up the pastry to make a nest shape approximately 12.5 cm/5 inches in diameter.

4 Place on a lightly oiled baking sheet and cook in the preheated oven for 10 minutes until golden and crisp.

5 Blanch the spinach in a pan of lightly salted boiling water for 2 minutes. Drain thoroughly and keep warm.

6 Mix the fromage frais, mustard and dill together, then warm gently. Season to taste with salt and pepper. Divide the spinach between the filo pastry nests and flake the salmon onto the spinach.

7 Spoon the mustard and dill sauce over the filo baskets and serve immediately.

1

3

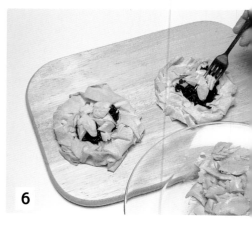
6

Griddled Garlic & Lemon Squid

INGREDIENTS

Serves 4

125 g/4 oz long-grain rice
300 ml/¹/₂ pint fish stock
225 g/8 oz squid, cleaned
finely grated rind of 1 lemon
1 garlic clove, peeled
  and crushed
1 shallot, peeled and
  finely chopped
2 tbsp freshly
  chopped coriander
2 tbsp lemon juice
salt and freshly ground
  black pepper

HELPFUL HINT

To prepare squid, peel the tentacles from the squid's pouch and cut away the head just below the eye. Discard the head. Remove the quill and the soft innards from the squid and discard. Peel off any dark skin that covers the squid and discard. Rinse the tentacles and pouch thoroughly. The squid is now ready to use.

1 Rinse the rice until the water runs clear, then place in a saucepan with the stock.

2 Bring to the boil, then reduce the heat. Cover and simmer gently for 10 minutes.

3 Turn off the heat and leave the pan covered so the rice can steam while you cook the squid.

4 Remove the tentacles from the squid and reserve.

5 Cut the body cavity in half. Using the tip of a small sharp knife, score the inside flesh of the body cavity in a diamond pattern. Do not cut all the way through.

6 Mix the lemon rind, crushed garlic and chopped shallot together.

7 Place the squid in a shallow bowl and sprinkle over the lemon mixture and stir.

8 Heat a griddle pan until almost smoking. Cook the squid for 3–4 minutes until cooked through, then slice.

9 Sprinkle with the coriander and lemon juice. Season to taste with salt and pepper. Drain the rice and serve immediately with the squid.

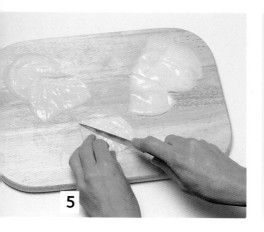

5

7

8

Garlic Fish Soup

INGREDIENTS

Serves 4

2 tsp olive oil
1 large onion, chopped
1 small fennel bulb, chopped
1 leek, sliced
3–4 large garlic cloves, thinly sliced
120 ml / 4 fl oz dry white wine
1.2 litres/2 pints fish stock
4 tbsp white rice
1 strip pared lemon rind
1 bay leaf
450 g/1 lb skinless white fish fillets,
  cut into 4 cm/1½ inch pieces
50 ml/2 fl oz double cream
2 tbsp fresh parsley, chopped
salt and pepper

1 Heat the oil in a large saucepan over a medium-low heat. Add the onion, fennel, leek and garlic and cook for 4–5 minutes, stirring frequently, until the onion is softened.

2 Add the wine and bubble briefly. Add the stock, rice, lemon rind and bay leaf. Bring to the boil, reduce the heat to medium-low and simmer for 20–25 minutes, or until the rice and vegetables are soft. Remove the lemon rind and bay leaf.

3 Allow the soup to cool slightly, then transfer to a blender or food processor and purée until smooth, working in batches if necessary. (If using a food processor, strain off the cooking liquid and reserve. Purée the soup solids with enough cooking liquid to moisten them, then combine with the remaining liquid.)

4 Return the soup to the saucepan and bring to a simmer. Add the fish to the soup, cover and continue simmering gently, stirring occasionally, for 4–5 minutes, or until the fish is cooked and begins to flake.

5 Stir in the cream. Taste and adjust the seasoning, adding salt, if needed, and pepper. Ladle into warmed bowls and serve sprinkled with parsley.

1

2

4

Smoked Salmon Sushi

INGREDIENTS

Serves 4

175 g/6 oz sushi rice
2 tbsp rice vinegar
4 tsp caster sugar
½ tsp salt
2 sheets sushi nori
60 g/2½ oz smoked salmon
¼ cucumber, cut into fine strips

To serve:
wasabi
soy sauce
pickled ginger

TASTY TIP

If wasabi is unavailable, use a little horseradish. If unable to get sushi nori (seaweed sheets), shape the rice into small bite-size oblongs, then drape a piece of smoked salmon over each one and garnish with chives.

1 Rinse the rice thoroughly in cold water, until the water runs clear, then place in a pan with 300 ml/½ pint of water. Bring to the boil and cover with a tight-fitting lid. Reduce to a simmer and cook gently for 10 minutes. Turn the heat off, but keep the pan covered, to allow the rice to steam for a further 10 minutes.

2 In a small saucepan gently heat the rice vinegar, sugar and salt until the sugar has dissolved. When the rice has finished steaming, pour over the vinegar mixture and stir well to mix. Empty the rice out on to a large flat surface (a chopping board or large plate is ideal). Fan the rice to cool and to produce a shinier rice.

3 Lay one sheet of sushi nori on a sushi mat (if you do not have a sushi mat, improvise with a stiff piece of fabric that is a little larger than the sushi nori) and spread with half the cooled rice. Dampen the hands while doing this (this helps to prevent the rice from sticking to the hands). On the nearest edge place half the salmon and half the cucumber strips.

4 Roll up the rice and smoked salmon into a tight Swiss roll-like shape. Dampen the blade of a sharp knife and cut the sushi into slices about 2 cm/¾ inch thick. Repeat with the remaining sushi nori, rice, smoked salmon and cucumber. Serve with wasabi, soy sauce and pickled ginger.

2

3

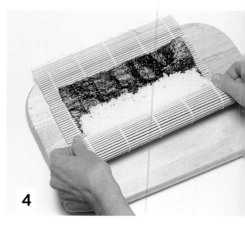
4

Honey & Ginger Prawns

INGREDIENTS

Serves 4

1 carrot
50 g/2 oz bamboo shoots
4 spring onions
1 tbsp clear honey
1 tbsp tomato ketchup
1 tsp soy sauce
2.5 cm/1 inch piece fresh root ginger,
   peeled and finely grated
1 garlic clove, peeled and crushed
1 tbsp lime juice
175 g/6 oz peeled prawns, thawed
   if frozen
2 heads little gem lettuce leaves
2 tbsp freshly chopped coriander
salt and freshly ground black pepper

To garnish:
fresh coriander sprigs
lime slices

HELPFUL HINT

This highly versatile dish can be adapted to suit any diet. If liked, raw tiger prawns can be used for this recipe – do make sure if using raw prawns that the black vein that runs along their back is removed.

1 Cut the carrot into matchstick-size pieces, roughly chop the bamboo shoots and finely slice the spring onions.

2 Combine the bamboo shoots with the carrot matchsticks and spring onions.

3 In a wok or large frying pan gently heat the honey, tomato ketchup, soy sauce, ginger, garlic and lime juice with 3 tablespoons of water. Bring to the boil.

4 Add the carrot mixture and stir-fry for 2–3 minutes until the vegetables are hot.

5 Add the prawns and continue to stir-fry for 2 minutes.

6 Remove the wok or frying pan from the heat and reserve until cooled slightly.

7 Divide the little gem lettuce into leaves and rinse lightly.

8 Stir the chopped coriander into the prawn mixture and season to taste with salt and pepper. Spoon into the lettuce leaves and serve immediately garnished with sprigs of fresh coriander and lime slices.

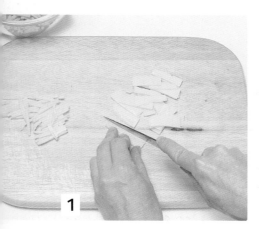

1

5

8

Crostini with Chicken Livers

INGREDIENTS

Serves 4

2 tbsp olive oil

2 tbsp butter

1 shallot, peeled and finely chopped

1 garlic clove, peeled and crushed

150 g/5 oz chicken livers

1 tbsp plain flour

2 tbsp dry white wine

1 tbsp brandy

50 g/2 oz mushrooms, sliced

salt and freshly ground black pepper

4 slices of ciabatta or similar bread

To garnish:

fresh sage leaves

lemon wedges

TASTY TIP

If you prefer a lower-fat alternative to the fried bread in this recipe, omit 1 tablespoon of the butter and brush the bread slices with the remaining 1 tablespoon of oil. Bake in a preheated oven 180°C/350°F/Gas Mark 4 for about 20 minutes, or until golden and crisp then serve as above.

1 Heat 1 tablespoon of the olive oil and 1 tablespoon of the butter in a frying pan, add the shallot and garlic and cook gently for 2–3 minutes.

2 Trim and wash the chicken livers thoroughly and pat dry on absorbent kitchen paper. Cut into slices, then toss in the flour. Add the livers to the frying pan with the shallot and garlic and continue to fry for a further 2 minutes, stirring continuously.

3 Pour in the white wine and brandy and bring to the boil. Boil rapidly for 1–2 minutes to allow the alcohol to evaporate, then stir in the sliced mushrooms and cook gently for about 5 minutes, or until the chicken livers are cooked, but just a little pink inside. Season to taste with salt and pepper.

4 Fry the slices of ciabatta or similar-style bread in the remaining oil and butter, then place on individual serving dishes. Spoon over the liver mixture and garnish with a few sage leaves and lemon wedges. Serve immediately.

2

3

3

Mussels with Creamy Garlic & Saffron Sauce

INGREDIENTS

Serves 4

700 g/1½ lb fresh live mussels

300 ml/½ pint good quality dry
  white wine

1 tbsp olive oil

1 shallot, peeled and finely chopped

2 garlic cloves, peeled and crushed

1 tbsp freshly chopped oregano

2 saffron strands

150 ml/¼ pint single cream

salt and freshly ground black pepper

fresh crusty bread, to serve

1 Clean the mussels thoroughly in plenty of cold water and remove any beards and barnacles from the shells. Discard any mussels that are open or damaged. Place in a large bowl and cover with cold water and leave in the refrigerator until required, if prepared earlier.

2 Pour the wine into a large saucepan and bring to the boil. Tip the mussels into the pan, cover and cook, shaking the saucepan periodically for 6–8 minutes, or until the mussels have opened completely.

3 Discard any mussels with closed shells, then using a slotted spoon, carefully remove the remaining open mussels from the saucepan and keep them warm. Reserve the cooking liquor.

4 Heat the olive oil in a small frying pan and cook the shallot and garlic gently for 2–3 minutes, until softened. Add the reserved cooking liquid and chopped oregano and cook for a further 3–4 minutes. Stir in the saffron and the cream and heat through gently. Season to taste with salt and pepper. Place a few mussels in individual serving bowls and spoon over the saffron sauce. Serve immediately with plenty of fresh crusty bread.

HELPFUL HINT

Mussels are now farmed and are available most of the year. However, always try to buy mussels the day you intend to eat them. Place them in a bowl of cold water in the refrigerator as soon as possible, changing the water at least every 2 hours. If live mussels are unavailable, use prepacked, cooked mussels.

Hot Tiger Prawns with Parma Ham

INGREDIENTS

Serves 4

½ cucumber, peeled if preferred

4 ripe tomatoes

12 raw tiger prawns

6 tbsp olive oil

4 garlic cloves, peeled and crushed

4 tbsp freshly chopped parsley

salt and freshly ground black pepper

6 slices of Parma ham, cut in half

4 slices flat Italian bread

4 tbsp dry white wine

HELPFUL HINT

The black intestinal vein needs to be removed from raw prawns because it can cause a bitter flavour. Remove the shell, then using a small, sharp knife, make a cut along the centre back of the prawn and open out the flesh. Using the tip of the knife, remove the thread that lies along the length of the prawn and discard.

1 Preheat oven to 180°C/350°F/Gas Mark 4. Slice the cucumber and tomatoes thinly, then arrange on 4 large plates and reserve. Peel the prawns, leaving the tail shell intact and remove the thin black vein running down the back.

2 Whisk together 4 tablespoons of the olive oil, garlic and chopped parsley in a small bowl and season to taste with plenty of salt and pepper. Add the prawns to the mixture and stir until they are well coated. Remove the prawns, then wrap each one in a piece of Parma ham and secure with a cocktail stick.

3 Place the prepared prawns on a lightly oiled baking sheet or dish with the slices of bread and cook in the preheated oven for 5 minutes.

4 Remove the prawns from the oven and spoon the wine over the prawns and bread. Return to the oven and cook for a further 10 minutes until piping hot.

5 Carefully remove the cocktail sticks and arrange 3 prawn rolls on each slice of bread. Place on top of the sliced cucumber and tomatoes and serve immediately.

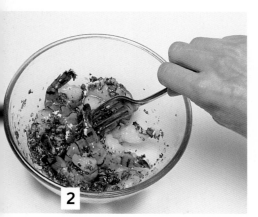
2

2

4

Mozzarella Parcels with Cranberry Relish

INGREDIENTS

Serves 6

125 g/4 oz mozzarella cheese
8 slices of thin white bread
2 medium eggs, beaten
salt and freshly ground black pepper
300 ml/½ pint olive oil

For the relish:

125 g/4 oz cranberries
2 tbsp fresh orange juice
grated rind of 1 small orange
50 g/2 oz soft light brown sugar
1 tbsp port

HELPFUL HINT

To test the temperature of the oil without a thermometer, drop a cube of bread into the frying pan. If the bread browns in 30 seconds the oil is at the right temperature. If it does not, try again in a couple of minutes or increase the heat. If the bread goes very dark, reduce the temperature under the pan and add about 150 ml/¼ pint of cold oil and test again.

1 Slice the mozzarella thinly, remove the crusts from the bread and make sandwiches with the bread and cheese. Cut into 5 cm/2 inch squares and squash them quite flat. Season the eggs with salt and pepper, then soak the bread in the seasoned egg for 1 minute on each side until well coated.

2 Heat the oil to 190°C/375°F and deep-fry the bread squares for 1–2 minutes, or until they are crisp and golden brown. Drain on absorbent kitchen paper and keep warm while the cranberry relish is prepared.

3 Place the cranberries, orange juice, rind, sugar and port into a small saucepan and add 5 tablespoons of water. Bring to the boil, then simmer for 10 minutes, or until the cranberries have 'popped'. Sweeten with a little more sugar if necessary.

4 Arrange the mozzarella parcels on individual serving plates. Serve with a little of the cranberry relish.

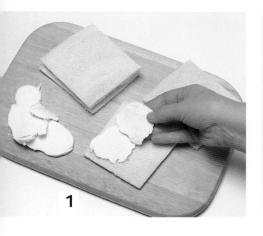

1

1

3

Fresh Tagliatelle with Courgettes

INGREDIENTS

Serves 4–6

225 g/8 oz strong plain bread flour
  or type oo pasta flour, plus extra
  for rolling
1 tsp salt
2 medium eggs
1 medium egg yolk
3 tbsp extra-virgin olive oil
2 small courgettes, halved
  lengthways and thinly sliced
2 garlic cloves, peeled and
  thinly sliced
large pinch chilli flakes
zest of ½ lemon
1 tbsp freshly shredded basil
salt and freshly ground black pepper
freshly grated Parmesan cheese,
  to serve

1. Sift the flour and salt into a large bowl, make a well in the centre and add the eggs and yolk, 1 tablespoon of oil with 1 teaspoon of water. Gradually mix to form a soft but not sticky dough, adding a little more flour or water as necessary. Turn out onto a lightly floured surface and knead for 5 minutes, or until smooth and elastic. Wrap in clingfilm and leave to rest at room temperature for about 30 minutes.

2. Divide the dough into 8 pieces. Feed a piece of dough through a pasta machine. Gradually decrease the settings on the rollers, feeding the pasta through each time, until the sheet is very long and thin. If the pasta seems sticky, dust the work surface and both sides of the pasta generously with flour. Cut in half crosswise and hang over a clean pole. Repeat with the remaining dough. Leave to dry for about 5 minutes. Feed each sheet through the tagliatelle cutter, hanging the cut pasta over the pole. Leave to dry for a further 5 minutes. Wind a handful of pasta strands into nests and leave on a floured tea towel. Repeat with the remaining dough and leave to dry for 5 minutes.

3. Cook the pasta in plenty of salted boiling water for 2–3 minutes, or until 'al dente'.

4. Meanwhile, heat the remaining oil in a large frying pan and add the courgettes, garlic, chilli and lemon zest. Cook over a medium heat for 3–4 minutes, or until the courgettes are lightly golden and tender.

5. Drain the pasta thoroughly, reserving 2 tablespoons of the cooking water. Add the pasta to the courgettes with the basil and seasoning. Mix well, adding the reserved cooking water. Serve with the Parmesan cheese.

1

2

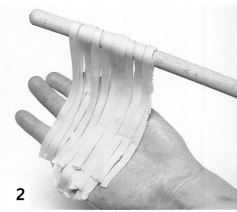

2

Beetroot Ravioli with Dill Cream Sauce

INGREDIENTS

Serves 4–6

fresh pasta (see Fresh Tagliatelle
   with Courgettes, page 46)

1 tbsp olive oil

1 small onion, peeled and
   finely chopped

½ tsp caraway seeds

175 g/6 oz cooked beetroot, chopped

175 g/6 oz ricotta cheese

25 g/1 oz fresh white breadcrumbs

1 medium egg yolk

2 tbsp grated Parmesan cheese

salt and freshly ground black pepper

4 tbsp walnut oil

4 tbsp freshly chopped dill

1 tbsp green peppercorns, drained
   and roughly chopped

6 tbsp crème fraîche

1 Make the pasta dough according to the recipe on page 46. Wrap in clingfilm and leave to rest for 30 minutes.

2 Heat the olive oil in a large frying pan, add the onion and caraway seeds and cook over a medium heat for 5 minutes, or until the onion is softened and lightly golden. Stir in the beetroot and cook for 5 minutes.

3 Blend the beetroot mixture in a food processor until smooth, then allow to cool. Stir in the ricotta cheese, breadcrumbs, egg yolk and Parmesan cheese. Season the filling to taste with salt and pepper and reserve.

4 Divide the pasta dough into 8 pieces. Roll out as for tagliatelle, but do not cut the sheets in half. Lay 1 sheet on a floured surface and place 5 heaped teaspoons of the filling 2.5 cm/1 inch apart.

5 Dampen around the heaps of filling and lay a second sheet of pasta over the top. Press around the heaps to seal.

6 Cut into squares using a pastry wheel or sharp knife. Put the filled pasta shapes onto a floured tea towel.

7 Bring a large pan of lightly salted water to a rolling boil. Drop the ravioli into the boiling water, return to the boil and cook for 3–4 minutes, until 'al dente'.

8 Meanwhile, heat the walnut oil in a small pan then add the chopped dill and green peppercorns. Remove from the heat, stir in the crème fraîche and season well. Drain the cooked pasta thoroughly and toss with the sauce. Tip into warmed serving dishes and serve immediately.

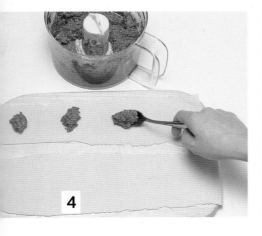

4

5

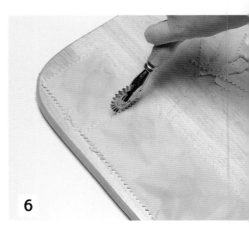

6

Tagliatelle with Brown Butter, Asparagus & Parmesan

INGREDIENTS

Serves 6

fresh pasta (see Fresh Tagliatelle with
  Courgettes, page 46) or 450 g/1 lb
  dried tagliatelle, such as the white
  and green variety
350 g/12 oz asparagus, trimmed and
  cut into short lengths
75 g/3 oz unsalted butter
1 garlic clove, peeled and sliced
25 g/1 oz flaked hazelnuts or whole
  hazelnuts, roughly chopped
1 tbsp freshly chopped parsley
1 tbsp freshly snipped chives
salt and freshly ground black pepper
50 g/2 oz freshly grated Parmesan
  cheese, to serve

FOOD FACT

Asparagus is available all year
round, but is at its best during
May and June. If you buy loose
asparagus, rather than prepacked, choose stems of similar
thickness so they will all cook in
the same time.

1. If using fresh pasta, prepare the dough according to the recipe on page 46. Cut into tagliatelle, wind into nests and reserve on a floured tea towel until ready to cook.

2. Bring a pan of lightly salted water to the boil. Add the asparagus and cook for 1 minute. Drain immediately, refresh under cold running water and drain again. Pat dry and reserve.

3. Melt the butter in a large frying pan, then add the garlic and hazelnuts and cook over a medium heat until the butter turns golden. Immediately remove from the heat and add the parsley, chives and asparagus. Leave for 2–3 minutes, until the asparagus is heated through.

4. Meanwhile, bring a large pan of lightly salted water to a rolling boil, then add the pasta nests. Cook until 'al dente': 2–3 minutes for fresh pasta and according to the packet instructions for dried pasta. Drain the pasta thoroughly and return to the pan. Add the asparagus mixture and toss together. Season to taste with salt and pepper and tip into a warmed serving dish. Serve immediately with grated Parmesan cheese.

2

3

4

Pasta with Raw Fennel, Tomato & Red Onions

INGREDIENTS

Serves 6

1 fennel bulb
700 g/1½ lb tomatoes
1 garlic clove
¼ small red onion
small handful fresh basil
small handful fresh mint
100 ml/3½ fl oz extra-virgin olive oil,
   plus extra to serve
juice of 1 lemon
salt and freshly ground black pepper
450 g/1 lb penne or pennette
freshly grated Parmesan cheese,
   to serve

1 Trim the fennel and slice thinly. Stack the slices and cut into sticks, then cut crosswise again into fine dice. Deseed the tomatoes and chop them finely. Peel and finely chop or crush the garlic. Peel and finely chop or grate the onion.

2 Stack the basil leaves then roll up tightly. Slice crosswise into fine shreds. Finely chop the mint.

3 Place the chopped vegetables and herbs in a medium bowl. Add the olive oil and lemon juice and mix together. Season well with salt and pepper then leave for 30 minutes to allow the flavours to develop.

4 Bring a large pan of salted water to a rolling boil. Add the pasta and cook according to the packet instructions, or until 'al dente'.

5 Drain the cooked pasta thoroughly. Transfer to a warmed serving dish, pour over the vegetable mixture and toss. Serve with the grated Parmesan cheese and extra olive oil to drizzle over.

HELPFUL HINT

The vegetables used in this dish are not cooked, but are tossed with the hot pasta. It is important, therefore, that they are chopped finely.

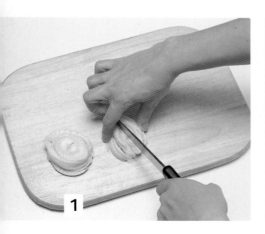

1

2

5

Louisiana Prawns & Fettuccine

INGREDIENTS

Serves 4

4 tbsp olive oil

450 g/1 lb raw tiger prawns, washed
  and peeled, shells and
  heads reserved

2 shallots, peeled and finely chopped

4 garlic cloves, peeled and
  finely chopped

large handful fresh basil leaves

1 carrot, peeled and finely chopped

1 onion, peeled and finely chopped

1 celery stick, trimmed and
  finely chopped

2–3 sprigs fresh parsley

2–3 sprigs fresh thyme

salt and freshly ground black pepper

pinch cayenne pepper

175 ml/6 fl oz dry white wine

450 g/1 lb ripe tomatoes,
  roughly chopped

juice of ½ lemon, or to taste

350 g/12 oz fettuccine

1 Heat 2 tablespoons of the olive oil in a large saucepan and add the reserved prawn shells and heads. Fry over a high heat for 2–3 minutes, until the shells turn pink and are lightly browned. Add half the shallots, half the garlic, half the basil and the carrot, onion, celery, parsley and thyme. Season lightly with salt, pepper and cayenne and sauté for 2–3 minutes, stirring often.

2 Pour in the wine and stir, scraping the pan well. Bring to the boil and simmer for 1 minute, then add the tomatoes. Cook for a further 3–4 minutes then pour in 200 ml/7 fl oz water. Bring to the boil, lower the heat and simmer for about 30 minutes, stirring often and using a wooden spoon to mash the prawn shells in order to release as much flavour as possible into the sauce. Lower the heat if the sauce is reducing very quickly.

3 Strain through a sieve, pressing well to extract as much liquid as possible; there should be about 450 ml/¾ pint. Pour the liquid into a clean pan and bring to the boil, then lower the heat and simmer gently until the liquid is reduced by about half.

4 Heat the remaining olive oil over a high heat in a clean frying pan and add the peeled prawns. Season lightly and add the lemon juice. Cook for 1 minute, lower the heat and add the remaining shallots and garlic. Cook for 1 minute. Add the sauce and adjust the seasoning.

5 Meanwhile, bring a large pan of lightly salted water to a rolling boil and add the fettuccine. Cook according to the packet instructions, or until 'al dente', and drain thoroughly. Transfer to a warmed serving dish. Add the sauce and toss well. Garnish with the remaining basil and serve immediately.

1

2

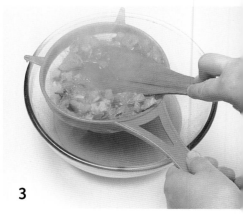

3

Pasta with Walnut Sauce

INGREDIENTS

Serves 4

50 g/2 oz walnuts, toasted

3 spring onions, trimmed
 and chopped

2 garlic cloves, peeled and sliced

1 tbsp freshly chopped parsley
 or basil

5 tbsp extra-virgin olive oil

salt and freshly ground black pepper

450 g/1 lb broccoli, cut into florets

350 g/12 oz pasta shapes

1 red chilli, deseeded and
 finely chopped

HELPFUL HINT

There is no hard-and-fast rule about which shape of pasta to use with this recipe; it is really a matter of personal preference. Spirali have been used here, but rigatoni, farfalle, garganelle or pipe rigate would all work well, or you could choose flavoured pasta, such as tomato, or a wholewheat variety for a change.

1 Place the toasted walnuts in a blender or food processor with the chopped spring onions, one of the garlic cloves and parsley or basil. Blend to a fairly smooth paste, then gradually add 3 tablespoons of the olive oil, until it is well mixed into the paste. Season the walnut paste to taste with salt and pepper and reserve.

2 Bring a large pan of lightly salted water to a rolling boil. Add the broccoli, return to the boil and cook for 2 minutes. Remove the broccoli, using a slotted draining spoon and refresh under cold running water. Drain again and pat dry on absorbent kitchen paper.

3 Bring the water back to a rolling boil. Add the pasta and cook according to the packet instructions, or until 'al dente'.

4 Meanwhile, heat the remaining oil in a frying pan. Add the remaining garlic and chilli. Cook gently for 2 minutes, or until softened. Add the broccoli and walnut paste. Cook for a further 3–4 minutes, or until heated through.

5 Drain the pasta thoroughly and transfer to a large warmed serving bowl. Pour over the walnut and broccoli sauce. Toss together, adjust the seasoning and serve immediately.

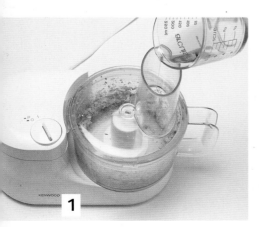

Linguine with Fennel, Crab & Chervil

INGREDIENTS

Serves 6

450g/1 lb linguine

25 g/1 oz butter

2 carrots, peeled and finely diced

2 shallots, peeled and finely diced

2 celery sticks, trimmed and
   finely diced

1 bulb fennel, trimmed and
   finely diced

6 spring onions, trimmed and
   finely chopped

300 ml/½ pint double cream

3 tbsp freshly chopped chervil

1 large cooked crab,
   plus extra for garnish

salt and freshly ground pepper

juice of ½ lemon, or to taste

sprig of dill, to garnish

HELPFUL HINT

When cooking pasta, use a very large saucepan so that the pasta has plenty of space to move around freely. Once the water has come to the boil, add the pasta, stir, cover and return to the boil. The lid can then be removed so that the water does not boil over.

1 Bring a large pan of lightly salted water to a rolling boil. Add the pasta and cook according to the packet instructions, or until 'al dente'.

2 Meanwhile, heat the butter in a large saucepan. Add the carrots, shallots, celery, fennel and three-quarters of the chopped spring onions. Cook the vegetables gently for 8–10 minutes, or until tender, stirring frequently and ensuring that they do not brown.

3 Add the double cream and chopped chervil to the vegetable mixture. Scrape the crab meat over the sauce, then stir to mix the sauce ingredients.

4 Season the sauce to taste with salt and pepper and stir in the lemon juice. Drain the pasta thoroughly and transfer to a large warmed serving dish. Pour over the sauce and toss. Garnish with extra chervil, the remaining spring onions and a sprig of dill. Serve immediately.

2

3

4

Poached Fish Dumplings with Creamy Chilli Sauce

INGREDIENTS

Serves 4

450 g/1 lb white fish fillet, skinned
    and boned
1 tsp dark soy sauce
1 tbsp cornflour
1 medium egg yolk
salt and freshly ground black pepper
3 tbsp freshly chopped coriander,
    plus extra, to garnish
1.6 litres/2³/₄ pints fish stock

For the creamy chilli sauce:

2 tsp groundnut oil
2 garlic cloves, peeled and
    finely chopped
4 spring onions, trimmed and
    finely sliced
2 tbsp dry sherry
1 tbsp sweet chilli sauce
1 tbsp light soy sauce
1 tbsp lemon juice
6 tbsp crème fraîche

To garnish:

sprigs of fresh coriander
fresh carrot sticks

1 Chop the fish into chunks and place in a food processor with the soy sauce, cornflour and egg yolk. Season to taste with salt and pepper. Blend until fairly smooth. Add the coriander and process for a few seconds until well mixed. Transfer to a bowl, cover and chill in the refrigerator for 30 minutes.

2 With damp hands shape the chilled mixture into walnut-sized balls and place on a baking tray lined with non-stick baking paper. Chill in the refrigerator for a further 30 minutes.

3 Pour the stock into a wide saucepan, bring to the boil, then reduce the heat until barely simmering. Add the fish balls and poach for 3–4 minutes or until cooked through.

4 Meanwhile, make the sauce. Heat the oil in a small saucepan, add the garlic and spring onions and cook until golden. Stir in the sherry, chilli and soy sauces and lemon juice, then remove immediately from the heat. Stir in the crème fraîche and season to taste with salt and pepper.

5 Using a slotted spoon, lift the cooked fish balls from the stock and place on a warmed serving dish. Drizzle over the sauce, garnish with sprigs of fresh coriander and serve immediately.

1

2

3

Smoked Mackerel Vol–au–Vents

INGREDIENTS

Makes 12

350 g/12 oz prepared puff pastry
1 small egg, beaten
2 tsp sesame seeds
225 g/8 oz peppered smoked
  mackerel, skinned and chopped
5 cm/2 inch piece cucumber
4 tbsp soft cream cheese
2 tbsp cranberry sauce
1 tbsp freshly chopped dill
1 tbsp finely grated lemon rind
dill sprigs, to garnish
mixed salad leaves, to serve

FOOD FACT

Mackerel is a relatively cheap fish and one of the richest sources of minerals, oils and vitamins available. This dish is an affordable way to incorporate all these essential nutrients into your diet.

1 Preheat the oven to 230°C/450°F/Gas Mark 8. Roll the pastry out on a lightly floured surface and using a 9 cm/3½ inch fluted cutter cut out 12 rounds.

2 Using a 1 cm/½ inch cutter mark a lid in the centre of each round.

3 Place on a damp baking sheet and brush the rounds with a little beaten egg.

4 Sprinkle the pastry with the sesame seeds and bake in the preheated oven for 10–12 minutes, or until golden brown and well risen.

5 Transfer the vol-au-vents to a chopping board and, when cool enough to touch, carefully remove the lids with a small sharp knife.

6 Scoop out any uncooked pastry from the inside of each vol-au-vent, then return to the oven for 5–8 minutes to dry out. Remove and allow to cool.

7 Flake the mackerel into small pieces and reserve. Peel the cucumber if desired, cut into very small dice and add to the mackerel.

8 Beat the soft cream cheese with the cranberry sauce, dill and lemon rind. Stir in the mackerel and cucumber and use to fill the vol-au-vents. Place the lids on top and garnish dill sprigs.

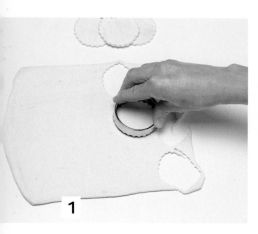

1

5

8

Garlic Wild Mushroom Galettes

INGREDIENTS

Serves 6

1 quantity quick flaky pastry
  (see page 66), chilled
1 onion, peeled
1 red chilli, deseeded
2 garlic cloves, peeled
275 g/10 oz mixed mushrooms,
  e.g. oysters, chestnuts, morels,
  ceps and chanterelles
25 g/1 oz butter
2 tbsp freshly chopped parsley
125 g/4 oz mozzarella cheese, sliced

To serve:
cherry tomatoes
mixed green salad leaves

HELPFUL HINT

Many supermarkets now stock a variety of wild mushrooms, all of which can be used in this recipe. It is important to maintain as much of the flavour of the mushrooms as possible, so do not peel mushrooms unless they appear old or tough. Either rinse lightly if covered with small pieces of soil or wipe well, trim the stalks and use.

1 Preheat the oven to 220°C/425°F/Gas Mark 7. On a lightly floured surface roll out the chilled pastry very thinly.

2 Cut out 6 x 15 cm/6 inch circles and place on a lightly oiled baking sheet.

3 Thinly slice the onion, then divide into rings and reserve.

4 Thinly slice the chilli and slice the garlic into wafer-thin slivers. Add to the onions and reserve.

5 Wipe or lightly rinse the mushrooms. Halve or quarter any large mushrooms and keep the small ones whole.

6 Heat the butter in a frying pan and sauté the onion, chilli and garlic gently for about 3 minutes. Add the mushrooms and cook for about 5 minutes, or until beginning to soften.

7 Stir the parsley into the mushroom mixture and drain off any excess liquid.

8 Pile the mushroom mixture on to the pastry circles within 5 mm/¼ inches of the edge. Arrange the sliced mozzarella cheese on top.

9 Bake in the preheated oven for 12–15 minutes, or until golden brown and serve with the tomatoes and salad.

2

5

8

French Onion Tart

INGREDIENTS

Serves 4

For the quick, flaky pastry:

125 g/4 oz butter
175 g/6 oz plain flour
pinch of salt

For the filling:

2 tbsp olive oil
4 large onions, peeled and
  thinly sliced
3 tbsp white wine vinegar
2 tbsp muscovado sugar
a little beaten egg or milk
175 g/6 oz Cheddar
  cheese, grated
salt and freshly ground
  black pepper

1. Preheat the oven to 200°C/400°F/Gas Mark 6. Place the butter in the freezer for 30 minutes. Sift the flour and salt into a large bowl. Remove the butter from the freezer and grate using the coarse side of a grater, dipping the butter in the flour every now and again as it makes it easier to grate.

2. Mix the butter into the flour, using a knife, making sure all the butter is coated thoroughly with flour.

3. Add 2 tablespoons of cold water and continue to mix, bringing the mixture together. Use your hands to complete the mixing. Add a little more water if needed to leave a clean bowl. Place the pastry in a polythene bag and chill in the refrigerator for 30 minutes.

4. Heat the oil in a large frying pan, then fry the onions for 10 minutes, stirring occasionally until softened.

5. Stir in the white wine vinegar and sugar. Increase the heat and stir frequently, for another 4–5 minutes until the onions turn a deep caramel colour. Cook for another 5 minutes, then reserve to cool.

6. On a lightly floured surface, roll out the pastry to a 35.5 cm/14 inch circle. Wrap over a rolling pin and move the circle onto a baking sheet.

7. Sprinkle half the cheese over the pastry, leaving a 5 cm/2 inch border around the edge, then spoon the caramelised onions over the cheese.

8. Fold the uncovered pastry edges over the edge of the filling to form a rim and brush the rim with beaten egg or milk.

9. Season to taste, sprinkle over the remaining Cheddar and bake for 20–25 minutes. Transfer to a large plate and serve immediately.

1

4

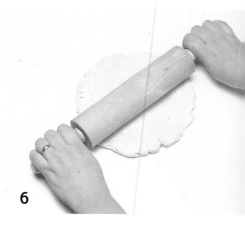

6

Olive & Feta Parcels

INGREDIENTS

Makes 30

1 small red pepper
1 small yellow pepper
125 g/4 oz assorted marinated green
   and black olives
125 g/4 oz feta cheese
2 tbsp pine nuts, lightly toasted
6 sheets filo pastry
3 tbsp olive oil
sour cream and chive dip, to serve

1 Preheat the oven to 180°C/350°F/Gas Mark 4. Preheat the grill, then line the grill rack with tinfoil.

2 Cut the peppers into quarters and remove the seeds. Place skin-side up on the foil-lined grill rack and cook under the preheated grill for 10 minutes, turning occasionally until the skins begin to blacken.

3 Place the peppers in a polythene bag and leave until cool enough to handle, then skin and thinly slice.

4 Chop the olives and cut the feta cheese into small cubes. Mix together the olives, feta, sliced peppers and pine nuts.

5 Cut 1 sheet of filo pastry in half then brush with a little of the oil. Place a spoonful of the olive and feta mix about one-third of the way up the pastry.

6 Fold over the pastry and wrap to form a square parcel encasing the filling completely.

7 Place this parcel in the centre of the second half of the pastry sheet. Brush the edges lightly with a little oil, bring up the corners to meet in the centre and twist them loosely to form a purse.

8 Brush with a little more oil and repeat with the remaining filo pastry and filling.

9 Place the parcels on a lightly oiled baking sheet and bake in the preheated oven for 10–15 minutes, or until crisp and golden brown. Serve with the dip.

HELPFUL HINT

Feta is generally made from goats' milk and has quite a salty taste. To make the cheese less salty simply soak it in milk, then drain before eating.

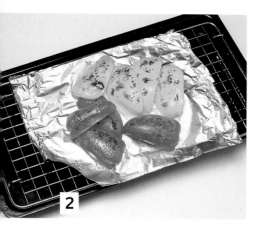

2

5

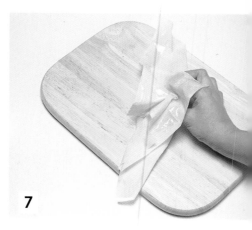

7

Fettuccine with Wild Mushrooms & Prosciutto

INGREDIENTS

Serves 6

15 g/½ oz dried porcini mushrooms
150 ml/¼ pint hot chicken stock
2 tbsp olive oil
1 small onion, peeled and
   finely chopped
2 garlic cloves, peeled and
   finely chopped
4 slices prosciutto, chopped or torn
225 g/8 oz mixed wild or cultivated
   mushrooms, wiped and sliced
   if necessary
450 g/1 lb fettuccine
3 tbsp crème fraîche
2 tbsp freshly chopped parsley
salt and freshly ground black pepper
freshly grated Parmesan cheese,
   to serve (optional)

FOOD FACT

Prosciutto is produced from pigs fed on whey. The ham is dry cured, then weighted to flatten it and give it a dense texture. The delicious flavour develops during the year it is allowed to mature.

1 Place the dried mushrooms in a small bowl and pour over the hot chicken stock. Leave to soak for 15–20 minutes, or until the mushrooms have softened.

2 Meanwhile, heat the olive oil in a large frying pan. Add the onion and cook for 5 minutes over a medium heat, or until softened. Add the garlic and cook for 1 minute, then add the prosciutto and cook for a further minute.

3 Drain the dried mushrooms, reserving the soaking liquid. Roughly chop and add to the frying pan together with the fresh mushrooms. Cook over a high heat for 5 minutes, stirring often, or until softened. Strain the mushroom soaking liquid into the pan.

4 Meanwhile, bring a large pan of lightly salted water to a rolling boil. Add the pasta and cook according to the packet instructions, or until 'al dente'.

5 Stir the crème fraîche and chopped parsley into the mushroom mixture and heat through gently. Season to taste with salt and pepper. Drain the pasta well, transfer to a large warmed serving dish and pour over the sauce. Serve immediately with grated Parmesan cheese.

1

2

3

Prunes Stuffed with Mussels

INGREDIENTS

Serves 6

3 tbsp port
1 tbsp clear honey
2 cloves garlic, crushed
24 large stoned prunes
24 live mussels
12 rashers smoked streaky bacon
salt and pepper

1 Mix together the port, honey and garlic then season. Put the prunes into a small bowl and pour over the port mixture. Cover and leave to marinate for at least 4 hours and preferably overnight.

2 Next day, clean the mussels by scrubbing or scraping the shells and pulling out any beards. Put the mussels in a large saucepan with just the water that clings to their shells. Cook, covered, over a high heat for 3–4 minutes until all the mussels have opened. Discard any mussels that remain closed.

3 Drain the mussels, reserving the cooking liquid. Allow to cool then remove the mussels from their shells.

4 Using the back of a knife, stretch the bacon rashers then cut in half widthways. Lift the prunes from their marinade, reserving any that remains.

5 Stuff each prune with a mussel then wrap with a piece of bacon. Secure with a cocktail stick. Repeat to make 24.

6 In a saucepan, simmer together the mussel cooking liquid and remaining marinade until reduced and syrupy. Brush the stuffed prunes with this mixture. Place under a preheated hot grill and cook for 3–4 minutes each side, turning regularly and brushing with the marinade, until the bacon is crisp and golden. Serve while still hot.

3

4

5

Stuffed Squid

INGREDIENTS

Serves 4

12 baby squid, cleaned

1 tsp salt

4 tbsp olive oil

1 small onion, finely chopped

1 garlic clove, finely chopped

40g /1¾ oz basmati rice

1 tbsp seedless raisins

1 tbsp pine nuts, toasted

1 tbsp fresh flat-leaf parsley, chopped

400 g/14 oz can chopped tomatoes

25 g/1 oz sun-dried tomatoes in oil,
  drained and finely chopped

120 ml/4 fl oz dry white wine

salt and pepper

crusty bread, to serve

1 Separate the tentacles from the body of the squid. Chop the tentacles and set aside. Rub the squid tubes inside and out with the salt and set aside while you prepare the stuffing.

2 Heat 1 tablespoon of the olive oil in a frying pan and add the onion and garlic. Cook for 4–5 minutes until softened and lightly browned. Add the chopped tentacles and fry for 2–3 minutes. Add the rice, raisins, pine nuts, parsley and seasoning. Remove from the heat.

3 Allow the rice mixture to cool slightly and spoon it into the squid tubes, about three quarters full to allow the rice to expand. You may need to open the squid tubes a little by making a small cut. Secure each filled squid with a cocktail stick.

4 Heat the remaining oil in a large flameproof casserole dish. Add the squid and fry for a few minutes on all sides until lightly browned. Add the tomatoes, sun-dried tomatoes, wine and seasoning. Bake in a preheated oven at 180°C/350°F/Gas Mark 4, for 45 minutes. Serve hot or cold with plenty of crusty bread.

TASTY TIP

If you have difficulty finding baby squid, larger ones work very well and the cooking time is the same. Use cleaned squid weighing 8 oz in total for the amount of stuffing in this recipe.

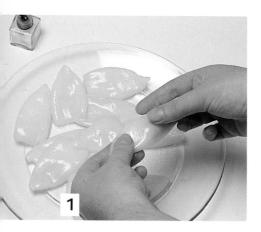

1

2

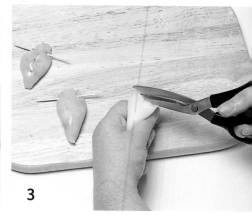

3

Dim Sum Pork Parcels

INGREDIENTS

Makes about 40

125 g/4 oz canned water chestnuts, drained and finely chopped

125 g/4 oz raw prawns, peeled, deveined and coarsely chopped

350 g/12 oz fresh pork mince

2 tbsp smoked bacon, finely chopped

1 tbsp light soy sauce, plus extra, to serve

1 tsp dark soy sauce

1 tbsp Chinese rice wine

2 tbsp fresh root ginger, peeled and finely chopped

3 spring onions, trimmed and finely chopped

2 tsp sesame oil

1 medium egg white, lightly beaten

salt and freshly ground black pepper

2 tsp sugar

40 wonton skins, thawed if frozen

toasted sesame seeds, to garnish

soy sauce, to serve

FOOD FACT

These steamed dumplings are known as shao mai in China, meaning 'cook and sell' and are a popular street food.

1 Place the water chestnuts, prawns, pork mince and bacon in a bowl and mix together. Add the soy sauces, Chinese rice wine, ginger, chopped spring onion, sesame oil and egg white. Season to taste with salt and pepper, sprinkle in the sugar and mix the filling thoroughly.

2 Place a spoonful of filling in the centre of a wonton skin. Bring the sides up and press around the filling to make a basket shape. Flatten the base of the skin, so the wonton stands solid. The top should be wide open, exposing the filling.

3 Place the parcels on a heatproof plate, on a wire rack inside a wok or on the base of a muslin-lined bamboo steamer. Place over a wok, half-filled with boiling water, cover, then steam the parcels for about 20 minutes. Do this in 2 batches. Transfer to a warmed serving plate, sprinkle with toasted sesame seeds, drizzle with soy sauce and serve immediately.

1

2

3

Vitello Tonnato

INGREDIENTS

Serves 6

1 boned and rolled piece of veal leg,
   about 900 g/2 lb boned weight
olive oil
salt and pepper

For the tuna mayonnaise:

150 g/5½ oz can tuna in olive oil
2 large eggs
3 tbsp lemon juice
olive oil

To garnish:

8 black olives, stoned and halved
1 tbsp capers in brine, rinsed and
   drained
fresh flat-leaf parsley, finely chopped
lemon wedges

1 Rub the veal all over with oil and pepper and place in a roasting tin. Cover the meat with a piece of foil if there is not any fat on it, then roast in a preheated oven at 230°C/450°F/Gas Mark 8 for 10 minutes. Lower the heat to 180°C/350°F/Gas Mark 4 and continue roasting for 1 hour for medium, or 1¼ hours for well-done. Set the veal aside and leave to cool completely, reserving any juices in the roasting tin.

2 Meanwhile, drain the tuna, reserving the oil. Blend the eggs in a food processor with 1 teaspoon of the lemon juice and a pinch of salt. Add enough olive oil to the tuna oil to make up to 300 ml/10 fl oz.

3 With the motor running, add the oil to the eggs, drop by drop, until a thin mayonnaise forms. Add the tuna and process until smooth. Blend in the lemon juice to taste. Adjust the seasoning.

4 Slice the cool meat very thinly. Add any juices to the reserved pan juices. Gradually pour the veal juices into the tuna mayonnaise, whisking until a thin, pouring consistency.

5 Layer the veal slices with the sauce on a platter, ending with a layer of sauce. Cover and leave to chill overnight. Garnish with olives, capers and a light sprinkling of parsley. Arrange lemon wedges around the edge and serve.

3

4

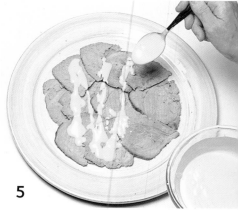

5

Noisettes of Salmon

INGREDIENTS

Serves 4

4 salmon steaks
50 g/13/4 oz butter, softened
1 garlic clove, crushed
2 tsp mustard seeds
2 tbsp fresh thyme, chopped
1 tbsp fresh parsley, chopped
2 tbsp vegetable oil
4 tomatoes, skinned, deseeded
  and chopped
salt and pepper

To serve:

new potatoes
green vegetables or salad

1 Carefully remove the central bone from the salmon steaks and cut them in half. Curl each piece around to form a medallion and tie with string. Blend together the butter, garlic, mustard seeds, thyme, parsley and seasoning and set aside.

2 Heat the oil in a ridged pan or frying pan and brown the salmon noisettes on both sides, in batches if necessary. Drain on paper towels and leave to cool.

3 Cut 4 pieces of baking parchment into 30 cm/12 inch squares. Place 2 salmon noisettes on top of each square and top with a little of the flavoured butter and tomato. Draw up the edges of the paper and fold together to enclose the fish. Place on a baking sheet.

4 Cook in a preheated oven at 200°C/400°F/Gas Mark 6 for 10–15 minutes or until the salmon is cooked through. Serve immediately while still warm with new potatoes and a green vegetable of your choice.

HELPFUL HINT

You can make cod steaks into noisettes in the same way. Cook them with butter flavoured with chives and basil.

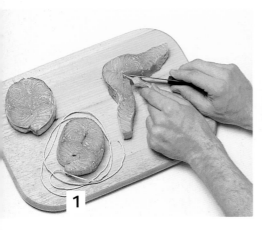
1

2

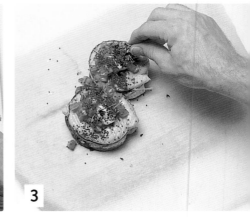
3

Stuffed Monkfish Tail

INGREDIENTS

Serves 4

750 g/1 lb 10 oz monkfish tail,
  skinned and trimmed
6 slices Parma ham
4 tbsp chopped mixed herbs such as
  parsley, chives, basil, sage
1 tsp finely grated lemon rind
2 tbsp olive oil
salt and pepper

To serve:

shredded stir-fried vegetables
new potatoes

1 Using a sharp knife, carefully cut down each side of the central bone of the monkfish to leave 2 fillets. Wash and dry the fillets.

2 Lay the Parma ham slices widthways on a clean work surface so that they overlap slightly. Lay the fish fillets lengthways on top of the ham so that the two cut sides face each other.

3 Mix together the chopped herbs and lemon rind. Season well. Pack this mixture on to the cut surface of one monkfish fillet. Press the 2 fillets together and wrap tightly with the Parma ham slices. Secure with string or cocktail sticks.

4 Heat the olive oil in a large ovenproof frying pan and place the fish in the pan, seam-side down first, and brown the wrapped monkfish tail all over.

5 Cook in a preheated oven, at 200°C/400°F/Gas Mark 6, for 25 minutes until golden and the fish is tender. Remove from the oven and allow to rest for 10 minutes before slicing thickly. Serve with shredded stir-fried vegetables and new potatoes.

TASTY TIP

It is possible to remove the central bone from a monkfish tail without separating the two fillets completely. This makes it easier to stuff, but takes some practice.

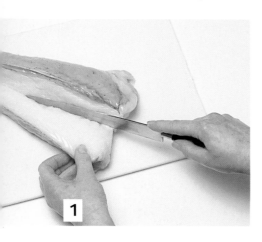
1

2

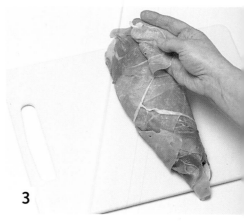
3

Parmesan & Garlic Lobster

INGREDIENTS

Serves 2

1 large cooked lobster
25 g/1 oz unsalted butter
4 garlic cloves, peeled and crushed
1 tbsp plain flour
300 ml/½ pint milk
125 g/4 oz Parmesan cheese, grated
sea salt and freshly ground
    black pepper
assorted salad leaves, to serve

FOOD FACT

Nowadays we consider lobster to be a luxury, however, up until the end of 19th century lobster was so plentiful that it was used as fish bait.

HELPFUL HINT

This impressive-looking dish makes a wonderful meal for two. Make the sauce in advance and cover the surface with a layer of clingfilm. Refrigerate until ready to serve.

1 Preheat oven to 180°C/350°F/Gas Mark 4, 10 minutes before cooking. Halve the lobster and crack the claws. Remove the gills, green sac behind the head and the black vein running down the body. Place the 2 lobster halves in a shallow ovenproof dish.

2 Melt the butter in a small saucepan and gently cook the garlic for 3 minutes, until softened. Add the flour and stir over a medium heat for 1 minute. Draw the saucepan off the heat then gradually stir in the milk, stirring until the sauce thickens. Return to the heat and cook for 2 minutes, stirring throughout until smooth and thickened. Stir in half the cheese and continue to cook for 1 minute, then season to taste with salt and pepper.

3 Pour the cheese sauce over the lobster halves and sprinkle with the remaining Parmesan cheese. Bake in the preheated oven for 20 minutes, or until heated through and the cheese sauce is golden brown. Serve with assorted salad leaves.

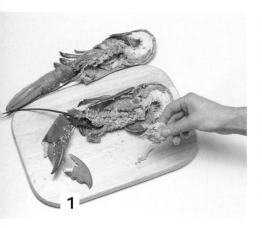

1

2

3

Seared Pancetta–wrapped Cod

INGREDIENTS

Serves 4

4 x 175 g/6 oz thick cod fillets
4 very thin slices of pancetta
3 tbsp capers in vinegar
1 tbsp of vegetable or sunflower oil
2 tbsp lemon juice
1 tbsp olive oil
freshly ground black pepper
1 tbsp freshly chopped parsley,
  to garnish

To serve:

freshly cooked vegetables
new potatoes

FOOD FACT

Pancetta is Italian-cured belly pork, which is often delicately smoked and sold either finely sliced or chopped roughly into small cubes. The slices of pancetta can be used to encase poultry and fish, whereas chopped pancetta is often used in sauces. To cook chopped pancetta, fry for 2–3 minutes and reserve. Use the oil to seal meat or to fry onions, then return the pancetta to the pan.

1 Wipe the cod fillets and wrap each one with the pancetta. Secure each fillet with a cocktail stick and reserve.

2 Drain the capers and soak in cold water for 10 minutes to remove any excess salt, then drain and reserve.

3 Heat the oil in a large frying pan and sear the wrapped pieces of cod fillet for about 3 minutes on each side, turning carefully with a fish slice so as not to break up the fish.

4 Lower the heat then continue to cook for 2–3 minutes or until the fish is cooked thoroughly.

5 Meanwhile, place the reserved capers, lemon juice and olive oil into a small saucepan. Grind over the black pepper.

6 Place the saucepan over a low heat and bring to a gentle simmer, stirring continuously for 2–3 minutes.

7 Once the fish is cooked, garnish with the parsley and serve with the warm caper dressing, freshly cooked vegetables and new potatoes.

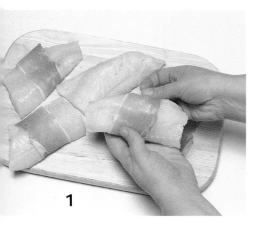

1

3

6

Mussels Linguine

INGREDIENTS

Serves 4

2 kg/4½ lb fresh mussels, washed
  and scrubbed
knob of butter
1 onion, peeled and finely chopped
300 ml/½ pint medium dry
  white wine

For the sauce:

1 tbsp sunflower oil
4 baby onions, peeled and quartered
2 garlic cloves, peeled and crushed
400 g can chopped tomatoes
large pinch of salt
225 g/8 oz dried linguine
  or tagliatelle
2 tbsp freshly chopped parsley

TASTY TIP

Serving mussels in their shells is a fantastic way to eat them. Every mussel is surrounded with the delicious sauce, adding flavour to every mouthful. Clams, which often have a sweeter flavour, could also be used in this recipe.

1 Soak the mussels in plenty of cold water. Leave in the refrigerator until required. When ready to use, scrub the mussel shells, removing any barnacles or beards. Discard any open mussels.

2 Melt the butter in a large pan. Add the mussels, onion and wine. Cover with a close-fitting lid and steam for 5–6 minutes, shaking the pan gently to ensure even cooking. Discard any mussels that have not opened, then strain and reserve the liquor.

3 To make the sauce, heat the oil in a medium-sized saucepan, and gently fry the quartered onion and garlic for 3–4 minutes until soft and transparent. Stir in the tomatoes and half the reserved mussel liquor. Bring to the boil and simmer for 7–10 minutes until the sauce begins to thicken.

4 Cook the pasta in boiling salted water for 7 minutes or or until 'al dente'. Drain the pasta, reserving 2 tablespoons of the cooking liquor, then return the pasta and liquor to the pan.

5 Remove the meat from half the mussel shells. Stir into the sauce along with the remaining mussels. Pour the hot sauce over the cooked pasta and toss gently. Garnish with the parsley and serve immediately.

1

2

5

Cod with Fennel & Cardamom

INGREDIENTS

Serves 4

1 garlic clove, peeled and crushed
finely grated rind of 1 lemon
1 tsp lemon juice
1 tbsp olive oil
1 fennel bulb
1 tbsp cardamom pods
salt and freshly ground black pepper
4 x 175 g/6 oz thick cod fillets

FOOD FACT

When buying fresh fish, look for fish that does not smell. Any ammonia-type smelling fish should be avoided. The flesh should be plump and firm-looking. The eyes should be bright, not sunken. If in doubt, choose frozen fish. This is cleaned and packed almost as soon as it is caught. It is often fresher and contains more nutrients than its fresh counterparts.

1 Preheat the oven to 190°C/375°F/Gas Mark 5. Place the garlic in a small bowl with the lemon rind, juice and olive oil and stir well.

2 Cover and leave to infuse for at least 30 minutes. Stir well before using.

3 Trim the fennel bulb, thinly slice and place in a bowl.

4 Place the cardamom pods in a pestle and mortar and lightly pound to crack the pods.

5 Alternatively, place in a polythene bag and pound gently with a rolling pin. Add the crushed cardamom to the fennel slices.

6 Season the fish with salt and pepper and place on to 4 separate 20.5 x 20.5 cm/8 x 8 inch parchment paper squares.

7 Spoon the fennel mixture over the fish and drizzle with the infused oil.

8 Place the parcels on a baking sheet and bake in the preheated oven for 8–10 minutes or until cooked. Serve immediately in the paper parcels.

1

4

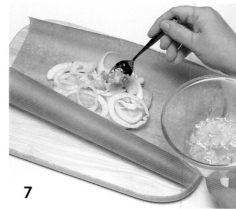

7

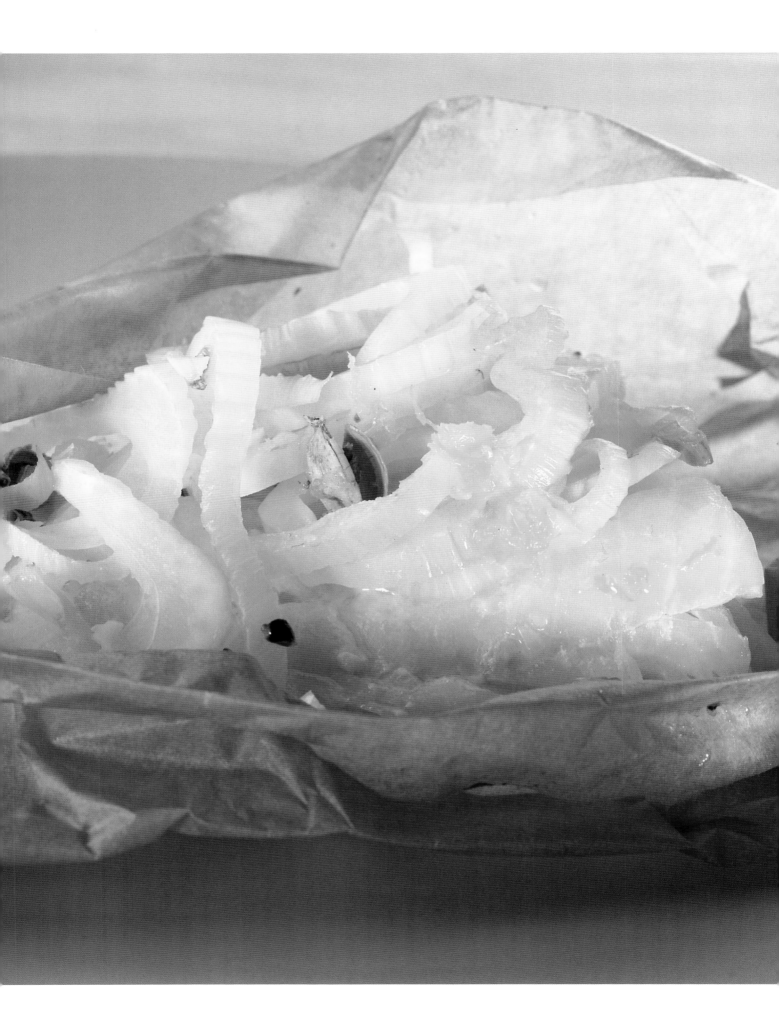

Seared Tuna with Pernod & Thyme

INGREDIENTS

Serves 4

4 tuna or swordfish steaks
salt and freshly ground
  black pepper
3 tbsp Pernod
1 tbsp olive oil
zest and juice of 1 lime
2 tsp fresh thyme leaves
4 sun-dried tomatoes

To serve:
freshly cooked mixed rice
tossed green salad

HELPFUL HINT

Tuna is now widely available all year round at fishmongers and in supermarkets. Tuna is an oily fish rich in Omega-3 fatty acids which help in the prevention of heart disease by lowering blood cholesterol levels. Tuna is usually sold in steaks, and the flesh should be dark red in colour.

1 Wipe the fish steaks with a damp cloth or dampened kitchen paper.

2 Season both sides of the fish to taste with salt and pepper, then place in a shallow bowl and reserve.

3 Mix together the Pernod, olive oil, lime zest and juice with the fresh thyme leaves.

4 Finely chop the sun-dried tomatoes and add to the Pernod mixture.

5 Pour the Pernod mixture over the fish and chill in the refrigerator for about 2 hours, spooning the marinade occasionally over the fish.

6 Heat a griddle or heavy-based frying pan. Drain the fish, reserving the marinade. Cook the fish for 3–4 minutes on each side for a steak that is still slightly pink in the middle. Or, if liked, cook the fish for 1–2 minutes longer on each side if you prefer your fish cooked through.

7 Place the remaining marinade in a small saucepan and bring to the boil. Pour the marinade over the fish and serve immediately, with the mixed rice and salad.

2

5

6

Steamed Monkfish with Chilli & Ginger

INGREDIENTS

Serves 4

700 g/1½ lb skinless monkfish tail
1–2 red chillies
4 cm/1½ inch piece fresh root ginger
1 tsp sesame oil
4 spring onions, trimmed and thinly
   sliced diagonally
2 tbsp soy sauce
2 tbsp Chinese rice wine or dry sherry
freshly steamed rice, to serve

To garnish:

sprigs of fresh coriander
lime wedges

1 Place the monkfish on a chopping board. Using a sharp knife, cut down each side of the central bone and remove. Cut the fish into 2.5cm/1 inch pieces and reserve.

2 Make a slit down the side of each chilli, remove and discard the seeds and the membrane, then slice thinly. Peel the ginger and either chop finely or grate.

3 Brush a large heatproof plate with the sesame oil and arrange the monkfish pieces in one layer on the plate. Sprinkle over the spring onions and pour over the soy sauce and Chinese rice wine or sherry.

4 Place a wire rack or inverted ramekin in a large wok. Pour in enough water to come about 2.5 cm/1 inch up the side of the wok and bring to the boil over a high heat.

5 Fold a long piece of tinfoil lengthways to about 5–7.5 cm/2–3 inches wide and lay it over the rack or ramekin. It must extend beyond the plate edge when it is placed in the wok.

6 Place the plate with the monkfish on the rack or ramekin and cover tightly. Steam over a medium-low heat for 5 minutes, or until the fish is tender and opaque. Using the tinfoil as a hammock, lift out the plate. Garnish with sprigs of coriander and lime wedges and serve immediately with steamed rice.

FOOD FACT

Chillies immediately transformed Chinese cooking when they were introduced to China about 100 years ago. They are used extensively in Szechuan and in Hunan.

2

3

6

Stir-fried Squid with Asparagus

INGREDIENTS

Serves 4

450 g/1 lb squid, cleaned and cut
　into 1 cm/½ inch rings
225 g/8 oz fresh asparagus, sliced
　diagonally into 6.5 cm/
　2½ inch pieces
2 tbsp groundnut oil
2 garlic cloves, peeled and
　thinly sliced
2.5 cm/1 inch piece fresh root ginger,
　peeled and thinly sliced
225 g/8 oz pak choi, trimmed
75 ml/3 fl oz chicken stock
2 tbsp soy sauce
2 tbsp oyster sauce
1 tbsp Chinese rice wine or dry sherry
2 tsp cornflour, blended with
　1 tbsp water
1 tbsp sesame oil
1 tbsp toasted sesame seeds
freshly cooked rice, to serve

TASTY TIP

Pak choi is a member of the
cabbage family. If available, use
baby pak choi for this recipe or
Shanghai pak choi, which is
slightly smaller and more
delicately flavoured.

1　Bring a medium saucepan of water to the boil over a high heat. Add the squid, return to the boil and cook for 30 seconds. Using a wide wok strainer or slotted spoon, transfer to a colander, drain and reserve.

2　Add the asparagus pieces to the boiling water and blanch for 2 minutes. Drain and reserve.

3　Heat a wok or large frying pan, add the groundnut oil and when hot, add the garlic and ginger and stir-fry for 30 seconds. Add the pak choi, stir-fry for 1–2 minutes, then pour in the stock and cook for 1 minute.

4　Blend the soy sauce, oyster sauce and Chinese rice wine or sherry in a bowl or jug, then pour into the wok.

5　Add the reserved squid and asparagus to the wok and stir-fry for 1 minute. Stir the blended cornflour into the wok. Stir-fry for 1 minute, or until the sauce thickens and all the ingredients are well coated.

6　Stir in the sesame oil, give a final stir and turn into a warmed serving dish. Sprinkle with the toasted sesame seeds and serve immediately with freshly cooked rice.

1

2

4

Ginger Lobster

INGREDIENTS

Serves 4

1 celery stalk, trimmed and
   finely chopped
1 onion, peeled and chopped
1 small leek, trimmed and chopped
10 black peppercorns
1 x 550 g/1¼ lb live lobster
25 g/1 oz butter
75 g/3 oz raw prawns, peeled and
   finely chopped
6 tbsp fish stock
50 g/2 oz fresh root ginger, peeled
   and cut into matchsticks
2 shallots, peeled and finely chopped
4 shiitake mushrooms, wiped and
   finely chopped
1 tsp green peppercorns, drained
   and crushed
2 tbsp oyster sauce
freshly ground black pepper
¼ tsp cornflour
sprigs of fresh coriander, to garnish
freshly cooked Thai rice and mixed
   shredded leek, celery, and red chilli,
   to serve

1 Place the celery, onion and leek in a large saucepan with the black peppercorns. Pour in 2 litres/3½ pints of hot water, bring to the boil and boil for 5 minutes, then immerse the lobster and boil for a further 8 minutes.

2 Remove the lobster. When cool enough to handle, sit it on its back. Using a sharp knife, halve the lobster neatly along its entire length. Remove and discard the intestinal vein from the tail, the stomach, (which lies near the head) and the inedible gills or dead man's fingers. Remove the meat from the shell and claws and cut into pieces.

3 Heat a wok or large frying pan, add the butter and when melted, add the raw prawns and fish stock. Stir-fry for 3 minutes or until the prawns change colour. Add the ginger, shallots, mushrooms, green peppercorns and oyster sauce. Season to taste with black pepper. Stir in the lobster. Stir-fry for 2–3 minutes.

4 Blend the cornflour with 1 teaspoon of water to form a thick paste, stir into the wok and cook, stirring, until the sauce thickens. Place the lobster on a warmed serving platter and tip the sauce over. Garnish and serve immediately.

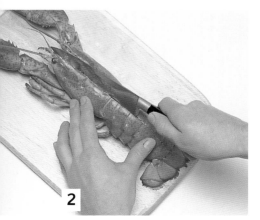
2

3

3

Smoked Haddock Tart

INGREDIENTS

Serves 6

For the shortcrust pastry:

150 g/5 oz plain flour

pinch of salt

25 g/1 oz lard or white vegetable fat, cut into small cubes

40 g/1½ oz butter or hard margarine, cut into small cubes

For the filling:

225 g/8 oz smoked haddock, skinned and cubed

2 large eggs, beaten

300 ml/½ pint double cream

1 tsp Dijon mustard

freshly ground black pepper

125 g/4 oz Gruyère cheese, grated

1 tbsp freshly snipped chives

To serve:

lemon wedges

tomato wedges

fresh green salad leaves

1 Preheat the oven to 190°C/375°F/Gas Mark 5. Sift the flour and salt into a large bowl. Add the fats and mix lightly. Using the fingertips rub into the flour until the mixture resembles breadcrumbs.

2 Sprinkle 1 tablespoon of cold water into the mixture and with a knife, start bringing the dough together. (It may be necessary to use the hands for the final stage.) If the dough does not form a ball instantly, add a little more water.

3 Put the pastry in a polythene bag and chill for at least 30 minutes.

4 On a lightly floured surface, roll out the pastry and use to line a 18 cm/7 inch lightly oiled quiche or flan tin. Prick the base all over with a fork and bake blind in the preheated oven for 15 minutes.

5 Carefully remove the pastry from the oven, brush with a little of the beaten egg.

6 Return to the oven for a further 5 minutes, then place the fish in the pastry case.

7 For the filling, beat together the eggs and cream. Add the mustard, black pepper and cheese and pour over the fish.

8 Sprinkle with the chives and bake for 35–40 minutes or until the filling is golden brown and set in the centre. Serve hot or cold with the lemon and tomato wedges and salad leaves.

2

5

7

Squid & Prawns with Saffron Rice

INGREDIENTS

Serves 4

2 tbsp groundnut oil

1 large onion, peeled and sliced

2 garlic cloves, peeled and chopped

450 g/1 lb tomatoes, skinned,
  deseeded and chopped

225 g/8 oz long-grain rice

1/4 tsp saffron strands

600 ml/1 pint fish stock

225 g/8 oz firm fish fillets, such as
  monkfish or cod

225 g/8 oz squid, cleaned

225 g/8 oz mussels with shells

75 g/3 oz frozen or shelled fresh peas

225 g/8 oz peeled prawns, thawed
  if frozen

salt and freshly ground black pepper

To garnish:

8 whole cooked prawns

lemon wedges

HELPFUL HINT

Skin tomatoes by making a cross on the top of each one, cover with boiling water, the leave for 2 minutes. Drain and peel.

1 Heat a large wok, add the oil and when hot, stir-fry the onion and garlic for 3 minutes. Add the tomatoes and continue to stir-fry for 1 minute before adding the rice, saffron and stock. Bring to the boil, reduce the heat, cover and simmer for 10 minutes, stirring occasionally.

2 Meanwhile, remove any skin from the fish fillets, rinse lightly and cut into small cubes. Rinse the squid, pat dry with absorbent kitchen paper, then cut into rings and reserve. Scrub the mussels, discarding any that stay open after being tapped on the work surface. Cover with cold water and reserve until required.

3 Add the peas to the wok together with the fish and return to a gentle simmer. Cover and simmer for 5–10 minutes, or until the rice is tender and most of the liquid has been absorbed.

4 Uncover and stir in the squid, the drained prepared mussels and the peeled prawns. Re-cover and simmer for 5 minutes, or until the mussels have opened. Discard any unopened ones. Season to taste with salt and pepper. Garnish with whole cooked prawns and lemon wedges, then serve immediately.

Prawn Skewers with Tomato Salsa

INGREDIENTS

Serves 4

32 large tiger prawns
olive oil, for brushing
sordalia or aïoli, to serve

For the marinade:

120 ml/4 fl oz extra-virgin olive oil
2 tbsp lemon juice
1 tsp red chilli, finely chopped
1 tsp balsamic vinegar
black pepper

For the tomato salsa:

2 large sun-ripened tomatoes,
  skinned, cored, deseeded
  and chopped
4 spring onions, white parts only,
  very finely chopped
1 red pepper, skinned, deseeded and
  chopped
1 orange or yellow pepper, skinned,
  deseeded and chopped
1 tbsp extra-virgin olive oil
2 tsp balsamic vinegar
4 sprigs fresh basil

1 To make the marinade, place all the ingredients in a non-metallic bowl and whisk together. Set aside.

2 To prepare the prawns, break off the heads. Peel off the shells, leaving the tails intact. Using a small knife, make a slit along the back and remove the thin black vein. Add the prawns to the marinade and stir until well coated. Cover and chill for 15 minutes.

3 Make the salsa. Put all the ingredients, except the basil, in a non-metallic bowl and toss together. Season to taste with salt and pepper.

4 Thread 4 prawns onto a metal skewer, bending each in half. Repeat with 7 more skewers. Brush with marinade.

5 Brush a grill rack with oil. Place the skewers on the rack, then position under a preheated hot grill, about 7.5 cm/3 inches from the heat and cook for 1 minute. Turn the skewers over, brush again and continue to cook for 1–1½ minutes until the prawns turn pink and opaque.

6 Tear the basil leaves and toss with the salsa. Arrange each skewer on a plate with some salsa and garnish with parsley. Serve with skordalia or aïoli dip.

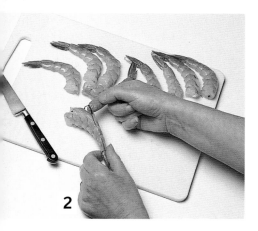

2

3

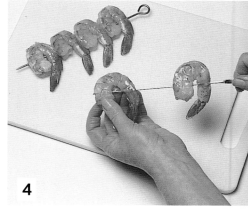

4

Rice with Smoked Salmon & Ginger

INGREDIENTS

Serves 4

225 g/8 oz basmati rice
600 ml/1 pint fish stock
1 bunch spring onions, trimmed
   and diagonally sliced
3 tbsp freshly chopped coriander
1 tsp grated fresh root ginger
200 g/7 oz sliced smoked salmon
2 tbsp soy sauce
1 tsp sesame oil
2 tsp lemon juice
4–6 slices pickled ginger
2 tsp sesame seeds
rocket leaves, to serve

FOOD FACT

Good smoked salmon should look moist and firm and have a peachy pink colour. If you buy it from a delicatessan counter, ask for it to be freshly sliced as any that has already been sliced may be dried out. Vacuum-packed salmon will keep for about 2 weeks in the refrigerator (check the use-by date), but once opened should be used within 3 days.

1 Place the rice in a sieve and rinse under cold water until the water runs clear. Drain, then place in a large saucepan with the stock and bring gently to the boil. Reduce to a simmer and cover with a tight-fitting lid. Cook for 10 minutes, then remove from the heat and leave, covered, for a further 10 minutes.

2 Stir the spring onions, coriander and fresh ginger into the cooked rice and mix well.

3 Spoon the rice into 4 tartlet tins, each measuring 10 cm/4 inches, and press down firmly with the back of a spoon to form cakes. Invert a tin onto an individual serving plate, then tap the base firmly and remove the tin. Repeat with the rest of the filled tins.

4 Top the rice with the salmon, folding if necessary, so the sides of the rice can still be seen in places. Mix together the soy sauce, sesame oil and lemon juice to make a dressing, then drizzle over the salmon. Top with the pickled ginger and a sprinkling of sesame seeds. Scatter the rocket leaves around the edge of the plates and serve immediately.

3

3

4

Salmon & Filo Parcels

INGREDIENTS

Serves 4

1 tbsp sunflower oil
1 bunch of spring onions, trimmed
   and finely chopped
1 tsp paprika
175 g/6 oz long-grain white rice
300 ml/½ pint fish stock
salt and freshly ground black pepper
450 g/1 lb salmon fillet, cubed
1 tbsp freshly chopped parsley
grated rind and juice of 1 lemon
150 g/5 oz rocket
150 g/5 oz spinach
12 sheets filo pastry
50 g/2 oz butter, melted

1. Preheat the oven to 200°C/400°F/Gas Mark 6. Heat the oil in a small frying pan and gently cook the spring onions for 2 minutes. Stir in the paprika and continue to cook for 1 minute, then remove from the heat and reserve.

2. Put the rice in a sieve and rinse under cold running water until the water runs clear; drain. Put the rice and stock in a saucepan, bring to the boil, then cover and simmer for 10 minutes, or until the liquid is absorbed and the rice is tender. Add the spring onion mixture and fork through. Season to taste with salt and pepper, then leave to cool.

3. In a non-metallic bowl, mix together the salmon, parsley, lemon rind and juice and salt and pepper. Reserve.

4. Blanch the rocket and spinach for 30 seconds in a large saucepan of boiling water, or until just wilted. Drain well in a colander and refresh in plenty of cold water, then squeeze out as much moisture as possible.

5. Brush 3 sheets of filo pastry with melted butter and lay them on top of one another. Take a quarter of the rice mixture and arrange it in an oblong in the centre of the pastry. On top of this place a quarter of the salmon followed by a quarter of the rocket and spinach.

6. Draw up the pastry around the filling and twist at the top to create a parcel. Repeat with the remaining pastry and filling until you have 4 parcels. Brush with the remaining butter.

7. Place the parcels on a lightly oiled baking tray and cook in the preheated oven for 20 minutes, or until golden brown and cooked. Serve immediately.

1

2

3

Fish Roulades with Rice & Spinach

INGREDIENTS

Serves 4

4 x 175 g/6 oz lemon sole, skinned
salt and freshly ground black pepper
1 tsp fennel seeds
75 g/3 oz long-grain rice, cooked
150 g/5 oz white crab meat, fresh
  or canned
125 g/4 oz baby spinach, washed
  and trimmed
5 tbsp dry white wine
5 tbsp half-fat crème fraîche
2 tbsp freshly chopped parsley, plus
  extra to garnish
asparagus spears, to serve

1 Wipe each fish fillet with either a clean damp cloth or kitchen paper. Place on a chopping board, skinned side up and season lightly with salt and black pepper.

2 Place the fennel seeds in a pestle and mortar and crush lightly. Transfer to a small bowl and stir in the cooked rice. Drain the crab meat thoroughly. Add to the rice mixture and mix lightly.

3 Lay 2–3 spinach leaves over each fillet and top with a quarter of the crab meat mixture. Roll up and secure with a cocktail stick if necessary. Place into a large pan and pour over the wine. Cover and cook on a medium heat for 5–7 minutes or until cooked.

4 Remove the fish from the cooking liquor, and transfer to a serving plate and keep warm. Stir the crème fraîche into the cooking liquor and season to taste. Heat for 3 minutes, then stir in the chopped parsley.

5 Spoon the sauce on to the base of a plate. Cut each roulade into slices and arrange on top of the sauce. Serve with freshly cooked asparagus spears.

FOOD FACT

Spinach is one of the healthiest, leafy green vegetables to be eaten. It also acts as an antioxidant and it is suggested that it can reduce risks of certain cancers. Why not use whole-grain rice to add nutritional value and to give the dish a nuttier taste?

2

3

4

Orange Roasted Whole Chicken

INGREDIENTS

Serves 6

1 small orange, thinly sliced
50 g/2 oz sugar
1.4 kg/3 lb oven-ready chicken
1 small bunch fresh coriander
1 small bunch fresh mint
2 tbsp olive oil
1 tsp Chinese five spice powder
1/2 tsp paprika
1 tsp fennel seeds, crushed
salt and freshly ground black pepper
sprigs of fresh coriander, to garnish
freshly cooked vegetables, to serve

TASTY TIP

To make oven-baked rice, soften a chopped onion in 1 tablespoon sunflower oil in an ovenproof casserole. Stir in 250 g/9 oz long-grain rice, then remove from the heat. Pour in 750 ml/1¼ pints chicken or vegetable stock, 1 star anise, ½ cinnamon stick, 1 bay leaf, salt and pepper. Cover and cook for 45 minutes or until tender. Fluff up with a fork and remove the spices.

1 Preheat the oven to 190°C/375°F/Gas Mark 5, 10 minutes before cooking. Place the orange slices in a small saucepan, cover with water, bring to the boil, then simmer for 2 minutes and drain. Place the sugar in a clean saucepan with 150 ml/¼ pint fresh water. Stir over a low heat until the sugar dissolves, then bring to the boil, add the drained orange slices and simmer for 10 minutes. Remove from the heat and leave in the syrup until cold.

2 Remove any excess fat from inside the chicken. Starting at the neck end, carefully loosen the skin of the chicken over the breast and legs without tearing. Push the orange slices under the loosened skin with the coriander and mint.

3 Mix together the olive oil, Chinese five spice powder, paprika and crushed fennel seeds and season to taste with salt and pepper. Brush the chicken skin generously with this mixture. Transfer to a wire rack set over a roasting tin and roast in the preheated oven for 1½ hours, or until the juices run clear when a skewer is inserted into the thickest part of the thigh. Remove from the oven and leave to rest for 10 minutes. Garnish with sprigs of fresh coriander and serve with freshly cooked vegetables.

1

2

3

Roast Chicken with Ginger & Lime

INGREDIENTS

Serves 4

3 cm/1 inch piece fresh ginger root, finely chopped

2 garlic cloves, finely chopped

1 small onion, finely chopped

1 lemon grass stalk, finely chopped

½ tsp salt

1 tsp black peppercorns

1.5 kg/3 lb 5 oz roasting chicken

1 tbsp coconut cream

2 tbsp lime juice

2 tbsp clear honey

1 tsp cornflour

2 tsp water

stir-fried vegetables, to serve

1 Put the ginger, garlic, onion, lemon grass, salt and peppercorns in a pestle and mortar and crush to form a smooth paste.

2 Cut the chicken in half lengthways, using poultry shears or strong kitchen scissors. Spread the paste all over the chicken, both inside and out, and spread it on to the flesh under the breast skin. Cover and chill overnight, or at least several hours.

3 In a small pan, heat the coconut cream, lime juice and honey together, stirring until smooth. Brush a little of the mixture evenly over the chicken.

4 Place the chicken halves on a tray over a roasting tin half-filled with boiling water. Roast in an oven preheated to 180°C/ 350°F/Gas Mark 4 for about 1 hour, or until the chicken is a rich golden brown, basting occasionally with the reserved lime and honey mixture.

5 When the chicken is cooked, boil the water from the roasting tin to reduce it to about 100 ml/3½ fl oz. Blend the cornflour and water and stir into the reduced liquid. Heat gently to the boil, then stir until slightly thickened and clear. Serve the chicken with the sauce and stir-fried vegetables.

1

2

5

Sauvignon Chicken & Mushroom Filo Pie

INGREDIENTS

Serves 4

1 onion, peeled and chopped

1 leek, trimmed and chopped

225 ml/8 fl oz chicken stock

3 x 175 g/6 oz chicken breasts

150 ml/¼ pint dry white wine

1 bay leaf

175 g/6 oz baby
   button mushrooms

2 tbsp plain flour

1 tbsp freshly chopped tarragon

salt and freshly ground black pepper

sprig of fresh parsley, to garnish

seasonal vegetables, to serve

For the topping:

75 g/3 oz (about 5 sheets)
   filo pastry

1 tbsp sunflower oil

1 tsp sesame seeds

1. Preheat the oven to 190°C/375°F/Gas Mark 5. Put the onion and leek in a heavy-based saucepan with 125 ml/4 fl oz of the stock.

2. Bring to the boil, cover and simmer for 5 minutes, then uncover and cook until all the stock has evaporated and the vegetables are tender.

3. Cut the chicken into bite-sized cubes. Add to the pan with the remaining stock, wine and bay leaf. Cover and gently simmer for 5 minutes. Add the mushrooms and simmer for a further 5 minutes.

4. Blend the flour with 3 tablespoons of cold water. Stir into the pan and cook, stirring all the time until the sauce has thickened.

5. Stir the tarragon into the sauce and season with salt and pepper.

6. Spoon the mixture into a 1.2 litre/2 pint pie dish, discarding the bay leaf.

7. Lightly brush a sheet of filo pastry with a little of the oil.

8. Crumple the pastry slightly. Arrange on top of the filling. Repeat with the remaining filo sheets and oil, then sprinkle the top of the pie with the sesame seeds.

9. Bake the pie on the middle shelf of the preheated oven for 20 minutes until the filo pastry topping is golden and crisp. Garnish with a sprig of parsley. Serve the pie immediately with the seasonal vegetables.

3

6

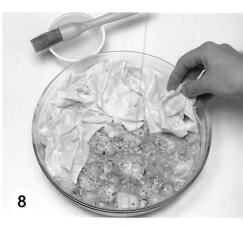

8

Guinea Fowl with Calvados & Apples

INGREDIENTS

Serves 4

4 guinea fowl supremes, each
  about 150 g/5 oz, skinned
1 tbsp plain flour
1 tbsp sunflower oil
1 onion, peeled and finely sliced
1 garlic clove, peeled and crushed
1 tsp freshly chopped thyme
150 ml/¼ pint dry cider

salt and freshly ground
  black pepper
3 tbsp Calvados brandy
sprigs of fresh thyme, to garnish

For the caramalised apples:

15 g/½ oz unsalted butter
2 red-skinned eating apples,
  quartered, cored and sliced
1 tsp caster sugar

1 Lightly dust the guinea fowl supremes with the flour.

2 Heat 2 teaspoons of the oil in a large non-stick frying pan and cook the supremes for 2–3 minutes on each side until browned. Remove from the pan and reserve.

3 Heat the remaining teaspoon of oil in the pan and add the onion and garlic. Cook over a medium heat for 10 minutes, stirring occasionally until soft and just beginning to colour.

4 Stir in the chopped thyme and cider. Return the guinea fowl to the pan, season with salt and pepper and bring to a very gentle simmer. Cover and cook over a low heat for 15–20 minutes or until the guinea fowl is tender.

5 Remove the guinea fowl and keep warm. Turn up the heat and boil the sauce until thickened and reduced by half.

6 Meanwhile, prepare the caramelised apples. Melt the butter in a small non-stick pan, add the apple slices in a single layer and sprinkle with the sugar. Cook until the apples are tender and beginning to caramelise, turning once.

7 Put the Calvados in a metal ladle or small saucepan and gently heat until warm. Carefully set alight with a match, let the flames die down, then stir into the sauce.

8 Serve the guinea fowl with the sauce spooned over and garnished with the caramelised apples and sprigs of fresh thyme.

2

4

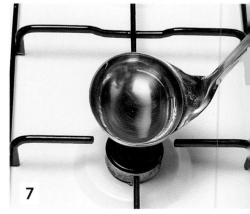
7

Chicken with Roasted Fennel & Citrus Rice

INGREDIENTS

Serves 4

2 tsp fennel seeds
1 tbsp freshly chopped oregano
1 garlic clove, peeled and crushed
salt and freshly ground black pepper
4 chicken quarters,
   about 175 g/6 oz each
½ lemon, finely sliced
1 fennel bulb, trimmed
2 tsp olive oil
4 plum tomatoes
25 g/1 oz stoned green olives

To garnish:
fennel fronds,
orange slices

For the citrus rice:
225 g/8 oz long-grain rice
finely grated rind and juice
   of ½ lemon
150 ml/¼ pint orange juice
450 ml/¾ pint boiling chicken
   or vegetable stock

1 Preheat the oven to 200°C/400°F/Gas Mark 6. Lightly crush the fennel seeds and mix with oregano, garlic, salt and pepper. Place between the skin and flesh of the chicken breasts, careful not to tear the skin. Arrange the lemon slices on top of the chicken.

2 Cut the fennel into 8 wedges. Place on baking tray with the chicken. Lightly brush the fennel with the oil. Cook the chicken and fennel on the top shelf of the preheated oven for 10 minutes.

3 Meanwhile, put the rice in a 2.3 litre/4 pint ovenproof dish. Stir in the lemon rind and juice, orange juice and stock. Cover with a lid and put on the middle shelf of the oven.

4 Reduce the oven temperature to 180°C/350°F/Gas Mark 4. Cook the chicken for a further 40 minutes, turning the fennel wedges and lemon slices once. Deseed and chop the tomatoes. Add to the tray and cook for 5–10 minutes. Remove from the oven.

5 When cooled slightly, remove the chicken skin and discard. Fluff the rice, scatter olives over the dish. Garnish with fennel fronds, orange slices and serve.

1

3

4

Turkey Escalopes with Apricot Chutney

INGREDIENTS

Serves 4

4 x 175–225 g/6–8 oz turkey steaks
1 tbsp plain flour
salt and freshly ground black pepper
1 tbsp olive oil
flat-leaf parsley sprigs, to garnish
orange wedges, to serve

For the apricot chutney:

125 g/4 oz no-need-to-soak dried
  apricots, chopped
1 red onion, peeled and
  finely chopped
1 tsp grated fresh root ginger
2 tbsp caster sugar
finely grated rind of ½ orange
125 ml/4 fl oz fresh orange juice
125 ml/4 fl oz ruby port
1 whole clove

1   Put a turkey steak onto a sheet of non-pvc clingfilm or non-stick baking parchment. Cover with a second sheet.

2   Using a rolling pin, gently pound the turkey until the meat is flattened to about 5 mm/¼ inch thick. Repeat to make 4 escalopes.

3   Mix the flour with the salt and pepper and use to lightly dust the turkey escalopes.

4   Put the turkey escalopes on a board or baking tray and cover with a piece of non-pvc clingfilm or non-stick baking parchment. Chill in the refrigerator until ready to cook.

5   For the apricot chutney, put the apricots, onion, ginger, sugar, orange rind, orange juice, port and clove into a saucepan.

6   Slowly bring to the boil and simmer, uncovered for 10 minutes, stirring occasionally, until thick and syrupy.

7   Remove the clove and stir in the chopped coriander.

8   Heat the oil in a pan and chargriddle the turkey escalopes, in two batches if necessary, for 3–4 minutes on each side until golden brown and tender.

9   Spoon the chutney onto four individual serving plates. Place a turkey escalope on top of each spoonful of chutney. Garnish with sprigs of parsley and serve immediately with orange wedges.

2

5

8

Duck with Berry Sauce

INGREDIENTS

Serves 4

4 x 175 g/6 oz boneless
   duck breasts
salt and freshly ground
   black pepper
1 tsp sunflower oil

For the sauce:

juice of 1 orange
1 bay leaf
3 tbsp redcurrant jelly
150 g/5 oz fresh or frozen
   mixed berries
2 tbsp dried cranberries or cherries
1/2 tsp soft light brown sugar
1 tbsp balsamic vinegar
1 tsp freshly chopped mint
sprigs of fresh mint, to garnish

To serve:

freshly cooked potatoes
freshly cooked green beans

HELPFUL HINT

Duck breasts are best served slightly pink in the middle. Whole ducks, however, should be thoroughly cooked.

1 Remove the skins from the duck breasts and season with a little salt and pepper. Brush a griddle pan with the oil, then heat on the stove until smoking hot.

2 Place the duck, skinned-side down in the pan. Cook over a medium-high heat for 5 minutes, or until well browned. Turn the duck and cook for 2 minutes. Lower the heat and cook for a further 5–8 minutes, or until cooked, but still slightly pink in the centre. Remove from the pan and keep warm.

3 While the duck is cooking, make the sauce. Put the orange juice, bay leaf, redcurrant jelly, fresh or frozen and dried berries and sugar in a small griddle pan. Add any juices left in the griddle pan to the small pan. Slowly bring to the boil, lower the heat and simmer uncovered for 4–5 minutes, until the fruit is soft.

4 Remove the bay leaf. Stir in the vinegar and chopped mint and season to taste with salt and pepper.

5 Slice the duck breasts on the diagonal and arrange on serving plates. Spoon over the berry sauce and garnish with sprigs of fresh mint. Serve immediately with the potatoes and green beans.

2

3

5

Sticky–glazed Spatchcocked Poussins

INGREDIENTS

Serves 4

2 poussins, each about 700 g/1½ lb
salt and freshly ground black pepper
4 kumquats, thinly sliced
assorted salad leaves, crusty bread
  or new potatoes, to serve

For the glaze:

zest of 1 small lemon, finely grated
1 tbsp lemon juice
1 tbsp dry sherry
2 tbsp clear honey
2 tbsp dark soy sauce
2 tbsp whole-grain mustard
1 tsp tomato purée
½ tsp Chinese five spice powder

1 Preheat the grill just before cooking. Place one of the poussins breast-side down on a board. Using poultry shears, cut down one side of the backbone. Cut down the other side of the backbone. Remove the bone.

2 Open out the poussin and press down hard on the breast bone with the heel of your hand to break it and to flatten the poussin.

3 Thread two skewers crosswise through the bird to keep it flat, ensuring that each skewer goes through a wing and out through the leg on the opposite side. Repeat with the other bird. Season both sides of the bird with salt and pepper.

4 To make the glaze, mix together the lemon zest and juice, sherry, honey, soy sauce, mustard, tomato purée and Chinese five spice powder and use to brush all over the poussins.

5 Place the poussins skin-side down on a grill rack and grill under a medium heat for 15 minutes, brushing halfway through with more glaze.

6 Turn the poussins over and grill for 10 minutes. Brush again with glaze and arrange the kumquat slices on top. Grill for a further 15 minutes until well-browned and cooked through. If they start to brown too quickly, turn down the grill a little.

7 Remove the skewers and cut each poussin in half along the breastbone. Serve immediately with the salad, crusty bread or new potatoes.

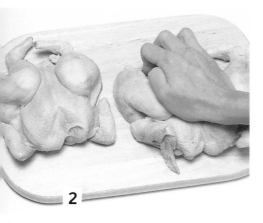
2

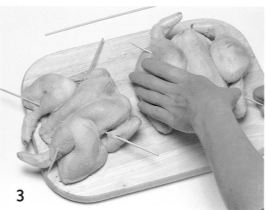
3

6

Chicken & White Wine Risotto

INGREDIENTS

Serves 4–6

2 tbsp oil

125 g/4 oz unsalted butter

2 shallots, peeled and finely chopped

300 g/11 oz Arborio rice

600 ml/1 pint dry white wine

750 ml/1¼ pints chicken
   stock, heated

350 g/12 oz skinless chicken breast
   fillets, thinly sliced

50 g/2 oz Parmesan cheese, grated

2 tbsp freshly chopped dill or parsley

salt and freshly ground black pepper

1   Heat the oil and half the butter in a large heavy-based saucepan over a medium-high heat. Add the shallots and cook for 2 minutes, or until softened, stirring frequently. Add the rice and cook for 2–3 minutes, stirring frequently, until the rice is translucent and well coated.

2   Pour in half the wine; it will bubble and steam rapidly. Cook, stirring constantly, until the liquid is absorbed. Add a ladleful of the hot stock and cook until the liquid is absorbed. Carefully stir in the chicken.

3   Continue adding the stock, about half a ladleful at a time, allowing each addition to be absorbed before adding the next; never allow the rice to cook dry. This process should take about 20 minutes. The risotto should have a creamy consistency and the rice should be tender, but firm to the bite.

4   Stir in the remaining wine and cook for 2–3 minutes. Remove from the heat and stir in the remaining butter with the Parmesan cheese and half the chopped herbs. Season to taste with salt and pepper. Spoon into warmed shallow bowls and sprinkle each with the remaining chopped herbs. Serve immediately.

HELPFUL HINT

Keep the stock to be added to the risotto at a low simmer in a separate saucepan, so that it is piping hot when added to the rice. This will ensure that the dish is kept at a constant heat during cooking, which is important to achieve a perfect creamy texture.

2

3

4

Potato-stuffed Roast Poussin

INGREDIENTS

Serves 4

4 oven-ready poussins
salt and freshly ground black pepper
1 lemon, cut into quarters
450 g/1 lb floury potatoes, peeled and
  cut into 4 cm/1½ inch pieces
1 tbsp freshly chopped thyme
  or rosemary
3–4 tbsp olive oil
4 garlic cloves, unpeeled and
  lightly smashed
8 slices streaky bacon or Parma ham
125 ml/4 fl oz white wine
2 spring onions, trimmed and
  thinly sliced
2 tbsp double cream or crème fraîche
lemon wedges, to garnish

1 Preheat the oven to 220°C/425°F/Gas Mark 7. Place a roasting tin in the oven to heat. Rinse the poussin cavities and pat dry with absorbent kitchen paper. Season the cavities with salt and pepper and a squeeze of lemon. Push a lemon quarter into each cavity.

2 Put the potatoes in a saucepan of lightly salted water and bring to the boil. Reduce the heat to low and simmer until just tender; do not overcook. Drain and cool slightly. Sprinkle the chopped herbs over the potatoes and drizzle with 2–3 tablespoons of the oil.

3 Spoon half the seasoned potatoes into the poussin cavities; do not pack too tightly. Rub each poussin with a little more oil and season with pepper. Carefully spoon 1 tablespoon of oil into the hot roasting tin and arrange the poussins in the tin. Spoon the remaining potatoes around the edge. Sprinkle over the garlic.

4 Roast the poussins in the preheated oven for 30 minutes, or until the skin is golden and beginning to crisp. Carefully lay the bacon slices over the breast of each poussin and continue to roast for 15–20 minutes until crisp and the poussins are cooked through.

5 Transfer the poussins and potatoes to a serving platter and cover loosely with tinfoil. Skim off the fat from the juices. Place the tin over a medium heat, add the wine and spring onions. Cook briefly, scraping the bits from the bottom of the tin. Whisk in the cream or crème fraîche and bubble for 1 minute, or until thickened. Garnish the poussins with lemon wedges, and serve with the creamy gravy.

2

3

4

Spicy Chicken with Open Ravioli & Tomato Sauce

INGREDIENTS

Serves 2–3

2 tbsp olive oil

1 onion, peeled and finely chopped

1 tsp ground cumin

1 tsp hot paprika pepper

1 tsp ground cinnamon

175 g/6 oz boneless and skinless
  chicken breasts, chopped

salt and freshly ground black pepper

1 tbsp smooth peanut butter

50 g/2 oz butter

1 shallot, peeled and finely chopped

2 garlic cloves, peeled and crushed

400 g can chopped tomatoes

125 g/4 oz fresh egg lasagne

2 tbsp freshly chopped coriander

1. Heat the olive oil in a frying pan, add the onion and cook gently for 2–3 minutes then add the cumin, paprika pepper and cinnamon and cook for a further 1 minute. Add the chicken, season to taste with salt and pepper and cook for 3–4 minutes, or until tender. Add the peanut butter and stir until well mixed and reserve.

2. Melt the butter in the frying pan, add the shallot and cook for 2 minutes. Add the tomatoes and garlic and season to taste. Simmer gently for 20 minutes, or until thickened, then keep the sauce warm.

3. Cut each sheet of lasagne into 6 squares. Bring a large pan of lightly salted water to a rolling boil. Add the lasagne squares and cook according to the packet instructions, about 3–4 minutes, or until 'al dente'. Drain the lasagne pieces thoroughly, reserve and keep warm.

4. Layer the pasta squares with the spicy filling on individual warmed plates. Pour over a little of the hot tomato sauce and sprinkle with chopped coriander. Serve immediately.

HELPFUL HINT

Because fresh pasta contains fresh eggs it should always be stored in the refrigerator, kept in its packet or wrapped in non-stick baking parchment, then in clingfilm.

1

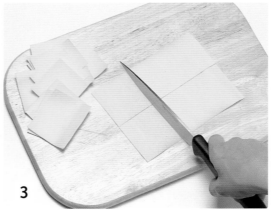

3

4

Garlic Mushrooms with Crispy Bacon & Chicken Liver Sauté

INGREDIENTS

Serves 4

4 large field mushrooms
40 g/1½ oz butter, melted and cooled
2 garlic cloves, peeled and crushed
1 tbsp sunflower oil
3 rashers smoked streaky bacon,
  derinded and chopped
4 shallots, peeled and thinly sliced
450 g/1 lb chicken livers, halved
2 tbsp marsala or sweet sherry
4 tbsp chicken or vegetable stock
6 tbsp double cream
2 tsp freshly chopped thyme
salt and freshly ground black pepper

FOOD FACT

Mushrooms are an extremely nutritious food, rich in vitamins and minerals, which help to boost our immune system. This recipe could be adapted to include shitake mushrooms which can significantly boost and protect the body's immune system and can go some way to boost the body's protection against cancer.

1 Remove the stalks from the mushrooms and roughly chop. Mix together 25 g/1 oz of the butter and garlic and brush over both sides of the mushroom caps. Place on the rack of a grill pan.

2 Heat a wok, add the oil and when hot, add the bacon and stir-fry for 2–3 minutes, or until crispy. Remove and reserve. Add the remaining butter to the wok and stir-fry the shallots and chopped mushroom stalks for 4–5 minutes until they are softened.

3 Add the chicken livers and cook for 3–4 minutes, or until well browned on the outside, but still pink and tender inside. Pour in the marsala or sherry and the stock. Simmer for 1 minute, then stir in the cream, thyme, salt and pepper and half the bacon. Cook for about 30 seconds to heat through.

4 While the livers are frying, cook the mushroom caps under a hot grill for 3–4 minutes each side, until tender.

5 Place the mushrooms on warmed serving plates, allowing 1 per person. Spoon the chicken livers over and around the mushrooms. Scatter with the remaining bacon and serve immediately.

Pork Loin Stuffed with Orange & Hazelnut Rice

INGREDIENTS

Serves 4

15 g/½ oz butter
1 shallot, peeled and finely chopped
50 g/2 oz long-grain brown rice
175 ml/6 fl oz vegetable stock
½ orange
25 g/1 oz ready-to-eat dried prunes, stoned and chopped
25 g/1 oz hazelnuts, roasted and roughly chopped
1 small egg, beaten
1 tbsp freshly chopped parsley
salt and freshly ground pepper
450 g/1 lb boneless pork tenderloin or fillet, trimmed

To serve:

steamed courgettes
carrots

1 Preheat the oven to 190°C/375°F/Gas Mark 5, 10 minutes before required. Heat the butter in a small saucepan, add the shallot and cook gently for 2–3 minutes until softened. Add the rice and stir well for 1 minute. Add the stock, stir well and bring to the boil. Cover tightly and simmer gently for 30 minutes until the rice is tender and all the liquid is absorbed. Leave to cool.

2 Grate the orange rind and reserve. Remove the white pith and chop the orange flesh finely. Mix together the orange rind and flesh, prunes, hazelnuts, cooled rice, egg and parsley. Season to taste with salt and pepper.

3 Cut the fillet in half, then using a sharp knife, split the pork fillet lengthways almost in two, forming a pocket, leaving it just attached. Open out the pork and put between 2 pieces of clingfilm. Flatten using a meat mallet until about half its original thickness. Spoon the filling into the pocket and close the fillet over. Tie along the length with kitchen string at regular intervals.

4 Put the pork fillet in a small roasting tray and cook in the top of the preheated oven for 25–30 minutes, or until the meat is just tender. Remove from the oven and allow to rest for 5 minutes. Slice into rounds and serve with steamed courgettes and carrots.

TASTY TIP

For an alternative stuffing try adding pine nuts and thyme.

2

3

3

Seared Calves' Liver with Onions & Mustard Mash

INGREDIENTS

Serves 2

2 tbsp olive oil

100 g/3½ oz butter

3 large onions, peeled and
finely sliced

pinch of sugar

salt and freshly ground black pepper

1 tbsp sprigs of fresh thyme

1 tbsp balsamic vinegar

700 g/1½ lb potatoes, peeled and cut
into chunks

6–8 tbsp milk

1 tbsp wholegrain mustard

3–4 fresh sage leaves

550 g/1¼ lb thinly sliced calves' liver

1 tsp lemon juice

HELPFUL HINT

Lambs' liver may be used for this recipe instead, but tone down the slightly stronger flavour by soaking in milk for up to 1 hour before cooking.

1. Preheat the oven to 150°C/300°F/Gas Mark 2. Heat half the oil and 25 g/1 oz of the butter in a flameproof casserole. When foaming, add the onions. Cover and cook over a low heat for 20 minutes until softened and beginning to collapse. Add the sugar and season with salt and pepper. Stir in the thyme. Cover the casserole and transfer to the preheated oven. Cook for a further 30–45 minutes until softened completely, but not browned. Remove from the oven and stir in the balsamic vinegar.

2. Meanwhile, boil the potatoes in boiling salted water for 15–18 minutes until tender. Drain well, then return to the pan. Place over a low heat to dry completely, remove from the heat and stir in 50 g/ 2 oz of the butter, the milk, mustard and salt and pepper to taste. Mash thoroughly until creamy and keep warm.

3. Heat a large frying pan and add the remaining butter and oil. When it is foaming, add the mustard and sage leaves and stir for a few seconds, then add the liver. Cook over a high heat for 1–2 minutes on each side. It should remain slightly pink: do not overcook. Remove the liver from the pan. Add the lemon juice to the pan and swirl around to deglaze.

4. To serve, place a large spoonful of the mashed potato on each plate. Top with some of the melting onions, the liver and finally the pan juices.

1

3

3

Fettuccine with Calves' Liver & Calvados

INGREDIENTS

Serves 4

450 g/1 lb calves' liver, trimmed and
 thinly sliced
50 g/2 oz plain flour
salt and freshly ground black pepper
1 tsp paprika
50 g/2 oz butter
11½ tbsp olive oil
2 tbsp Calvados
150 ml/¼ pint cider
150 ml/¼ pint whipping cream
350 g/12 oz fresh fettuccine
fresh thyme sprigs, to garnish

HELPFUL HINT

Calvados is made from apples and adds a fruity taste to this dish, although you can, of course, use ordinary brandy instead. Calves' liver is very tender, with a delicate flavour. It should be cooked over a high heat until the outside is brown and crusty and the centre still slightly pink.

1 Season the flour with the salt, black pepper and paprika, then toss the liver in the flour until well coated.

2 Melt half the butter and 1 tablespoon of the olive oil in a large frying pan and fry the liver in batches for 1 minute, or until just browned but still slightly pink inside. Remove using a slotted spoon and place in a warmed dish.

3 Add the remaining butter to the pan, stir in 1 tablespoon of the seasoned flour and cook for 1 minute. Pour in the Calvados and cider and cook over a high heat for 30 seconds. Stir the cream into the sauce and simmer for 1 minute to thicken slightly, then season to taste. Return the liver to the pan and heat through.

4 Bring a large pan of lightly salted water to a rolling boil. Add the fettuccine and cook according to the packet instructions, about 3–4 minutes, or until 'al dente'.

5 Drain the fettuccine thoroughly, return to the pan and toss in the remaining olive oil. Divide among 4 warmed plates and spoon the liver and sauce over the pasta. Garnish with thyme sprigs and serve immediately.

1

3

3

Red Wine Risotto with Lambs' Kidneys & Caramelised Shallots

INGREDIENTS

Serves 4

8 lambs' kidneys, halved and
  cores removed
150 ml/¼ pint milk
2 tbsp olive oil
50 g/2 oz butter
275 g/10 oz shallots, peeled and
  halved if large
1 onion, peeled and finely chopped
2 garlic cloves, peeled and
  finely chopped
350 g/12 oz Arborio rice
225 ml/8 fl oz red wine
1 litre/13¾ pints chicken or vegetable
  stock, heated
1 tbsp sprigs of fresh thyme
50 g/2 oz Parmesan cheese, grated
salt and freshly ground black pepper
fresh herbs, to garnish

1 Place the lambs' kidneys in a bowl and pour the milk over. Leave to soak for 15–20 minutes, then drain and pat dry on absorbent kitchen paper. Discard the milk.

2 Heat 1 tablespoon of the oil with 25 g/1 oz of the butter in a medium saucepan. Add the shallots, cover and cook for 10 minutes over a gentle heat. Remove the lid and cook for a further 10 minutes, or until tender and golden.

3 Meanwhile, heat the remaining oil with the remaining butter in a deep-sided frying pan. Add the onion and cook over a medium heat for 5–7 minutes until starting to brown. Add the garlic and cook briefly.

4 Stir in the rice and cook for a further minute until glossy and well coated in oil and butter. Add half the red wine and stir until absorbed. Add a ladleful or two of the stock and stir well until the stock is absorbed. Continue adding the stock, a ladleful at a time, and stirring well between additions, until all of the stock is added and the rice is just tender, but still firm. Remove from the heat.

5 Meanwhile, when the rice is nearly cooked, increase the heat under the shallots, add the thyme and kidneys. Cook for 3–4 minutes, then add the wine.

6 Bring to the boil, then simmer rapidly until the red wine is reduced and syrupy. Stir the cheese into the rice with the caramelised shallots and kidneys. Season to taste, garnish and serve.

1

4

5

Brandied Lamb Chops

INGREDIENTS

Serves 4

8 lamb loin chops

3 tbsp groundnut oil

5 cm/2 inch piece fresh root ginger,
  peeled and cut into matchsticks

2 garlic cloves, peeled and chopped

225 g/8 oz button mushrooms, wiped
  and halved if large

2 tbsp light soy sauce

2 tbsp dry sherry

1 tbsp brandy

1 tsp Chinese five spice powder

1 tsp soft brown sugar

200 ml/7 fl oz lamb or chicken stock

1 tsp sesame oil

To serve:
freshly cooked rice
freshly stir-fried vegetables

FOOD FACT
Lamb is not widely eaten in China, but Chinese Muslims (who are forbidden to eat pork) often cook it as do Mongols and people from Sinkiang.

1 Using a sharp knife, trim the lamb chops, discarding any sinew or fat. Heat a wok or large frying pan, add the oil and when hot, add the lamb chops and cook for 3 minutes on each side or until browned. Using a fish slice, transfer the lamb chops to a plate and keep warm.

2 Add the ginger, garlic and button mushrooms to the wok and stir-fry for 3 minutes or until the mushrooms have browned.

3 Return the lamb chops to the wok together with the soy sauce, sherry, brandy, five spice powder and sugar. Pour in the stock, bring to the boil, then reduce the heat slightly and simmer for 4–5 minutes, or until the lamb is tender, ensuring that the liquid does not evaporate completely. Add the sesame oil and heat for a further 30 seconds. Turn into a warmed serving dish and serve immediately with freshly cooked rice and stir-fried vegetables.

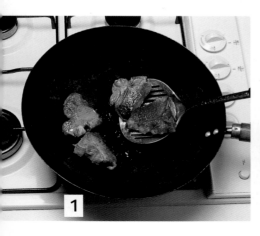

Beef & Red Wine Pie

INGREDIENTS

Serves 4

1 quantity quick flaky pastry
  (see page 66), chilled
700 g/1½ lb stewing
  beef, cubed
4 tbsp seasoned plain flour
2 tbsp sunflower oil
2 onions, peeled and chopped
2 garlic cloves, peeled and crushed
1 tbsp freshly chopped thyme
300 ml/½ pint red wine
150 ml/¼ pint beef stock
1–2 tsp Worcestershire sauce
2 tbsp tomato ketchup
2 bay leaves
a knob of butter
225 g/8 oz button mushrooms
beaten egg or milk, to glaze
sprig of parsley, to garnish

HELPFUL HINT

Shortcrust or puff pastry could also be used to top the pie in this recipe. It is important though, whichever pastry is used, to brush the pie with beaten egg or milk before baking, as this will result in an appetising golden crust.

1. Preheat the oven to 200°C/400°F/Gas Mark 6. Toss the beef cubes in the seasoned flour.

2. Heat the oil in a large heavy-based frying pan. Fry the beef in batches for about 5 minutes until golden brown.

3. Return all of the beef to the pan and add the onions, garlic and thyme. Fry for about 10 minutes, stirring occasionally. If the beef begins to stick, add a little water.

4. Add the red wine and stock and bring to the boil. Stir in the Worcestershire sauce, tomato ketchup and bay leaves.

5. Cover and simmer on a very low heat for about 1 hour or until the beef is tender.

6. Heat the butter and gently sauté the mushrooms until golden brown. Add to the stew. Simmer uncovered for a further 15 minutes. Remove the bay leaves. Spoon the beef into a 1.1 litre/2 pint pie dish and reserve.

7. Roll out the pastry on a lightly floured surface. Cut out the lid to 5 mm/¼ inch wider than the dish. Brush the rim with the beaten egg and lay the pastry lid on top. Press to seal, then knock the edges with the back of the knife.

8. Cut a slit in the lid and brush with the beaten egg or milk to glaze. Bake in the preheated oven for 30 minutes, or until golden brown. Garnish with the sprig of parsley and serve immediately.

2

4

8

Lamb Skewers on Rosemary

INGREDIENTS

Serves 4

500 g/1 lb 2 oz boneless leg of lamb
4 long, thick branches fresh rosemary
1 or 2 red peppers, depending
  on the size
12 large garlic cloves, peeled
olive oil
Spiced Pilau with Saffron, to serve

For the marinade:

2 tbsp olive oil
2 tbsp dry white wine
$\frac{1}{2}$ tsp ground cumin
1 sprig fresh oregano, chopped

1 At least 4 hours before cooking, cut the lamb into 5 cm/2 inch cubes. Mix all the marinade ingredients together in a bowl. Add the lamb cubes, stir well to coat and leave to marinate for at least 4 hours, or up to 12.

2 An hour before cooking, put the rosemary in a bowl of cold water and leave to soak.

3 Slice the tops off the peppers, cut them in half, quarter and remove the cores and seeds. Cut the halves into 5 cm/2 inch pieces.

4 Bring a small saucepan of water to the boil, blanch the pepper pieces and garlic cloves for 1 minute. Drain and refresh under cold water. Pat dry and set aside.

5 Remove the rosemary from the water and pat dry. To make the skewers, remove the rosemary needles from about the first 4 cm/ $1\frac{3}{4}$ inches of the branches so you have a 'handle' to turn them over with while grilling.

6 Thread alternate pieces of lamb, garlic and red pepper pieces on to the 4 rosemary skewers: the meat should be tender enough to push the sprig through it, but, if not, use a metal skewer to poke a hole in the centre of each cube.

7 Lightly oil the grill rack. Place the skewers on the rack about 12.5 cm/5 inches under a preheated hot grill and grill for 10–12 minutes, brushing with any leftover marinade or olive oil and turning, until the meat is cooked. Serve with the pilau.

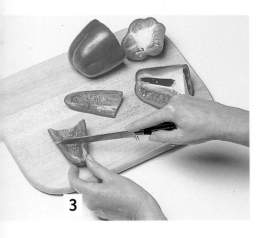

3

5

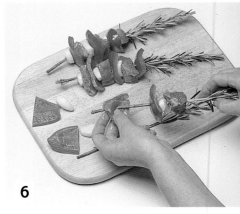

6

Leg of Lamb with Minted Rice

INGREDIENTS

Serves 4

1 tbsp olive oil

1 medium onion, peeled and
  finely chopped

1 garlic clove, peeled and crushed

1 celery stalk, trimmed and chopped

1 large mild red chilli, deseeded
  and chopped

75 g/3 oz long-grain rice

150 ml/¼ pint lamb or chicken stock

2 tbsp freshly chopped mint

salt and freshly ground black pepper

1.4 kg/3 lb boned leg of lamb

freshly cooked vegetables, to serve

HELPFUL HINT

Use a meat thermometer to check whether the joint is cooked, or push a fine skewer into the thickest part: for rare meat the juices will be slightly red, for medium they will be pink and when well-done, the juices will run clear.

1 Preheat the oven to 190°C/375°F/Gas Mark 5, 10 minutes before roasting. Heat the oil in a frying pan and gently cook the onion for 5 minutes. Stir in the garlic, celery and chilli and continue to cook for 3–4 minutes.

2 Place the rice and the stock in a large saucepan and cook, covered, for 10–12 minutes or until the rice is tender and all the liquid is absorbed. Stir in the onion and celery mixture, then leave to cool. Once the rice mixture is cold, stir in the chopped mint and season to taste with salt and pepper.

3 Place the boned lamb skin-side down and spoon the rice mixture along the centre of the meat. Roll up the meat to enclose the stuffing and tie securely with string. Weigh the lamb after stuffing and allow it to come to room temperature before roasting. For medium-cooked lamb, allow 25 minutes per 450 g/ 1 lb plus 25 minutes; for well-done, allow 30 minutes per 450 g/1 lb plus 30 minutes. Place in a roasting tin and roast in the preheated oven until cooked to personal preference. Remove from the oven and leave to rest in a warm place for 20 minutes, before carving. Serve with a selection of cooked vegetables.

1

2

3

Potato & Goats' Cheese Tart

INGREDIENTS

Serves 6

275 g/10 oz prepared shortcrust
  pastry, thawed if frozen
550 g/1¼ lb small waxy potatoes
salt and freshly ground black pepper
beaten egg, for brushing
2 tbsp sun-dried tomato paste
¼ tsp chilli powder, or to taste
1 large egg
150 ml/¼ pint soured cream
150 ml/¼ pint milk
2 tbsp freshly snipped chives
300 g/11 oz goats' cheese, sliced
salad and warm crusty bread,
  to serve

HELPFUL HINT

Using ready-made shortcrust pastry is a good way to save time, but always remove it from the refrigerator 10–15 minutes before rolling out, otherwise it may be difficult to handle. Brushing the base with egg helps seal the pastry and keeps it crisp when filled.

1 Preheat the oven to 190°C/375°F/Gas Mark 5, about 10 minutes before cooking. Roll the pastry out on a lightly floured surface and use to line a 23 cm/9 inch fluted flan tin. Chill in the refrigerator for 30 minutes.

2 Scrub the potatoes, place in a large saucepan of lightly salted water and bring to the boil. Simmer for 10–15 minutes, or until the potatoes are tender. Drain and reserve until cool enough to handle.

3 Line the pastry case with greaseproof paper and baking beans or crumpled tinfoil and bake blind in the preheated oven for 15 minutes. Remove from the oven and discard the paper and beans or tinfoil. Brush the base with a little beaten egg, then return to the oven and cook for a further 5 minutes. Remove from the oven.

4 Cut the potatoes into 1 cm/ ½ inch thick slices and reserve. Spread the sun-dried tomato paste over the base of pastry case, sprinkle with the chilli powder, then arrange the potato slices on top in a decorative pattern.

5 Beat together the egg, soured cream, milk and chives, then season to taste with salt and pepper. Pour over the potatoes. Arrange the goats' cheese on top of the potatoes. Bake in the preheated oven for 30 minutes until golden brown and set. Serve immediately with salad and warm bread.

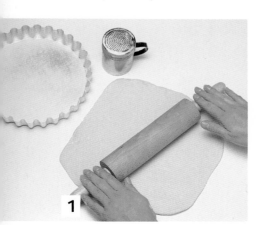

1

3

4

Wild Mushroom Risotto

INGREDIENTS

Serves 6

60 g/2 oz dried porcini or morel
 mushrooms
about 500 g/1 lb 2 oz mixed fresh
 wild mushrooms, such as porcini,
 girolles, horse mushrooms and
 chanterelles, cleaned and halved if
 large
4 tbsp olive oil
3–4 garlic cloves, finely chopped
60 g/2 oz unsalted butter
1 onion, finely chopped
350 g/12 oz arborio or carnaroli rice
50 ml/2 fl oz dry white vermouth
1.2 litres/2 pints chicken
 stock, simmering
115 g/4 oz freshly grated
 Parmesan cheese
4 tbsp fresh flat-leaf parsley, chopped
salt and pepper

1 Cover the dried mushrooms with boiling water. Leave to soak for 30 minutes, then carefully lift out and pat dry. Strain the soaking liquid through a sieve lined with a paper towel, and set aside.

2 Trim the wild mushrooms and gently brush clean.

3 Heat 3 tablespoons of the oil in a large frying pan until hot. Add the fresh mushrooms, and stir-fry for 1–2 minutes. Add the garlic and the soaked mushrooms and cook for 2 minutes, stirring frequently. Scrape on to a plate and set aside.

4 Heat the remaining oil and half the butter in a large heavy based saucepan. Add the onion and cook for about 2 minutes until softened. Add the rice and cook, stirring frequently, for about 2 minutes until translucent and well coated.

5 Add the vermouth to the rice. When almost absorbed, add a ladleful (about 225 ml/8 fl oz) of the simmering stock. Cook, stirring constantly, until the liquid is absorbed.

6 Continue adding the stock, about half a ladleful at a time, allowing each addition to be absorbed before adding the next. This should take 20–25 minutes. The risotto should have a creamy consistency and the rice should be tender, but firm to the bite.

7 Add half the dried mushroom soaking liquid to the risotto and stir in the mushrooms. Season with salt and pepper, and add more mushroom liquid if necessary. Remove from the heat; stir in the remaining butter, Parmesan and parsley. Serve immediately.

2

3

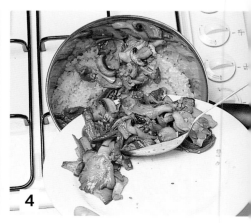

4

Vegetables Braised in Olive Oil & Lemon

INGREDIENTS

Serves 4

small strip of pared rind and
  juice of ½ lemon
4 tbsp olive oil
1 bay leaf
large sprig of thyme
150 ml/¼ pint water
4 spring onions, trimmed and
  finely chopped
175 g/6 oz baby button mushrooms
175 g/6 oz broccoli, cut into
  small florets
175 g/6 oz cauliflower, cut into
  small florets
1 medium courgette, sliced on
  the diagonal
2 tbsp freshly snipped chives
salt and freshly ground black pepper
lemon zest, to garnish

TASTY TIP

Serve these vegetables as an accompaniment to roasted or grilled chicken, fish or turkey. Alternatively, toast some crusty bread, rub with a garlic clove and drizzle with a little olive oil and top with a spoonful of vegetables.

1 Put the pared lemon rind and juice into a large saucepan. Add the olive oil, bay leaf, thyme and the water. Bring to the boil. Add the spring onions and mushrooms. Top with the broccoli and cauliflower, trying to add them so that the stalks are submerged in the water and the tops are just above it. Cover and simmer for 3 minutes.

2 Scatter the courgettes on top, so that they are steamed rather than boiled. Cook, covered, for a further 3–4 minutes, until all the vegetables are tender. Using a slotted spoon, transfer the vegetables from the liquid into a warmed serving dish. Increase the heat and boil rapidly for 3–4 minutes, or until the liquid is reduced to about 8 tablespoons. Remove the lemon rind, bay leaf and thyme sprig and discard.

3 Stir the chives into the reduced liquid, season to taste with salt and pepper and pour over the vegetables. Sprinkle with lemon zest and serve immediately.

Spinach Dumplings with Rich Tomato Sauce

INGREDIENTS

Serves 4

For the sauce:

2 tbsp olive oil

1 onion, peeled and chopped

1 garlic clove, peeled and crushed

1 red chilli, deseeded and chopped

150 ml/¼ pint dry white wine

400 g can chopped tomatoes

pared strip of lemon rind

For the dumplings:

450 g/1 lb fresh spinach

50 g/2 oz ricotta cheese

25 g/1 oz fresh white breadcrumbs

25 g/1 oz Parmesan cheese, grated

1 medium egg yolk

¼ tsp freshly grated nutmeg

salt and freshly ground black pepper

5 tbsp plain flour

2 tbsp olive oil, for frying

fresh basil leaves, to garnish

freshly cooked tagliatelle, to serve

1 To make the tomato sauce, heat the olive oil in a large saucepan and fry the onion gently for 5 minutes. Add the garlic and chilli and cook for a further 5 minutes, until softened.

2 Stir in the wine, chopped tomatoes and lemon rind. Bring to the boil, cover and simmer for 20 minutes, then uncover and simmer for 15 minutes, or until the sauce has thickened. Remove the lemon rind and season to taste with salt and pepper.

3 To make the spinach dumplings, wash the spinach thoroughly and remove any tough stalks. Cover and cook in a large saucepan over a low heat with just the water clinging to the leaves. Drain, then squeeze out all the excess water. Finely chop and put in a large bowl.

4 Add the ricotta, breadcrumbs, Parmesan cheese and egg yolk to the spinach. Season with nutmeg and salt and pepper. Mix together and shape into 20 walnut-sized balls.

5 Toss the spinach balls in the flour. Heat the olive oil in a large non-stick frying pan and fry the balls gently for 5–6 minutes, carefully turning occasionally. Garnish with fresh basil leaves and serve immediately with the tomato sauce and tagliatelle.

2

4

5

Hot Grilled Chicory & Pears

INGREDIENTS

Serves 4

50 g/2 oz unblanched almonds,
    roughly chopped
4 small heads of chicory
2 tbsp olive oil
1 tbsp walnut oil
2 firm ripe dessert pears
2 tsp lemon juice
1 tsp freshly chopped oregano
salt and freshly ground black pepper
freshly chopped oregano, to garnish
warmed ciabatta bread, to serve

1 Preheat grill. Spread the chopped almonds in a single layer on the grill pan. Cook under a hot grill for about 3 minutes, moving the almonds around occasionally, until lightly browned. Reserve.

2 Halve the chicory lengthways and cut out the cores. Mix together the olive and walnut oils. Brush about 2 tablespoons all over the chicory.

3 Put the chicory in a grill pan, cut-side up and cook under a hot grill for 2–3 minutes, or until beginning to char. Turn and cook for a further 1–2 minutes, then turn again.

4 Peel, core and thickly slice the pears. Brush with 1 tablespoon of the oils, then place the pears on top of the chicory. Grill for a further 3–4 minutes, or until both the chicory and pears are soft.

5 Transfer the chicory and pears to 4 warmed serving plates. Whisk together the remaining oil, lemon juice and oregano and season to taste with salt and pepper.

6 Drizzle the dressing over the chicory and pears and scatter with the toasted almonds. Garnish with fresh oregano and serve with ciabatta bread.

HELPFUL HINT

If preparing the pears ahead of time for this recipe, dip or brush them with some lemon juice to ensure that they do not discolour before cooking.

1

2

4

Roasted Butternut Squash

INGREDIENTS

Serves 4

2 small butternut squash
4 garlic cloves, peeled
  and crushed
1 tbsp olive oil
salt and freshly ground black pepper
1 tbsp walnut oil
4 medium-sized leeks, trimmed,
  cleaned and thinly sliced
1 tbsp black mustard seeds
300 g can cannellini beans, drained
  and rinsed
125 g/4 oz fine French beans, halved
150 ml/¼ pint vegetable stock
50 g/2 oz rocket
2 tbsp freshly snipped chives
fresh chives, to garnish

To serve:
4 tbsp low-fat fromage frais
mixed salad

1 Preheat the oven to 200°C/400°F/Gas Mark 6. Cut the butternut squash in half lengthways and scoop out all of the seeds.

2 Score the squash in a diamond pattern with a sharp knife. Mix the garlic with the olive oil and brush over the cut surfaces of the squash. Season well with salt and pepper. Put on a baking sheet and roast for 40 minutes until tender.

3 Heat the walnut oil in a saucepan and fry the leeks and mustard seeds for 5 minutes.

4 Add the drained cannellini beans, French beans and vegetable stock. Bring to the boil and simmer gently for 5 minutes until the French beans are tender.

5 Remove from the heat and stir in the rocket and chives. Season well. Remove the squash from the oven and allow to cool for 5 minutes. Spoon in the bean mixture. Garnish with a few snipped chives and serve immediately with the fromage frais and a mixed salad.

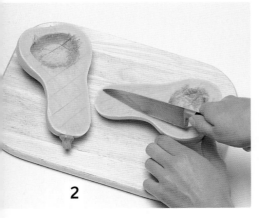
2

3

5

Peperonata

INGREDIENTS

Serves 6

2 red peppers

2 yellow peppers

450 g/1 lb waxy potatoes

1 large onion

2 tbsp good quality virgin olive oil

700 g/1½ lb tomatoes, peeled,
  deseeded and chopped

2 small courgettes

50 g/2 oz pitted black
  olives, quartered

small handful basil leaves

salt and freshly ground black pepper

crusty bread, to serve

FOOD FACT

This dish is delicious served with Parmesan melba toasts. To make simply remove the crusts from 4 slices of thin white bread. Lightly toast and allow to cool before splitting each piece in half by slicing horizontally. Cut diagonally into triangles, place under a hot grill and toast each side for a few minutes until golden and curling at the edges. Sprinkle with finely grated fresh Parmesan cheese and melt under the grill.

1 Prepare the peppers by halving them lengthways and removing the stems, seeds, and membranes.

2 Cut the peppers lengthways into strips about 1 cm/½ inch wide. Peel the potatoes and cut into rough dice, about 2.5–3 cm/1–1¼ inch across. Cut the onion lengthways into 8 wedges.

3 Heat the olive oil in a large saucepan over a medium heat.

4 Add the onion and cook for about 5 minutes, or until starting to brown.

5 Add the peppers, potatoes, tomatoes, courgettes, black olives and about 4 torn basil leaves. Season to taste with salt and pepper.

6 Stir the mixture, cover and cook over a very low heat for about 40 minutes, or until the vegetables are tender but still hold their shape. Garnish with the remaining basil. Transfer to a serving bowl and serve immediately, with chunks of crusty bread.

1

4

5

Marinated Vegetable Kebabs

INGREDIENTS

Serves 4

2 small courgettes, cut into
  2 cm/³/₄ inch pieces
¹/₂ green pepper, deseeded and cut
  into 2.5 cm/1 inch pieces
¹/₂ red pepper, deseeded and cut into
  2.5 cm /1 inch pieces
¹/₂ yellow pepper, deseeded and cut
  into 2.5 cm/1 inch pieces
8 baby onions, peeled
8 button mushrooms
8 cherry tomatoes
freshly chopped parsley,
  to garnish
freshly cooked couscous,
  to serve

For the marinade:

1 tbsp light olive oil
4 tbsp dry sherry
2 tbsp light soy sauce
1 red chilli, deseeded and
  finely chopped
2 garlic cloves, peeled and crushed
2.5 cm/1 inch piece root ginger,
  peeled and finely grated

1   Place the courgettes, peppers and baby onions in a pan of just boiled water. Bring back to the boil and simmer for about 30 seconds.

2   Drain and rinse the cooked vegetables in cold water and dry on absorbent kitchen paper.

3   Thread the cooked vegetables and the mushrooms and tomatoes alternately on to skewers and place in a large shallow dish.

4   Make the marinade by whisking all the ingredients together until thoroughly blended. Pour the marinade evenly over the kebabs, then chill in the refrigerator for at least 1 hour. Spoon the marinade over the kebabs occasionally during this time.

5   Place the kebabs in a hot griddle pan or on a hot barbecue and cook gently for 10–12 minutes. Turn the kebabs frequently and brush with the marinade when needed. When the vegetables are tender, sprinkle over the chopped parsley and serve immediately with couscous.

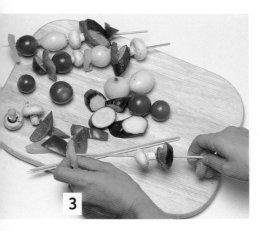
3

4

5

Stuffed Onions with Pine Nuts

INGREDIENTS

Serves 4

4 medium onions, peeled

2 garlic cloves, peeled
   and crushed

2 tbsp fresh brown breadcrumbs

2 tbsp white breadcrumbs

25 g/1 oz sultanas

25 g/1 oz pine nuts

50 g/2 oz low-fat hard cheese such
   as Edam, grated

2 tbsp freshly chopped parsley

1 medium egg, beaten

salt and freshly ground
   black pepper

salad leaves, to serve

1 Preheat the oven to 200°C/400°F/Gas Mark 6. Bring a pan of water to the boil, add the onions and cook gently for about 15 minutes.

2 Drain well. Allow the onions to cool, then slice each one in half horizontally.

3 Scoop out most of the onion flesh but leave a reasonably firm shell.

4 Chop up 4 tablespoons of the onion flesh and place in a bowl with the crushed garlic, breadcrumbs, sultanas, pine nuts, grated cheese and parsley.

5 Mix the breadcrumb mixture together thoroughly. Bind together with as much of the beaten egg as necessary to make a firm filling. Season to taste with salt and pepper.

6 Pile the mixture back into the onion shells and top with the grated cheese. Place on a oiled baking tray and cook in the preheated oven for 20–30 minutes or until golden brown. Serve immediately with the salad leaves.

FOOD FACT

While this dish is delicious on its own, it also compliments barbecued meat and fish. The onion takes on a mellow, nutty flavour when baked.

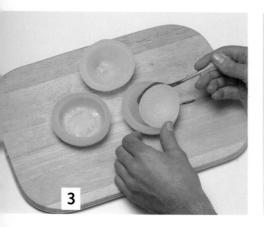

3

4

6

Beetroot & Potato Medley

INGREDIENTS

Serves 4

350 g/12 oz raw baby beetroot

½ tsp sunflower oil

225 g/8 oz new potatoes

½ cucumber, peeled

3 tbsp white wine vinegar

150 ml/5 fl oz natural low-fat yogurt

salt and freshly ground black pepper

fresh salad leaves

1 tbsp freshly snipped chives,
  to garnish

HELPFUL HINT

Beetroot can also be cooked in the microwave. Place in a microwaveable bowl. Add sufficient water to come halfway up the sides of the bowl. Cover and cook for 10–15 minutes on high. Leave for 5 minutes before removing the paper. Cook before peeling.

FOOD FACT

Like other fruits and vegetables which are red in colour, beetroot has particularly high levels of antioxidants which are essential to the body to fight disease.

1 Preheat the oven to 180°C/350°F/Gas Mark 4. Scrub the beetroot thoroughly and place on a baking tray.

2 Brush the beetroot with a little oil and cook for 1½ hours or until a skewer easily slides insertable into the beetroot. Allow to cool a little, then remove the skins.

3 Cook the potatoes in boiling water for about 10 minutes. Rinse in cold water and drain. Reserve the potatoes until cool. Dice evenly.

4 Cut the cucumber into cubes and place in a mixing bowl. Chop the beetroot into small cubes and add to the bowl with the reserved potatoes. Gently mix the vegetables together.

5 Mix together the vinegar and yogurt and season to taste with a little salt and pepper. Pour over the vegetables and combine gently.

6 Arrange on a bed of salad leaves garnished with the snipped chives and serve.

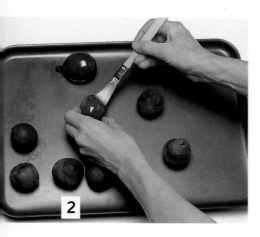

2

3

4

Carrot, Celeriac & Sesame Seed Salad

INGREDIENTS

Serves 6

225 g/8 oz celeriac
225 g/8 oz carrots, peeled
50 g/2 oz seedless raisins
2 tbsp sesame seeds
freshly chopped parsley,
   to garnish

For the lemon & chilli dressing:

grated rind of 1 lemon
4 tbsp lemon juice
2 tbsp sunflower oil
2 tbsp clear honey
1 red bird's eye chilli, deseeded
   and finely chopped
salt and freshly ground
   black pepper

FOOD FACT

Celeriac is a root vegetable that is similar in taste to fennel, but with a texture closer to parsnip. This versatile vegetable has a creamy taste and is also delicious in soups and gratins.

1 Slice the celeriac into thin matchsticks. Place in a small saucepan of boiling salted water and boil for 2 minutes.

2 Drain and rinse the celeriac in cold water and place in a mixing bowl.

3 Finely grate the carrot. Add the carrot and the raisins to the celeriac in the bowl.

4 Place the sesame seeds under a hot grill or dry-fry in a frying pan for 1–2 minutes until golden brown, then leave to cool.

5 Make the dressing by whisking together the lemon rind, lemon juice, oil, honey, chilli and seasoning or by shaking thoroughly in a screw-topped jar.

6 Pour 2 tablespoons of the dressing over the salad and toss well. Turn into a serving dish and sprinkle over the toasted sesame seeds and chopped parsley. Serve the remaining dressing separately.

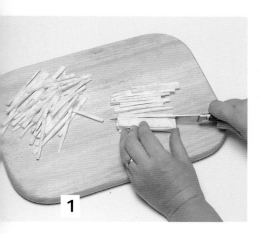

1

3

4

Orange & Fennel Salad

INGREDIENTS

Serves 4

4 large oranges
1 large bulb fennel
2 tsp fennel seeds
2 tbsp extra-virgin olive oil
orange juice, freshly squeezed,
 to taste
fresh parsley, finely chopped,
 to garnish

1 Using a small serrated knife, remove the rind and pith from one orange, cutting carefully from the top to the bottom of the orange so it retains its shape. Work over a bowl to catch the juices.

2 Peel the remaining oranges the same way, reserving all the juices. Cut the oranges horizontally into 5 mm/¼ inch slices and arrange in an attractive serving bowl and reserve the juices.

3 Place the fennel bulb on a chopping board and cut off the fronds. Cut the bulb in half lengthways and then into quarters. Cut crossways into the thinnest slices you can manage. Immediately transfer to the bowl with the oranges and toss with a little of the reserved orange juice to prevent browning.

4 Sprinkle the fennel seeds over the oranges and fennel.

5 Place the olive oil in a small bowl and whisk in the rest of the reserved orange juice, plus extra fresh orange juice to taste. Pour over the oranges and fennel and toss gently. Cover with clingfilm and chill until ready to serve.

6 Just before serving, remove from the refrigerator and sprinkle with parsley. Serve chilled.

2

3

4

Tortellini & Summer Vegetable Salad

INGREDIENTS

Serves 6

350 g/12 oz plain cheese-filled
   fresh tortellini
150 ml/¼ pint extra-virgin olive oil
225 g/8 oz fine green beans, trimmed
175 g/6 oz broccoli florets
1 yellow or red pepper, deseeded and
   thinly sliced
1 red onion, peeled and sliced
175 g jar marinated artichoke hearts,
   drained and halved
2 tbsp capers
75 g/3 oz dry-cured pitted black olives
3 tbsp raspberry or balsamic vinegar
1 tbsp Dijon mustard
1 tsp soft brown sugar
salt and freshly ground black pepper
2 tbsp freshly chopped basil or flat-
   leaf parsley
2 quartered hard-boiled eggs,
   to garnish

1 Bring a large pan of lightly salted water to a rolling boil. Add the tortellini and cook according to the packet instructions, or until 'al dente'.

2 Using a large slotted spoon, transfer the tortellini to a colander to drain. Rinse under cold running water and drain again. Transfer to a large bowl and toss with 2 tablespoons of the olive oil.

3 Return the pasta water to the boil and drop in the green beans and broccoli florets; blanch them for 2 minutes, or until just beginning to soften. Drain, rinse under cold running water and drain again thoroughly. Add the vegetables to the reserved tortellini.

4 Add the pepper, onion, artichoke hearts, capers and olives to the bowl. Stir lightly.

5 Whisk together the vinegar, mustard and brown sugar in a bowl and season to taste with salt and pepper. Slowly whisk in the remaining olive oil to form a thick, creamy dressing. Pour over the tortellini and vegetables, add the chopped basil or parsley and stir until lightly coated. Transfer to a shallow serving dish or salad bowl. Garnish with the hard-boiled egg quarters and serve.

FOOD FACT

Black olives are picked when fully ripe and a brownish pink colour and then fermented and oxidised until they become black.

3

4

5

Rice & Papaya Salad

INGREDIENTS

Serves 4

175 g/6 oz easy-cook basmati rice

1 cinnamon stick, bruised

1 bird's-eye chilli, deseeded and
   finely chopped

rind and juice of 2 limes

rind and juice of 2 lemons

2 tbsp Thai fish sauce

1 tbsp soft light brown sugar

1 papaya, peeled and seeds removed

1 mango, peeled and stone removed

1 green chilli, deseeded and
   finely chopped

2 tbsp freshly chopped coriander

1 tbsp freshly chopped mint

250 g/9 oz cooked chicken

50 g/2 oz roasted peanuts, chopped

strips of pitta bread, to serve

1. Rinse and drain the rice and pour into a saucepan. Add 450 ml/ ³/₄ pint boiling salted water and the cinnamon stick. Bring to the boil, reduce the heat to a very low heat, cover and cook without stirring for 15–18 minutes, or until all the liquid is absorbed. The rice should be light and fluffy and have steam holes on the surface. Remove the cinnamon stick and stir in the rind from 1 lime.

2. To make the dressing, place the bird's-eye chilli, remaining rind and lime and lemon juice, fish sauce and sugar in a food processor, mix for a few minutes until blended. Alternatively, place all these ingredients in a screw-top jar and shake until well blended. Pour half the dressing over the hot rice and toss until the rice glistens.

3. Slice the papaya and mango into thin slices, then place in a bowl. Add the chopped green chilli, coriander and mint. Place the chicken on a chopping board, then remove and discard any skin or sinews. Cut into fine shreds and add to the bowl with the chopped peanuts.

4. Add the remaining dressing to the chicken mixture and stir until all the ingredients are lightly coated. Spoon the rice onto a platter, pile the chicken mixture on top and serve with warm strips of pitta bread.

HELPFUL HINT

The papaya or pawpaw's skin turns from green when unripe, through to yellow and orange. To prepare, cut in half lengthways, scoop out the black seeds with a teaspoon and discard. Cut away the thin skin before slicing.

2

3

3

Bulghur Wheat Salad with Minty Lemon Dressing

INGREDIENTS

Serves 4

125 g/4 oz bulghur wheat
10 cm /4 inch piece cucumber
2 shallots, peeled
125 g/4 oz baby sweetcorn
3 ripe but firm tomatoes

For the dressing:

grated rind of 1 lemon
3 tbsp lemon juice
3 tbsp freshly chopped mint
2 tbsp freshly chopped parsley
1–2 tsp clear honey
2 tbsp sunflower oil
salt and freshly ground
   black pepper

1 Place the bulghur wheat in a saucepan and cover with boiling water.

2 Simmer for about 10 minutes, then drain thoroughly and turn into a serving bowl.

3 Cut the cucumber into small dice, chop the shallots finely and reserve. Steam the sweetcorn over a pan of boiling water for 10 minutes or until tender. Drain and slice into thick chunks.

4 Cut a cross on the top of each tomato and place in boiling water until their skins start to peel away.

5 Remove the skins and the seeds and cut the tomatoes into small dice.

6 Make the dressing by briskly whisking all the ingredients in a small bowl until mixed well.

7 When the bulghur wheat has cooled a little, add all the prepared vegetables and stir in the dressing. Season to taste with salt and pepper and serve.

FOOD FACT

This dish is loosely based on the Middle Eastern dish tabbouleh, a type of salad in which all the ingredients are mixed together and served cold.

2

3

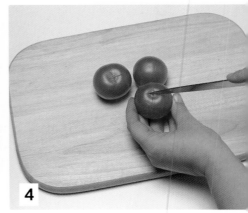

4

Warm Fruity Rice Salad

INGREDIENTS

Serves 4

175 g/6 oz mixed basmati and
   wild rice
125 g/4 oz skinless chicken breast
300 ml/½ pint chicken or
   vegetable stock
125 g/4 oz ready-to-eat
   dried apricots
125 g/4 oz ready-to-eat
   dried dates
3 sticks celery

For the dressing:

2 tbsp sunflower oil
1 tbsp white wine vinegar
4 tbsp lemon juice
1–2 tsp clear honey, warmed
1 tsp Dijon mustard
freshly ground black pepper

To garnish:

6 spring onions
sprigs of fresh coriander

1 Place the rice in a pan of boiling salted water and cook for 15–20 minutes or until tender. Rinse thoroughly with boiling water and reserve.

2 Meanwhile wipe the chicken and place in a shallow saucepan with the stock.

3 Bring to the boil, cover and simmer for about 15 minutes or until the chicken is cooked thoroughly and the juices run clear.

4 Leave the chicken in the stock until cool enough to handle, then cut into thin slices.

5 Chop the apricots and dates into small pieces. Peel any tough membranes from the outside of the celery and chop into dice. Fold the apricots, dates, celery and sliced chicken into the warm rice.

6 Make the dressing by whisking all the ingredients together in a small bowl until mixed thoroughly. Pour 2–3 tablespoons over the rice and stir in gently and evenly. Serve the remaining dressing separately.

7 Trim and chop the spring onions. Sprinkle the spring onions over the top of the salad and garnish with the sprigs of coriander. Serve while still warm.

2

5

6

Warm Leek & Tomato Salad

INGREDIENTS

Serves 4

450 g/1 lb trimmed baby leeks
225 g/8 oz ripe, but firm tomatoes
2 shallots, peeled and cut into
 thin wedges

For the honey and lime dressing:

2 tbsp clear honey
grated rind of 1 lime
4 tbsp lime juice
1 tbsp light olive oil
1 tsp Dijon mustard
salt and freshly ground
 black pepper

To garnish:

freshly chopped tarragon
freshly chopped basil

1 Trim the leeks so that they are all the same length. Place in a steamer over a pan of boiling water and steam for 8 minutes or until just tender.

2 Drain the leeks thoroughly and arrange in a shallow serving dish.

3 Make a cross in the top of the tomatoes, place in a bowl and cover them with boiling water until their skins start to peel away. Remove from the bowl and carefully remove the skins.

4 Cut the tomatoes into 4 and remove the seeds, then chop into small dice. Spoon over the top of the leeks together with the shallots.

5 In a small bowl make the dressing by whisking the honey, lime rind, lime juice, olive oil, mustard and salt and pepper. Pour 3 tablespoons of the dressing over the leeks and tomatoes and garnish with the tarragon and basil. Serve while the leeks are still warm, with the remaining dressing served separately.

HELPFUL HINT

An easy way to measure honey is to plunge a metal measuring spoon into boiling water. Drain the spoon, then dip into the honey.

1

3

5

Mediterranean Rice Salad

INGREDIENTS

Serves 4

250 g/9 oz Camargue red rice
2 sun-dried tomatoes, finely chopped
2 garlic cloves, peeled and
    finely chopped
4 tbsp oil from a jar of sun-
    dried tomatoes
2 tsp balsamic vinegar
2 tsp red wine vinegar
salt and freshly ground black pepper
1 red onion, peeled and thinly sliced
1 yellow pepper, quartered
    and deseeded
1 red pepper, quartered and deseeded
½ cucumber, peeled and diced
6 ripe plum tomatoes, cut
    into wedges
1 fennel bulb, halved and thinly sliced
fresh basil leaves, to garnish

FOOD FACT

Camargue red rice from the south of France is a reddish-brown colour and gives this salad a stunning appearance. It has a texture and cooking time similar to that of brown rice, which may be substituted in this recipe if Camargue red rice is unavailable.

1 Cook the rice in a saucepan of lightly salted boiling water for 35–40 minutes, or until tender. Drain well and reserve.

2 Whisk the sun-dried tomatoes, garlic, oil and vinegars together in a small bowl or jug. Season to taste with salt and pepper. Put the red onion in a large bowl, pour over the dressing and leave to allow the flavours to develop.

3 Put the peppers, skin-side up on a grill rack and cook under a preheated hot grill for 5–6 minutes, or until blackened and charred. Remove and place in a plastic bag. When cool enough to handle, peel off the skins and slice the peppers.

4 Add the peppers, cucumber, tomatoes, fennel and rice to the onions. Mix gently together to coat in the dressing. Cover and chill in the refrigerator for 30 minutes to allow the flavours to mingle.

5 Remove the salad from the refrigerator and leave to stand at room temperature for 20 minutes. Garnish with fresh basil leaves and serve.

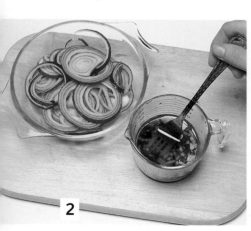

2

3

4

Winter Coleslaw

INGREDIENTS

Serves 6

175 g/6 oz white cabbage
1 medium red onion, peeled
175 g/6 oz carrot, peeled
175 g/6 oz celeriac, peeled
2 celery stalks, trimmed
75 g/3 oz golden sultanas

For the yogurt & herb dressing:

150 ml/¼ pint low-fat
  natural yogurt
1 garlic clove, peeled
  and crushed
1 tbsp lemon juice
1 tsp clear honey
1 tbsp freshly snipped chives

TASTY TIP

To make cheese coleslaw, simply replace the sultanas with 75 g/ 3 oz of reduced-fat cheese. Whether the winter or cheese variety, coleslaw is particularly good with baked potatoes and a little low-fat spread.

1   Remove the hard core from the cabbage with a small knife and shred finely.

2   Slice the onion finely and coarsely grate the carrot.

3   Place the raw vegetables in a large bowl and mix together.

4   Cut the celeriac into thin strips and simmer in boiling water for about 2 minutes.

5   Drain the celeriac and rinse thoroughly with cold water.

6   Chop the celery and add to the bowl with the celeriac and sultanas and mix well.

7   Make the yogurt and herb dressing by briskly whisking the yogurt, garlic, lemon juice, honey and chives together.

8   Pour the dressing over the top of the salad. Stir the vegetables thoroughly to coat evenly and serve.

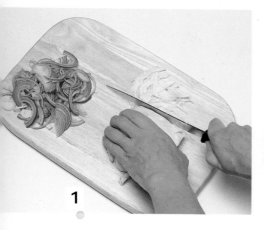

1

4

6

Warm Potato, Pear & Pecan Salad

INGREDIENTS

Serves 4

900 g/2 lb new potatoes, preferably
  red-skinned, unpeeled
salt and freshly ground black pepper
1 tsp Dijon mustard
2 tsp white wine vinegar
3 tbsp groundnut oil
1 tbsp hazelnut or walnut oil
2 tsp poppy seeds
2 firm ripe dessert pears
2 tsp lemon juice
175 g/6 oz baby spinach leaves
75 g/3 oz toasted pecan nuts

HELPFUL HINT

To toast the pecan nuts, place on a baking tray in a single layer and cook in a preheated oven at 180°C/350°F/Gas Mark 4 for 5 minutes, or under a medium grill for 3–4 minutes, turning frequently. Watch them carefully – they burn easily. If you can not get red-skinned new potatoes for this dish, add colour by using red-skinned pears instead. Look out for Red Bartlett and Red Williams.

1 Scrub the potatoes, then cook in a saucepan of lightly salted boiling water for 15 minutes, or until tender. Drain, cut into halves, or quarters if large, and place in a serving bowl.

2 In a small bowl or jug, whisk together the mustard and vinegar. Gradually add the oils until the mixture begins to thicken. Stir in the poppy seeds and season to taste with salt and pepper.

3 Pour about two-thirds of the dressing over the hot potatoes and toss gently to coat. Leave until the potatoes have soaked up the dressing and are just warm.

4 Meanwhile, quarter and core the pears. Cut into thin slices, then sprinkle with the lemon juice to prevent them from going brown. Add to the potatoes with the spinach leaves and toasted pecan nuts. Gently mix together.

5 Drizzle the remaining dressing over the salad. Serve immediately before the spinach starts to wilt.

1

2

4

Squid Salad

INGREDIENTS

Serves 4

900 g/2 lb small squid
120 ml/4 fl oz lemon juice
60 ml/2 fl oz extra-virgin olive oil
25 g/1 oz fresh flat-leaf parsley
8 spring onions
4 vine-ripened tomatoes, deseeded
  and chopped
salt and pepper

To garnish:

radicchio leaves
red chillies, finely chopped (optional)
capers or black olives (optional)
fresh flat-leaf parsley, finely chopped

1 To prepare each squid, pull the head and all the insides out of the body sac. Cut the tentacles off the head and discard the head. Remove the beak from the centre of the tentacles.

2 Pull out the thin, transparent quill that runs through the centre of the body. Rinse the body sac under running cold water and, using your fingers, rub off the thin, grey membrane. Cut the squid body sacs into 1 cm/½ inch slices. Rinse the tentacle pieces and set aside with the body slices.

3 Put the lemon juice and olive oil in a large bowl and stir together. Very finely chop the parsley and add to the bowl. Finely chop the white parts of the spring onions and add to the bowl with the tomatoes. Season with salt and pepper to taste.

4 Bring a pan of lightly salted water to the boil. Add all the squid and return to the boil.

5 As soon as the water returns to the boil, drain the squid. Add the squid to the bowl of dressing and gently toss all the ingredients together.

6 Leave the squid to cool completely, then cover and leave to marinate in the refrigerator for at least 6 hours, preferably overnight.

7 Line a serving bowl with radicchio leaves. Add the chopped chilli, capers or olives, to taste, if using. Mound the squid salad on top of the radicchio leaves and sprinkle with finely chopped parsley. Serve very chilled.

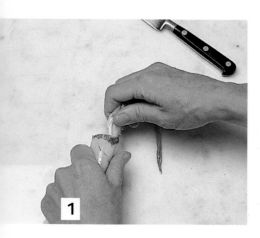

1

2

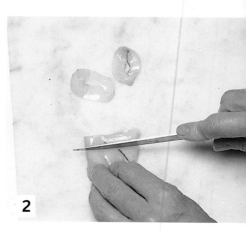

2

Lobster Salad

INGREDIENTS

Serves 2

2 raw lobster tails
salt and pepper

For the lemon–dill mayonnaise:

1 large lemon
1 large egg yolk
½ tsp Dijon mustard
150 ml/5 fl oz olive oil
1 tbsp fresh dill, chopped

To garnish:

radicchio leaves
lemon wedges
fresh dill sprigs

1 To make the lemon-dill mayonnaise, finely grate the rind from the lemon and squeeze the juice. Beat the egg yolk in a small bowl and beat in the mustard and 1 teaspoon of the lemon juice.

2 Using a balloon whisk or electric mixer, beat in the olive oil, drop by drop, until a thick mayonnaise forms. Stir in half the lemon rind and 1 tablespoon of the juice.

3 Season with salt and pepper, and add more lemon juice if desired. Stir in the dill and cover with clingfilm. Chill until required.

4 Bring a large saucepan of salted water to the boil. Add the lobster tails and continue to cook for 6 minutes until the flesh is opaque and the shells are red. Drain immediately and leave to cool completely.

5 Remove the lobster flesh from the shells and cut into bite-sized pieces. Arrange the radicchio leaves on individual plates and top with the lobster flesh. Place a spoonful of the lemon-dill mayonnaise on the side. Garnish with lemon wedges and dill sprigs and serve.

4

4

5

Tuna Bean Salad

INGREDIENTS

Serves 4

225 g/8 oz dried haricot beans
1 tbsp lemon juice
5 tbsp extra-virgin olive oil, plus
   extra for brushing
1 garlic clove, finely chopped
1 small red onion, very finely
   sliced (optional)
1 tbsp chopped fresh parsley
4 x 175 g/6 oz tuna steaks
salt and pepper

To Garnish:

parsley sprigs
lemon wedges

1 Soak the haricot beans for 8 hours or overnight in at least twice their volume of cold water.

2 When you are ready to cook, drain the beans and place in a saucepan with twice their volume of fresh water. Bring slowly to the boil, skimming off any scum that rises to the surface. Boil the beans rapidly for 10 minutes, then reduce the heat and simmer for a further $1\frac{1}{4}$–$1\frac{1}{2}$ hours until the beans are tender.

3 Meanwhile, mix together the lemon juice, olive oil, garlic and seasoning. Drain the beans thoroughly and mix together with the olive oil mixture, onion and parsley. Season to taste and set aside.

4 Wash and dry the tuna steaks. Brush lightly with olive oil and season. Cook on a preheated ridged grill pan for 2 minutes on each side until just pink in the centre.

5 Divide the bean salad between 4 serving plates. Top each with a tuna steak. Garnish with parsley sprigs and lemon wedges and serve immediately.

1

4

5

Mixed Salad with Anchovy Dressing & Ciabatta Croûtons

INGREDIENTS

Serves 4

1 small head endive
1 small head chicory
1 fennel bulb
400 g can artichokes, drained
   and rinsed
½ cucumber
125 g/4 oz cherry tomatoes
75 g/3 oz black olives

For the anchovy dressing:

50 g can anchovy fillets
1 tsp Dijon mustard
1 small garlic clove, peeled
   and crushed
4 tbsp olive oil
1 tbsp lemon juice
freshly ground black pepper

For the ciabatta croûtons:

2 thick slices ciabatta bread
2 tbsp olive oil

1 Divide the endive and chicory into leaves and reserve some of the larger ones. Arrange the smaller leaves in a wide salad bowl.

2 Cut the fennel bulb in half from the stalk to the root end, then cut across in fine slices. Quarter the artichokes, then quarter and slice the cucumber and halve the tomatoes. Add to the salad bowl with the olives.

3 To make the dressing, drain the anchovies and put in a blender with the mustard, garlic, olive oil, lemon juice, 2 tablespoons of hot water and black pepper. Whizz together until smooth and thickened.

4 To make the croûtons, cut the bread into 1 cm/½ inch cubes. Heat the oil in a frying pan, add the bread cubes and fry for 3 minutes, turning frequently until golden. Remove and drain on absorbent kitchen paper.

5 Drizzle half the anchovy dressing over the prepared salad and toss to coat. Arrange the reserved endive and chicory leaves around the edge, then drizzle over the remaining dressing. Scatter over the croûtons and serve immediately.

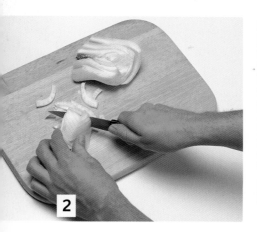
2

3

4

Seared Scallop Salad

INGREDIENTS

Serves 4

12 king (large) scallops
1 tbsp low-fat spread or butter
2 tbsp orange juice
2 tbsp balsamic vinegar
1 tbsp clear honey
2 ripe pears, washed
125 g/4 oz rocket
125 g/4 oz watercress
50 g/2 oz walnuts
freshly ground black pepper

FOOD FACT

As well as the king scallops which are used in this recipe, there are also the smaller queen scallops. It is worth noting that scallops are in season between September and March, when they will not only be at their best, but they may also be slightly cheaper in price. When buying, especially the larger king scallop, make sure that the orange roe is left intact.

1 Clean the scallops removing the thin black vein from around the white meat and coral. Rinse thoroughly and dry on absorbent kitchen paper.

2 Cut into 2–3 thick slices, depending on the scallop size.

3 Heat a griddle pan or heavy-based frying pan, then when hot, add the low-fat spread or butter and allow to melt.

4 Once melted, sear the scallops for 1 minute on each side or until golden. Remove from the pan and reserve.

5 Briskly whisk together the orange juice, balsamic vinegar and honey to make the dressing and reserve.

6 With a small sharp knife carefully cut the pears into quarters, core then cut into chunks.

7 Mix the rocket leaves, watercress, pear chunks and walnuts. Pile on to serving plates and top with the scallops.

8 Drizzle over the dressing and grind over plenty of black pepper. Serve immediately.

1

4

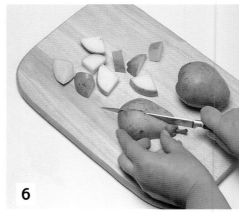

6

Curly Endive & Seafood Salad

INGREDIENTS

Serves 4

1 head of curly endive lettuce
2 green peppers
12.5 cm/5 inch piece cucumber
125 g/4 oz squid, cleaned and cut
  into thin rings
225 g/8 oz baby asparagus spears
125 g/4 oz smoked salmon slices,
  cut into wide strips
175 g/6 oz fresh cooked mussels
  in their shells

For the lemon Dressing:

2 tbsp sunflower oil
1 tbsp white wine vinegar
5 tbsp fresh lemon juice
1–2 tsp caster sugar
1 tsp mild whole-grain mustard
salt and freshly ground
  black pepper

To garnish:

slices of lemon
sprigs of fresh coriander

1 Rinse and tear the endive into small pieces and arrange on a serving platter.

2 Remove the seeds from the peppers and cut the peppers and the cucumber into small dice. Sprinkle over the endive.

3 Bring a saucepan of water to the boil and add the squid rings. Bring the pan up to the boil again, then switch off the heat and leave it to stand for 5 minutes. Then drain and rinse thoroughly in cold water.

4 Cook the asparagus in boiling water for 5 minutes or until tender but just crisp. Arrange with the squid, smoked salmon and mussels on top of the salad.

5 To make the lemon dressing, put all the ingredients into a screw-topped jar or into a small bowl and mix thoroughly until the ingredients are combined.

6 Spoon 3 tablespoons of the dressing over the salad and serve the remainder in a small jug. Garnish the salad with slices of lemon and sprigs of coriander and serve.

2

3

4

Coffee & Peach Creams

INGREDIENTS

Serves 4

4 peaches
50 g/2 oz caster sugar
2 tbsp coffee essence
200 g carton half-fat Greek
    set yogurt
300 g carton half-fat
    ready-made custard

To decorate:

peach slices
sprigs of mint
low-fat crème fraîche

1 Cut the peaches in half and remove the stones. Place the peaches in a large bowl, cover with boiling water and leave for 2–3 minutes.

2 Drain the peaches, then carefully remove the skin.

3 Place the caster sugar in a saucepan and add 50 ml/2 fl oz water.

4 Bring the sugar mixture to the boil, stirring occasionally, until the sugar has dissolved. Boil rapidly for about 2 minutes.

5 Add the peaches and coffee essence to the pan. Remove from the heat and allow the peach mixture to cool.

6 Meanwhile mix together the Greek yogurt and custard until well combined.

7 Divide the peaches between the 4 glass dishes.

8 Spoon over the custard mixture then top with remaining peach mixture.

9 Chill for 30 minutes and then serve, decorated with peach slices, mint sprigs and a little crème fraîche.

FOOD FACT

It is generally believed that peaches originated from China. There are over 2,000 varieties grown throughout the world.

2

5

6

Poached Pears

INGREDIENTS

Serves 4

2 small cinnamon sticks
125 g/4 oz caster sugar
300 ml/½ pint red wine
150 ml/¼ pint water
thinly pared rind and juice of
  1 small orange
4 firm pears
orange slices, to decorate
frozen vanilla yogurt, or
  low-fat ice cream, to serve

TASTY TIP

Poached pears are delicious served with a little half-fat crème fraîche and sprinkled with toasted almonds. To toast almonds, simply warm the grill and place whole, blanched almonds or flaked almonds on to a piece of tinfoil. Place under the grill and toast lightly on both sides for 1–2 minutes until golden. Remove and cool, chop if liked.

1 Place the cinnamon sticks on the work surface and with a rolling pin, slowly roll down the side of the cinnamon stick to bruise. Place in a large heavy-based saucepan.

2 Add the sugar, wine, water, pared orange rind and juice to the pan and bring slowly to the boil, stirring occasionally, until the sugar is dissolved.

3 Meanwhile peel the pears, leaving the stalks on.

4 Cut out the cores from the bottom of the pears and level them so that they stand upright.

5 Stand the pears in the syrup, cover the pan and simmer for 20 minutes or until tender.

6 Remove the pan from the heat and leave the pears to cool in the syrup, turning occasionally.

7 Arrange the pears on serving plates and spoon over the syrup. Decorate with the orange slices and serve with the yogurt or low-fat ice cream and any remaining juices.

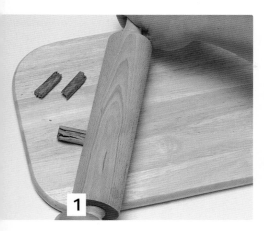
1

2

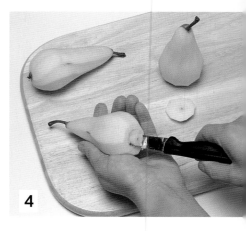
4

Caramelised Oranges in an Iced Bowl

INGREDIENTS

Serves 4

8 medium-sized oranges
225 g/8 oz caster sugar
4 tbsp Grand Marnier or Cointreau

For the ice bowl:

about 36 ice cubes
fresh flowers and fruits

1 Set freezer to rapid freeze. Place a few ice cubes in the base of a 1.7 litre/3 pint freezable glass bowl. Place a 900 ml /1½ pint glass bowl on top of the ice cubes. Arrange the flower heads and fruits in between the 2 bowls, wedging in position with the ice cubes.

2 Weigh down the smaller bowl with some heavy weights, then carefully pour cold water between the 2 bowls making sure that the flowers and the fruit are covered. Freeze for at least 6 hours or until the ice is frozen solid.

3 When ready to use, remove the weights and using a hot damp cloth rub the inside of the smaller bowl with the cloth until it loosens sufficiently for you to remove the bowl. Place the larger bowl in the sink or washing-up bowl, half filled with very hot water. Leave for about 30 seconds or until the ice loosens. Take care not to leave the bowl in the water for too long otherwise the ice will melt. Remove the bowl and leave in the refrigerator. Return the freezer to its normal setting.

4 Thinly pare the rind from 2 oranges and then cut into julienne strips. Using a sharp knife cut away the rind and pith from all the oranges, holding over a bowl to catch the juices. Slice the oranges, discarding any pips and reform each orange back to its original shape. Secure with cocktail sticks, then place in a bowl.

5 Heat 300 ml/½ pint water, orange rind and sugar together in a pan. Stir the sugar until dissolved. Bring to the boil. Boil for 15 minutes, until it is a caramel colour. Remove pan from heat.

6 Stir in the liqueur, pour over the oranges. Allow to cool. Chill for 3 hours, turning the oranges occasionally. Spoon into the ice bowl and serve.

HELPFUL HINT

This iced bowl can hold any dessert. Why not fill with flavoured ice creams?

1

2

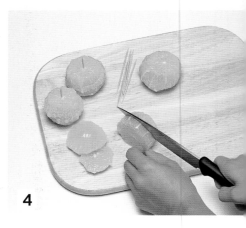

4

Raspberry Sorbet Crush

INGREDIENTS

Serves 4

225 g/8 oz raspberries, thawed
  if frozen
grated rind and juice of 1 lime
300 ml/½ pint orange juice
225 g/8 oz caster sugar
2 medium egg whites

1   Set the freezer to rapid freeze. If using fresh raspberries pick over and lightly rinse.

2   Place the raspberries in a dish and, using a masher, mash to a chunky purée.

3   Place the lime rind and juice, orange juice and half the caster sugar in a large heavy-based saucepan.

4   Heat gently stirring frequently until the sugar is dissolved. Bring to the boil and boil rapidly for about 5 minutes.

5   Remove the pan from the heat and pour carefully into a freezable container.

6   Leave to cool, then place in the freezer and freeze for 2 hours, stirring occasionally to break up the ice crystals.

7   Fold the ice mixture into the raspberry purée with a metal spoon and freeze for a further 2 hours, stirring occasionally.

8   Whisk the egg whites until stiff. Then gradually whisk in the remaining caster sugar a tablespoon at a time until the egg white mixture is stiff and glossy.

9   Fold into the raspberry sorbet with a metal spoon and freeze for 1 hour. Spoon into tall glasses and serve immediately. Remember to return the freezer to its normal setting.

FOOD FACT

This recipe contains raw egg and should not be given to babies, young children, pregnant women, the sick, the elderly and those suffering from a recurring illness.

2

7

9

Raspberry Soufflé

INGREDIENTS

Serves 4

125 g/4 oz redcurrants
50 g/2 oz caster sugar
1 sachet (3 tsp) powdered gelatine
3 medium eggs, separated
300 g/½ pint half-fat Greek yogurt
450 g/1 lb raspberries, thawed
    if frozen

To decorate:

mint sprigs
extra fruits

1. Wrap a band of double-thickness greaseproof paper around four ramekin dishes, making sure that 5 cm/2 inches of the paper stays above the top of each dish. Secure the paper to the dish with an elastic band or Sellotape.

2. Place the redcurrants and 1 tablespoon of the sugar in a small saucepan. Cook for 5 minutes until softened. Remove from the heat, sieve and reserve.

3. Place 3 tablespoons of water in a small bowl and sprinkle over the gelatine. Allow to stand for 5 minutes until spongy. Place the bowl over a pan of simmering water and leave until dissolved. Remove and allow to cool.

4. Beat together the remaining sugar and egg yolks until pale thick and creamy, then fold in the yogurt with a metal spoon or rubber spatula until well blended.

5. Sieve the raspberries and fold into the yogurt mixture with the gelatine. Whisk the egg whites until stiff and fold into the yogurt mixture. Pour into the prepared dishes and chill in the refrigerator for 2 hours until firm.

6. Remove the paper from the dishes and spread the redcurrant purée over the top of the soufflés. Decorate with mint sprigs and extra fruits and serve.

HELPFUL HINT

Soufflés rely on air, so it is important that the egg whites in this recipe are beaten until very stiff in order to support the mixture.

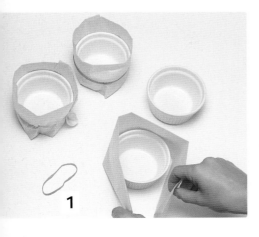
1

3

5

Fruity Roulade

INGREDIENTS

Serves 4

For the sponge:

3 medium eggs
75 g/3 oz caster sugar
75 g/3 oz plain flour, sieved
1–2 tbsp caster sugar for sprinkling

For the filling:

125 g/4 oz Quark
125 g/4 oz half-fat Greek yogurt
25 g/1 oz caster sugar
1 tbsp orange liqueur (optional)
grated rind of 1 orange
125 g/4 oz strawberries, hulled and
  cut into quarters

To decorate:

strawberries
sifted icing sugar

FOOD FACT

Quark is a soft unripened cheese with the flavour and texture of soured cream. It comes in 2 varieties, low fat and non-fat. Quark can be used as a sour cream substitute to top baked potatoes, or in dips and cheesecakes.

1 Preheat the oven to 220°C/425°F/Gas Mark 7. Lightly oil and line a 33 x 23 cm/13 x 9 inch Swiss roll tin with greaseproof or baking parchment paper.

2 Using an electric whisk, whisk the eggs and sugar until the mixture doubles in volume and leaves a trail across the top.

3 Fold in the flour with a metal spoon or rubber spatula. Pour into the prepared tin and bake in the preheated oven for 10–12 minutes, until well risen and golden.

4 Place a whole sheet of greaseproof or baking parchment paper out on a flat work surface and sprinkle evenly with caster sugar.

5 Turn the cooked sponge out on to the paper, discard the paper the sponge was baked on, trim the sponge and roll up encasing the paper inside. Reserve until cool.

6 To make the filling, mix together the Quark, yogurt, caster sugar, liqueur (if using) and orange rind. Unroll the roulade and spread over the mixture. Scatter over the strawberries and roll up.

7 Decorate the roulade with the strawberries. Dust with the icing sugar and serve.

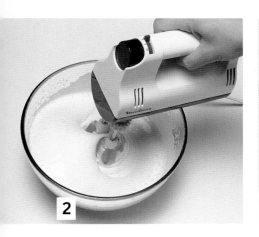

2

5

6

Chocolate Pear Pudding

INGREDIENTS

Serves 6

140 g/4½ oz butter, softened

2 tbsp soft brown sugar

400 g can of pear halves, drained and juice reserved

25 g/1 oz walnut halves

125 g/4 oz golden caster sugar

2 medium eggs, beaten

75 g/3 oz self-raising flour, sifted

50 g/2 oz cocoa powder

1 tsp baking powder

prepared chocolate custard, to serve

HELPFUL HINT

To soften butter or margarine quickly, pour hot water in a mixing bowl to warm, leave for a few minutes, then drain and dry. Cut the butter or margarine into small pieces and leave at room temperature for a short time. Do not attempt to melt in the microwave as this will make the fat oily and affect the texture of the finished cake.

1 Preheat the oven to 190°C/375°F/Gas Mark 5, 10 minutes before baking. Butter a 20.5 cm/8 inch sandwich tin with 15 g/½ oz of the butter and sprinkle the base with the soft brown sugar. Arrange the drained pear halves on top of the sugar, cut-side down. Fill the spaces between the pears with the walnut halves, flat-side upwards.

2 Cream the remaining butter with the caster sugar then gradually beat in the beaten eggs, adding 1 tablespoon of the flour after each addition. When all the eggs have been added, stir in the remaining flour.

3 Sift the cocoa powder and baking powder together, then stir into the creamed mixture with 1–2 tablespoons of the reserved pear juice to give a smooth dropping consistency.

4 Spoon the mixture over the pear halves, smoothing the surface. Bake in the preheated oven for 20–25 minutes, or until well risen and the surface springs back when lightly pressed.

5 Remove from the oven and leave to cool for 5 minutes. Using a palate knife, loosen the sides and invert onto a serving plate. Serve with custard.

1

2

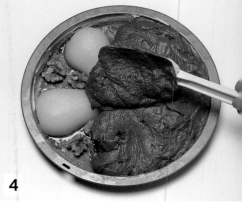

4

Spicy White Chocolate Mousse

INGREDIENTS

Serves 4–6

6 cardamom pods
125 ml/4 fl oz milk
3 bay leaves
200 g/7 oz white chocolate
300 ml/½ pint double cream
3 medium egg whites
1–2 tsp cocoa powder, sifted,
   for dusting

1 Tap the cardamom pods lightly so they split. Remove the seeds, then, using a pestle and mortar, crush lightly. Pour the milk into a small saucepan and add the crushed seeds and the bay leaves. Bring to the boil gently over a medium heat. Remove from the heat, cover and leave in a warm place for at least 30 minutes to infuse.

2 Break the chocolate into small pieces and place in a heatproof bowl set over a saucepan of gently simmering water. Ensure the water is not touching the base of the bowl. When the chocolate has melted remove the bowl from the heat and stir until smooth.

3 Whip the cream until it has slightly thickened and holds its shape, but does not form peaks. Reserve. Whisk the egg whites in a clean, grease-free bowl until stiff and standing in soft peaks.

4 Strain the milk through a sieve into the cooled, melted chocolate and beat until smooth. Spoon the chocolate mixture into the egg whites, then using a large metal spoon, fold gently. Add the whipped cream and fold in gently.

5 Spoon into a large serving dish or individual small cups. Chill in the refrigerator for 3–4 hours. Just before serving, dust with a little sifted cocoa powder and then serve.

TASTY TIP

Chocolate and spices go together very well as this recipe demonstrates. White chocolate has an affinity with spices such as cardamom, while dark and milk chocolate go very well with cinnamon.

2

3

4

White Chocolate Trifle

INGREDIENTS

Serves 6

1 homemade or bought chocolate
  Swiss roll, sliced
4 tbsp brandy
2 tbsp Irish cream liqueur
425 g can black cherries, drained
  and pitted, with 3 tbsp of the
  juice reserved
900 ml/1½ pints double cream
125 g/4 oz white chocolate, broken
  into pieces
6 medium egg yolks
50 g/2 oz caster sugar
2 tsp cornflour
1 tsp vanilla essence
50 g/2 oz plain dark chocolate, grated
50 g/2 oz milk chocolate, grated

HELPFUL HINT

It is critical that the custard is not allowed to boil once the eggs have been added. Otherwise, the mixture turns to sweet scrambled eggs and is unusable. Cook over a very gentle heat, stirring constantly and testing the mixture often.

1 Place the Swiss roll slices in the bottom of a trifle dish and pour over the brandy, Irish cream liqueur and a little of the reserved black cherry juice to moisten the Swiss roll. Arrange the black cherries on the top.

2 Pour 600 ml/1 pint of the cream into a saucepan and add the white chocolate. Heat gently to just below simmering point. Whisk together the egg yolks, caster sugar, cornflour and vanilla essence in a small bowl.

3 Gradually whisk the egg mixture into the hot cream, then strain into a clean saucepan and return to the heat.

4 Cook the custard gently, stirring throughout until thick and coats the back of a spoon.

5 Leave the custard to cool slightly, then pour over the trifle. Leave the trifle to chill in the refrigerator for at least 3–4 hours, or preferably overnight.

6 Before serving, lightly whip the remaining cream until soft peaks form, then spoon the cream over the set custard. Using the back of a spoon, swirl the cream in a decorative pattern. Sprinkle with grated plain and milk chocolate and serve.

2

3

5

White Chocolate Eclairs

INGREDIENTS

Serves 4–6

50 g/2 oz unsalted butter

60 g/2½ oz plain flour, sifted

2 medium eggs, lightly beaten

6 ripe passion fruit

300 ml/½ pint double cream

3 tbsp kirsch

1 tbsp icing sugar

125 g/4 oz white chocolate, broken
into pieces

HELPFUL HINT

Passion fruit are readily available in supermarkets. They are small, round purplish fruits that should have quite wrinkled skins. Smooth passion fruit are not ripe and will have little juice or flavour.

1 Preheat the oven to 190°C/375°F/Gas Mark 5, 10 minutes before baking. Lightly oil a baking sheet. Place the butter and 150 ml/¼ pint of water in a saucepan and gradually bring to the boil.

2 Remove the saucepan from the heat and immediately add the flour all at once, beating with a wooden spoon until the mixture forms a ball in the centre of the saucepan. Leave to cool for 3 minutes.

3 Add the eggs a little at a time, beating well after each addition until the paste is smooth, shiny and of a piping consistency.

4 Spoon the mixture into a piping bag fitted with a plain nozzle. Sprinkle the oiled baking sheet with water. Pipe the mixture onto the baking sheet in 7.5 cm/3 inch lengths.

5 Bake in the preheated oven for 18–20 minutes, or until well risen and golden. Make a slit along the side of each eclair.

6 Return the eclairs to the oven for a further 2 minutes to dry out. Transfer to a wire rack and leave to cool.

7 Halve the passion fruit and scoop the pulp of 4 of the fruits into a bowl. Add the cream, kirsch and icing sugar and whip until the cream holds it shape. Carefully spoon or pipe into the eclairs.

8 Melt the chocolate in a small heatproof bowl set over a saucepan of simmering water and stir until smooth.

9 Leave the chocolate to cool slightly, then spread over the top of the eclairs. Scoop the seeds and pulp out of the remaining passion fruit. Sieve. Use the juice to drizzle around the eclairs when serving.

2

5

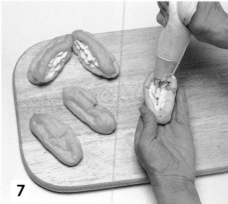

7

Chocolate Roulade

INGREDIENTS

Serves 8

150 g/5 oz golden caster sugar
5 medium eggs, separated
50 g/2 oz cocoa powder

For the filling:

300 ml/½ pint double cream
3 tbsp whisky
50 g/2 oz creamed coconut, chilled
2 tbsp icing sugar
coarsely shredded coconut, toasted

1 Preheat the oven to 180°C/350°F/Gas Mark 4, 10 minutes before baking. Oil and line a 33 x 23 cm /13 x 9 inch Swiss roll tin with a single sheet of non-stick baking parchment. Dust a large sheet of baking parchment with 2 tablespoons of the caster sugar.

2 Place the egg yolks in a bowl with the remaining sugar, set over a saucepan of gently simmering water and whisk until pale and thick. Sift the cocoa powder into the mixture and carefully fold in.

3 Whisk the egg whites in a clean, grease-free bowl until soft peaks form. Gently add 1 tablespoon of the whisked egg whites into the chocolate mixture then fold in the remaining whites. Spoon the mixture onto the prepared tin, smoothing the mixture into the corners. Bake in the preheated oven for 20–25 minutes, or until risen and springy to the touch.

4 Turn the cooked roulade out onto the sugar-dusted baking parchment and carefully peel off the lining paper. Cover with a clean damp tea towel and leave to cool.

5 To make the filling, pour the cream and whisky into a bowl and whisk until the cream holds its shape. Grate in the chilled creamed coconut, add the icing sugar and gently stir in. Uncover the roulade and spoon about three-quarters of coconut cream on the roulade and roll up. Spoon the remaining cream on the top and sprinkle with the coconut, then serve.

HELPFUL HINT

Take care when rolling up the roulade in this recipe as it can break up quite easily.

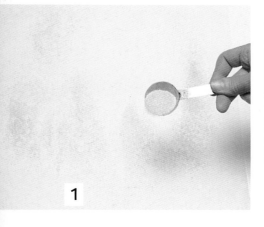

1

3

5

Chocolate Meringue Nest with Fruity Filling

INGREDIENTS

Serves 8

125 g/4 oz hazelnuts, toasted

125 g/4 oz golden caster sugar

75 g/3 oz plain dark chocolate, broken
   into pieces

2 medium egg whites

pinch of salt

1 tsp cornflour

¹/₂ tsp white wine vinegar

chocolate curls, to decorate

For the filling:

150 ml/¹/₄ pint double cream

150 g/5 oz mascarpone cheese

prepared summer fruits, such
   as strawberries, raspberries
   and redcurrants

HELPFUL HINT

To make chocolate curls, melt the
chocolate over hot water then
pour onto a cool surface,
preferably marble if available.
Leave until just set but not hard,
then using a large cook's knife or
a cheese parer, push the blade at
an angle across the surface of the
chocolate to form curls.

1   Preheat the oven to 110°C/225°F/Gas Mark 1, 5 minutes before
baking and line a baking sheet with non-stick baking parchment.
Place the hazelnuts and 2 tablespoons of the caster sugar in a food
processor and blend to a powder. Add the chocolate and blend
again until the chocolate is roughly chopped.

2   In a clean, grease-free bowl, whisk the egg whites and salt until soft
peaks form. Gradually whisk in the remaining sugar a teaspoonful
at a time and continue to whisk until the meringue is stiff and shiny.
Fold in the cornflour and the white wine vinegar with the chocolate
and hazelnut mixture.

3   Spoon the mixture into 8 mounds, about 10 cm/4 inches in
diameter, on the baking parchment. Do not worry if not perfect
shapes. Make a hollow in each mound, then place in the preheated
oven. Cook for 1¹/₂ hours, then switch the oven off and leave in the
oven until cool.

4   To make the filling, whip the cream until soft peaks form. In another
bowl, beat the mascarpone cheese until it is softened, then mix with
the cream. Spoon the mixture into the meringue nests and top with
the fresh fruits. Decorate with a few chocolate curls and serve.

1

2

3

Crème Brûlée with Sugared Raspberries

INGREDIENTS

Serves 6

600 ml/1 pint fresh whipping cream
4 medium egg yolks
75 g/3 oz caster sugar
½ tsp vanilla essence
25 g/1 oz demerara sugar
175 g/6 oz fresh raspberries

HELPFUL HINT

Most chefs use blow torches to brown the sugar in step 7, as this is the quickest way to caramelise the top of the dessert. Take great care if using a blow torch, especially when lighting. Otherwise use the grill, making sure that it is very hot and the dessert is thoroughly chilled before caramelising the sugar topping. This will prevent the custard underneath from melting.

1 Preheat the oven to 150°C/300°F/Gas Mark 2. Pour the cream into a bowl and place over a saucepan of gently simmering water. Heat gently but do not allow to boil.

2 Meanwhile, whisk together the egg yolks, 50 g/2 oz of the caster sugar and the vanilla essence. When the cream is warm, pour it over the egg mixture briskly whisking until it is mixed completely.

3 Pour into 6 individual ramekin dishes and place in a roasting tin.

4 Fill the tin with sufficient water to come halfway up the sides of the dishes.

5 Bake in the preheated oven for about 1 hour, or until the puddings are set. (To test if set, carefully insert a round bladed knife into the centre, if the knife comes out clean they are set.)

6 Remove the puddings from the roasting tin and allow to cool. Chill in the refrigerator, preferably overnight.

7 Sprinkle the sugar over the top of each dish and place the puddings under a preheated hot grill.

8 When the sugar has caramelised and turned deep brown, remove from the heat and cool. Chill the puddings in the refrigerator for 2–3 hours before serving.

9 Toss the raspberries in the remaining caster sugar and sprinkle over the top of each dish. Serve with a little extra cream if liked.

2

5

7

Chocolate, Orange & Pine Nut Tart

INGREDIENTS

Cuts into 8–10 slices

For the sweet shortcrust pastry:
150 g/5 oz plain flour

½ tsp salt

3–4 tbsp icing sugar

125 g/4 oz unsalted butter, diced

2 medium egg yolks, beaten

½ tsp vanilla essence

For the filling:
125 g/4 oz plain dark
   chocolate, chopped

60 g/2½ oz pine nuts,
   lightly toasted

2 large eggs

grated zest of 1 orange

1 tbsp Cointreau

225 ml/8 fl oz whipping cream

2 tbsp orange marmalade

FOOD FACT
Cointreau is an orange-flavoured liqueur and is used in many recipes. You could substitute Grand Marnier or any other orange liqueur, if you prefer.

1 Preheat the oven to 200°C/400°F/Gas Mark 6, 15 minutes before baking. Place the flour, salt and sugar in a food processor with the butter and blend briefly. Add the egg yolks, 2 tablespoons of iced water and the vanilla essence and blend until a soft dough is formed. Remove and knead until smooth, wrap in clingfilm and chill in the refrigerator for 1 hour.

2 Lightly oil a 23 cm/9 inch loose-based flan tin. Roll the dough out on a lightly floured surface to a 28 cm/11 inch round and use to line the tin. Press into the sides of the flan tin, crimp the edges, prick the base with a fork and chill in the refrigerator for 1 hour. Bake blind in the preheated oven for 10 minutes. Remove and place on a baking sheet. Reduce the oven temperature to 190°C/375°F/Gas Mark 5.

3 To make the filling, sprinkle the chocolate and the pine nuts evenly over the base of the pastry case. Beat the eggs, orange zest, Cointreau and cream in a bowl until well blended, then pour over the chocolate and pine nuts.

4 Bake in the oven for 30 minutes, or until the pastry is golden and the custard mixture is just set. Transfer to a wire rack to cool slightly. Heat the marmalade with 1 tablespoon of water and brush over the tart. Serve warm or at room temperature.

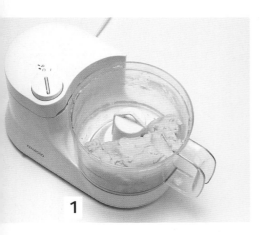

1

2

3

Pear & Chocolate Custard Tart

INGREDIENTS

Cuts into 6–8 slices

For the chocolate pastry:

125 g/4 oz unsalted butter, softened
60 g/2½ oz caster sugar
2 tsp vanilla essence
175 g/6 oz plain flour, sifted
40 g/1½ oz cocoa powder
whipped cream, to serve

For the filling:

125 g/4 oz plain dark
  chocolate, chopped
225 ml/8 fl oz whipping cream
50 g/2 oz caster sugar
1 large egg
1 large egg yolk
1 tbsp crème de cacao
3 ripe pears

HELPFUL HINT

The chocolate pastry is very soft so rolling it between sheets of clingfilm will make it much easier to handle without having to add a lot of extra flour.

1   Preheat the oven to 190°C/375°F/Gas Mark 5, 10 minutes before baking. To make the pastry, put the butter, sugar and vanilla essence into a food processor and blend until creamy. Add the flour and cocoa powder and process until a soft dough forms. Remove the dough, wrap in clingfilm and chill in the refrigerator for at least 1 hour.

2   Roll out the dough between 2 sheets of clingfilm to a 28 cm/11 inch round. Peel off the top sheet of clingfilm and invert the pastry round into a lightly oiled 23 cm/9 inch loose-based flan tin, easing the dough into the base and sides. Prick the base with a fork, then chill in the refrigerator for 1 hour.

3   Place a sheet of non-stick baking parchment and baking beans in the case and bake blind in the preheated oven for 10 minutes. Remove the parchment and beans and bake for a further 5 minutes. Remove and cool.

4   To make the filling, heat the chocolate, cream and half the sugar in a medium saucepan over a low heat, stirring until melted and smooth. Remove from the heat and cool slightly before beating in the egg, egg yolk and crème de cacao. Spread evenly over the pastry case base.

5   Peel the pears, then cut each pear in half and carefully remove the core. Cut each half crossways into thin slices and arrange over the custard, gently fanning the slices towards the centre and pressing into the chocolate custard. Bake in the oven for 10 minutes.

6   Reduce the oven temperature to 180°C/350°F/Gas Mark 4 and sprinkle the surface evenly with the remaining sugar. Bake in the oven for 20–25 minutes, or until the custard is set and the pears are tender and glazed. Remove from the oven and leave to cool slightly. Cut into slices, then serve with spoonfuls of whipped cream.

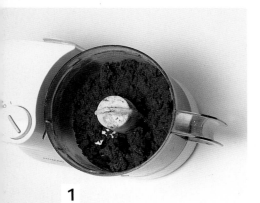

1

2

5

Double Chocolate Truffle Slice

INGREDIENTS

Cuts into 12–14 slices

1 quantity Chocolate Pastry
   (see page 232)
300 ml/½ pint double cream
300 g/11 oz plain dark
   chocolate, chopped
25–40 g/1–1½ oz unsalted
   butter, diced
50 ml/2 fl oz brandy or liqueur
icing sugar or cocoa powder
   for dusting

1 Preheat the oven to 200°C/400°F/Gas Mark 6, 15 minutes before baking. Prepare the chocolate pastry and chill in the refrigerator, according to instructions.

2 Roll the dough out to a rectangle about 38 x 15 cm/15 x 6 inches and use to line a rectangular loose-based flan tin, trim then chill in the refrigerator for 1 hour.

3 Place a sheet of non-stick baking parchment and baking beans in the pastry case, then bake blind in the preheated oven for 20 minutes. Remove the baking parchment and beans and bake for 10 minutes more. Leave to cool completely.

4 Bring the cream to the boil. Remove from the heat and add the chocolate all at once, stirring until melted and smooth. Beat in the butter, then stir in the brandy liqueur. Leave to cool slightly, then pour into the cooked pastry shell. Refrigerate until set.

5 Cut out 2.5 cm/1 inch strips of non-stick baking parchment. Place over the tart in a criss-cross pattern and dust with icing sugar or cocoa.

6 Arrange chocolate leaves, caraque or curls around the edges of the tart. Refrigerate until ready to serve. Leave to soften at room temperature for 15 minutes before serving.

TASTY TIP

Liqueurs that would work very well in this recipe include Tia Maria, Kahlua, Cointreau, Grand Marnier, Amaretto and Crème de Menthe.

3

4

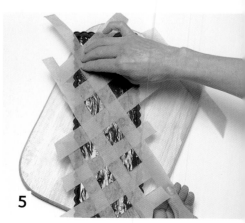

5

Chocolate Apricot Linzer Torte

INGREDIENTS

Cuts into 10–12 slices

For the chocolate almond pastry:

75 g/3 oz whole blanched almonds

125 g/4 oz caster sugar

215 g/7½ oz plain flour

2 tbsp cocoa powder

1 tsp ground cinnamon

½ tsp salt

grated zest of 1 orange

225 g/8 oz unsalted butter, diced

2–3 tbsp iced water

For the filling:

350 g/12 oz apricot jam

75 g/3 oz milk chocolate, chopped

icing sugar, for dusting

1 Preheat the oven to 375°C/190°F/Gas Mark 5, 10 minutes before baking. Lightly oil a 28 cm/11 inch flan tin. Place the almonds and half the sugar into a food processor and blend until finely ground. Add the remaining sugar, flour, cocoa powder, cinnamon, salt and orange zest and blend again. Add the diced butter and blend in short bursts to form coarse crumbs. Add the water 1 tablespoon at a time until the mixture starts to come together.

2 Turn onto a lightly floured surface and knead lightly, roll out, then using your fingertips, press half the dough onto the base and sides of the tin. Prick the base with a fork and chill in the refrigerator. Roll out the remaining dough between 2 pieces of clingfilm to a 28–30.5 cm/11–12 inch round. Slide the round onto a baking sheet and chill in the refrigerator for 30 minutes.

3 For the filling, spread the apricot jam evenly over the chilled pastry base and sprinkle with the chopped chocolate.

4 Slide the dough round onto a lightly floured surface and peel off the top layer of clingfilm. Using a straight edge, cut the round into 1 cm/½ inch strips; allow to soften until slightly flexible. Place half the strips, about 1 cm/½ inch apart, to create a lattice pattern. Press down on each side of each crossing to accentuate the effect. Press the ends of the strips to the edge, cutting off any excess. Bake in the preheated oven for 35 minutes, or until cooked. Leave to cool before dusting with icing sugar and serve cut into slices.

TASTY TIP

When making the pastry do not allow the dough to form into a ball or it will be tough.

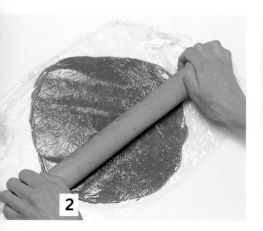

2

3

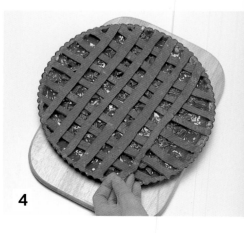

4

Mini Pistachio & Chocolate Strudels

INGREDIENTS
Makes 24

5 large sheets filo pastry
50 g/2 oz butter, melted
1–2 tbsp caster sugar for sprinkling
50 g/2 oz white chocolate, melted,
  to decorate

For the filling:
125 g/4 oz unsalted pistachios,
  finely chopped
3 tbsp caster sugar
50 g/2 oz plain dark chocolate,
  finely chopped
1–2 tsp rosewater
1 tbsp icing sugar for dusting

1 Preheat the oven to 170°C/325°F/Gas Mark 3, 10 minutes before baking. Lightly oil 2 large baking sheets. For the filling, mix the finely chopped pistachio nuts, the sugar and dark chocolate in a bowl. Sprinkle with the rosewater and stir lightly together and reserve.

2 Cut each filo pastry sheet into 4 to make 23 x 18 cm/ 9 x 7 inch rectangles. Place 1 rectangle on the work surface and brush with a little melted butter. Place another rectangle on top and brush with a little more butter. Sprinkle with a little caster sugar and spread about 1 dessertspoon of the filling along one short end. Fold the short end over the filling, then fold in the long edges and roll up. Place on the baking sheet seam-side down. Continue with the remaining pastry sheets and filling until both are used.

3 Brush each strudel with the remaining melted butter and sprinkle with a little caster sugar. Bake in the preheated oven for 20 minutes, or until golden brown and the pastry is crisp.

4 Remove from the oven and leave on the baking sheet for 2 minutes, then transfer to a wire rack. Dust with icing sugar. Place the melted white chocolate in a small piping bag fitted with a plain writing pipe and pipe squiggles over the strudel. Leave to set before serving.

TASTY TIP
Keep the unused filo pastry covered with a clean damp tea towel to prevent it from drying out.

1

2

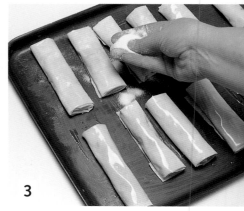
3

White Chocolate & Macadamia Tartlets

INGREDIENTS

Makes 10

1 quantity Sweet Shortcrust Pastry
  (see page 230)
2 medium eggs
50 g/2 oz caster sugar
250 ml/9 fl oz golden syrup
40 g/1½ oz butter, melted
50 ml/2 fl oz whipping cream
1 tsp vanilla or almond essence
225 g/8 oz unsalted macadamia nuts,
  coarsely chopped
150 g/5 oz white chocolate,
  coarsely chopped

1 Preheat the oven to 200°C/400°F/Gas Mark 6, 15 minutes before baking. Roll the pastry out on a lightly floured surface and use to line 10 x 7.5–9 cm/3–3½ inch tartlet tins. Line each tin with a small piece of tinfoil and fill with baking beans. Arrange on a baking sheet and bake blind in the preheated oven for 10 minutes. Remove the tinfoil and baking beans and leave to cool.

2 Beat the eggs with the sugar until light and creamy, then beat in the golden syrup, the butter, cream and vanilla or almond essence. Stir in the macadamia nuts. Sprinkle 100 g/3½ oz of the chopped white chocolate equally over the bases of the tartlet cases and divide the mixture evenly among them.

3 Reduce the oven temperature to 180°C/350°F/Gas Mark 4 and bake the tartlets for 20 minutes, or until the tops are puffy and golden and the filling is set. Remove from the oven and leave to cool on a wire rack.

4 Carefully remove the tartlets from their tins and arrange closely together on the wire rack. Melt the remaining white chocolate and, using a teaspoon or a small paper piping bag, drizzle the melted chocolate over the surface of the tartlets in a zig-zag pattern. Serve slightly warm or at room temperature.

FOOD FACT

Macadamia nuts come from Hawaii and are large, crisp, buttery flavoured nuts. They are readily available from supermarkets.

2

2

4

Chocolate Lemon Tartlets

INGREDIENTS

Makes 10

1 quantity Chocolate Pastry
   (see page 232)
175 ml/6 fl oz double cream
175 g/6 oz plain dark
   chocolate, chopped
2 tbsp butter, diced
1 tsp vanilla essence
350 g/12 oz lemon curd
225 ml/8 fl oz prepared custard sauce
225 ml/8 fl oz single cream
½ –1 tsp almond essence

To decorate:

grated chocolate
toasted flaked almonds

TASTY TIP

Lemon curd is very easy to make. In a medium-sized heatproof bowl, mix together 175 g/6 oz of caster sugar, the grated rind and juice of 2 large lemons and 4 large eggs. Add 125 g/4 oz cubed unsalted butter and place the bowl over a saucepan of gently simmering water. Stir often until thickened, about 20 minutes. Leave to cool and use as above.

1 Preheat the oven to 200°C/400°F/Gas Mark 6, 15 minutes before baking. Roll the prepared pastry out on a lightly floured surface and use to line 10 x 7.5 cm/3 inch tartlet tins. Place a small piece of crumpled tinfoil in each and bake blind in the preheated oven for 12 minutes. Remove from the oven and leave to cool.

2 Bring the cream to the boil, then remove from the heat and add the chocolate all at once. Stir until smooth and melted. Beat in the butter and vanilla essence and pour into the tartlets and leave to cool.

3 Beat the lemon curd until soft and spoon a thick layer over the chocolate in each tartlet, spreading gently to the edges. Do not chill in the refrigerator or the chocolate will be too firm.

4 Place the prepared custard sauce into a large bowl and gradually whisk in the cream and almond essence until the custard is smooth and runny.

5 To serve, spoon a little custard onto a plate and place a tartlet in the centre. Sprinkle with grated chocolate and almonds, then serve.

1

2

3

Raspberry Chocolate Ganache & Berry Tartlets

INGREDIENTS

Makes 10

1 quantity Chocolate Pastry
600 ml/1 pint whipping cream
275 g/10 oz seedless raspberry jam
225 g/8 oz plain dark chocolate, chopped
700 g/1½ lb raspberries or other summer berries
50 ml/2 fl oz framboise liqueur
1 tbsp caster sugar
crème fraîche, to serve

1 Preheat the oven to 200°C/400°F/Gas Mark 6, 15 minutes before cooking. Make the chocolate pastry and use to line 8 x 7.5 cm/3 inch tartlet tins. Bake blind in the preheated oven for 12 minutes.

2 Place 400 ml/14 fl oz of the cream and half of the raspberry jam in a saucepan and bring to the boil, whisking constantly to dissolve the jam. Remove from the heat and add the chocolate all at once, stirring until the chocolate has melted.

3 Pour into the pastry-lined tartlet tins, shaking gently to distribute the ganache evenly. Chill in the refrigerator for 1 hour or until set.

4 Place the berries in a large shallow bowl. Heat the remaining raspberry jam with half the framboise liqueur over a medium heat until melted and bubbling. Drizzle over the berries and toss gently to coat.

5 Divide the berries among the tartlets, piling them up if necessary. Chill in the refrigerator until ready to serve.

6 Remove the tartlets from the refrigerator for at least 30 minutes before serving. Using an electric whisk, whisk the remaining cream with the caster sugar and the remaining framboise liqueur until it is thick and softly peaking. Serve with the tartlets and crème fraîche.

1

2

3

Chocolate Raspberry Mille Feuille

INGREDIENTS

Serves 6

450 g/1 lb puff pastry, thawed
  if frozen
1 quantity Chocolate Raspberry
  Ganache (see page 244), chilled
700 g/1½ lbs fresh raspberries, plus
  extra for decorating
icing sugar for dusting

For the raspberry sauce:

225 g/8 oz fresh raspberries
2 tbsp seedless raspberry jam
1–2 tbsp caster sugar, or to taste
2 tbsp lemon juice or
  framboise liqueur

HELPFUL HINT

If you prefer, make 1 big mille feuille by leaving the 3 strips whole in step 2. Slice the finished mille feuille with a sharp serrated knife.

1. Preheat the oven to 200°C/400°F/Gas Mark 6, 15 minutes before baking. Lightly oil a large baking sheet and sprinkle with a little water. Roll out the pastry on a lightly floured surface to a rectangle about 43 x 28 cm/17 x 11 inches. Cut into 3 long strips. Mark each strip crossways at 6.5 cm/2½ inch intervals using a sharp knife; this will make cutting the baked pastry easier and neater. Carefully transfer to the baking sheet, keeping the edges as straight as possible.

2. Bake in the preheated oven for 20 minutes or until well risen and golden brown. Place on a wire rack and leave to cool. Carefully transfer each rectangle to a work surface and, using a sharp knife, trim the long edges straight. Cut along the knife marks to make 18 rectangles.

3. Place all the ingredients for the raspberry sauce in a food processor and blend until smooth. If the purée is too thick, add a little water. Taste and adjust the sweetness if necessary. Strain into a bowl, cover and chill in the refrigerator.

4. Place 1 pastry rectangle on the work surface flat-side down, spread with a little chocolate ganache and sprinkle with a few fresh raspberries. Spread a second rectangle with a little ganache, place over the first, pressing gently, then sprinkle with a few raspberries. Place a third rectangle on top, flat-side up, and spread with a little chocolate ganache.

5. Arrange some raspberries on top and dust lightly with a little icing sugar. Repeat with the remaining pastry rectangles, chocolate ganache and fresh raspberries.

6. Chill in the refrigerator until required and serve with the raspberry sauce and any remaining fresh raspberries.

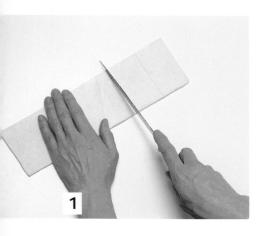

1

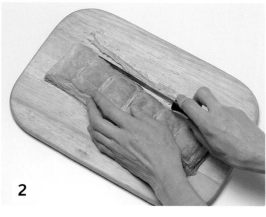

2

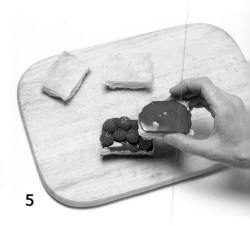

5

Sachertorte

INGREDIENTS

Cuts into 10–12 slices

150 g/5 oz plain dark chocolate

150 g/5 oz unsalted butter, softened

125 g/4 oz caster sugar, plus
  2 tbsp

3 medium eggs, separated

150 g/5 oz plain flour, sifted

To decorate:

225 g/8 oz apricot jam

125 g/4 oz plain dark
  chocolate, chopped

125 g/4 oz unsalted butter

25 g/1 oz milk chocolate

FOOD FACT

In 1832, the Viennese foreign minister asked a Vienna hotel to prepare an especially tempting cake. The head pastry chef was ill and so the task fell to second-year apprentice, Franz Sacher, who presented this delightful cake.

1 Preheat the oven to 180°C/350°F/Gas Mark 4, 10 minutes before baking. Lightly oil and line a deep 23 cm/9 inch cake tin.

2 Melt the 150 g/5 oz of chocolate in a heatproof bowl set over a pan of simmering water. Stir in 1 tablespoon of water and leave to cool.

3 Beat the butter and 125 g/4 oz of the sugar together until light and fluffy. Beat in the egg yolks, one at a time, beating well between each addition. Stir in the melted chocolate, then the flour.

4 In a clean grease-free bowl, whisk the egg whites until stiff peaks form, then whisk in the remaining sugar. Fold into the chocolate mixture and spoon into the prepared tin. Bake in the pre-heated oven for 30 minutes until firm. Leave for 5 minutes, then turn out onto a wire rack to cool. Leave the cake upside down.

5 To decorate the cake, split the cold cake in 2 and place one half on a serving plate. Heat the jam and rub through a fine sieve.

6 Spread half the jam onto the first cake half, then cover with the remaining cake layer and spread over the remaining jam. Leave at room temperature for 1 hour or until the jam has set.

7 Place the plain dark chocolate with the butter into a heatproof bowl set over a saucepan of simmering water and heat until the chocolate has melted. Stir until smooth, then leave until thickened. Use to cover the cake.

8 Melt the milk chocolate in a heatproof bowl set over a saucepan of simmering water. Place in a small greaseproof piping bag and snip a small hole at the tip. Pipe Sacher with a large 'S' on the top. Leave to set at room temperature.

3

4

5

White Chocolate & Raspberry Mousse Gateau

INGREDIENTS

Cuts 8 slices

4 medium eggs
125 g/4 oz caster sugar
75 g/3 oz plain flour, sifted
25 g/1 oz cornflour, sifted
3 gelatine leaves
450 g/1 lb raspberries, thawed
  if frozen
400 g/14 oz white chocolate
200 g/7 oz plain fromage frais
2 medium egg whites
25 g/1 oz caster sugar
4 tbsp raspberry or orange liqueur
200 ml/7 fl oz double cream
fresh raspberries, halved, to decorate

HELPFUL HINT

Do not try to wrap the chocolate-covered parchment around the cake before it is nearly set or it will run down and be uneven.

1 Preheat the oven to 190°C/375°F/Gas Mark 5, 10 minutes before baking. Oil and line 2 x 23 cm/9 inch cake tins. Whisk the eggs and sugar until thick and creamy and the whisk leaves a trail in the mixture. Fold in the flour and cornflour, then divide between the tins. Bake in the preheated oven for 12–15 minutes or until risen and firm. Cool in the tins, then turn out onto wire racks.

2 Place the gelatine with 4 tablespoons of cold water in a dish and leave to soften for 5 minutes. Purée half the raspberries, press through a sieve, then heat until nearly boiling. Squeeze out excess water from the gelatine, add to the purée and stir until dissolved. Reserve.

3 Melt 175 g/6 oz of the chocolate in a bowl set over a saucepan of simmering water. Leave to cool, then stir in the fromage frais and purée. Whisk the egg whites until stiff and whisk in the sugar. Fold into the raspberry mixture with the rest of the raspberries.

4 Line the sides of a 23 cm/9 inch springform tin with non-stick baking parchment. Place 1 layer of sponge in the base and sprinkle with half the liqueur. Pour in the raspberry mixture and top with the second sponge. Brush with the remaining liqueur. Press down and chill in the refrigerator for 4 hours. Unmould onto a plate.

5 Cut a strip of double thickness non-stick baking parchment to fit around the cake and stand 1 cm/½ inch higher. Melt the remaining white chocolate and spread thickly onto the parchment. Leave until just setting. Wrap around the cake and freeze for 15 minutes. Peel away the parchment. Whip the cream until thick and spread over the top. Decorate with raspberries.

1

2

4

French Chocolate Pecan Torte

INGREDIENTS

Cuts into 16 slices

200 g/7 oz plain dark
  chocolate, chopped
150 g/5 oz butter, diced
4 large eggs
100 g/3½ oz caster sugar
2 tsp vanilla essence
125 g/4 oz pecans, finely ground
2 tsp ground cinnamon
24 pecan halves, lightly toasted,
  to decorate

For the chocolate glaze:

125 g/4 oz plain dark
  chocolate, chopped
60 g/2½ oz butter, diced
2 tbsp clear honey
¼ tsp ground cinnamon

FOOD FACT

Although this recipe is French, the torte actually originates from Germany, and tends to be a very rich cake-like dessert. It is delicious served with a fruity mixed berry compote.

1 Preheat the oven to 180°C/350°F/Gas Mark 4, 10 minutes before baking. Lightly butter and line a 20.5 x 5 cm/8 x 2 inch springform tin with non-stick baking paper. Wrap the tin in a large sheet of tinfoil to prevent water seeping in.

2 Melt the chocolate and butter in a saucepan over a low heat and stir until smooth. Remove from the heat and cool.

3 Using an electric whisk, beat the eggs, sugar and vanilla essence until light and foamy. Gradually beat in the melted chocolate, ground nuts and cinnamon, then pour into the prepared tin.

4 Set the foil-wrapped tin in a large roasting tin and pour in enough boiling water to come 2 cm/¾ inches up the sides of the tin. Bake in the preheated oven until the edge is set, but the centre is still soft when the tin is gently shaken. Remove from the oven and place on a wire rack to cool.

5 For the glaze, melt all the ingredients over a low heat until melted and smooth, then remove from the heat. Dip each pecan halfway into the glaze and set on a sheet of non-stick baking paper until set. Allow the remaining glaze to thicken slightly.

6 Remove the cake from the tin and invert. Pour the glaze over the cake smoothing the top and spreading the glaze around the sides. Arrange the glazed pecans around the edge of the torte. Allow to set and serve.

3

4

5

Chocolate & Almond Daquoise with Summer Berries

INGREDIENTS

Serves 8

For the almond meringues:

6 large egg whites

¼ tsp cream of tartar

275 g/10 oz caster sugar

½ tsp almond essence

50 g/2 oz blanched or flaked almonds, lightly toasted and finely ground

For the chocolate buttercream:

75 g/3 oz butter, softened

450 g/1 lb icing sugar, sifted

50 g/2 oz cocoa powder, sifted

3–4 tbsp milk or single cream

550 g/1¼ lb mixed summer berries such as raspberries, strawberries and blackberries

To decorate:

toasted flaked almonds

icing sugar

1 Preheat the oven to 140°C/ 275°F/Gas Mark 1 10 minutes before baking. Line 3 baking sheets with non-stick baking paper and draw a 20.5 cm/8 inch round on each one.

2 Whisk the egg whites and cream of tartar until soft peaks form. Gradually beat in the sugar, 2 tablespoons at a time, beating well after each addition, until the whites are stiff and glossy.

3 Beat in the almond essence, then using a metal spoon or rubber spatula gently fold in the ground almonds.

4 Divide the mixture evenly between the 3 circles of baking paper, spreading neatly into the rounds and smoothing the tops evenly.

5 Bake in the preheated oven for about 1 1/4 hours or until crisp, rotating the baking sheets halfway through cooking. Turn off the oven, allow to cool for about 1 hour, then remove and cool completely before discarding the lining paper

6 Beat the butter, icing sugar and cocoa powder until smooth and creamy, adding the milk or cream to form a soft consistency.

7 Reserve about a quarter of the berries to decorate. Spread 1 meringue with a third of the buttercream and top with a third of the remaining berries. Repeat with the other meringue rounds, buttercream and berries.

8 Scatter with the toasted flaked almonds, the reserved berries and sprinkle with icing sugar and serve.

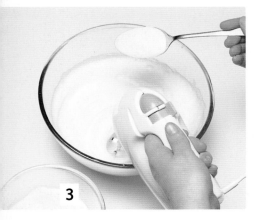

3

6

7

Index

C000320096

ALI

MUHAMMAD ALI

igloobooks

Published in 2014
by Igloo Books Ltd
Cottage Farm
Sywell
NN6 0BJ
www.igloobooks.com

Copyright © 2014 Igloo Books Ltd

All rights reserved. No part of this publication may be
reproduced or transmitted in any form or by any means,
electronic, or mechanical, including photocopying, recording,
or by any information storage and retrieval system,
without permission in writing from the publisher.

Writen by Louise Spilsbury

SHE001 0714
2 4 6 8 10 9 7 5 3 1
ISBN 978-1-78343-535-7

Printed and manufactured in China

CONTENTS

MUHAMMAD ALI

Muhammad Ali is probably the most famous boxer of all time and one of the most recognised athletes in the world. When he was still a skinny child with just one win under his belt, he started to boast about being the greatest, but he soon backed up his brash claims with ability, dedication and expertise, and proved them to be true. Ali was the first man to win the undisputed World Heavyweight boxing title three times and he beat more champions and top contenders than any other heavyweight champion in history.

At the height of his fame, Ali had it all. He was young, strong, handsome and charismatic. He enraged opponents and entertained fans with his arrogant proclamations and witty pre-match taunts. He lit up the ring with his quick reflexes, strong punches and unique fighting style: a style that went against many of the game's fundamental teachings. As well as being a sporting legend, Ali is almost as well-known for his actions outside the ring, as a thinker, poet and an artist.

The story of Muhammad Ali's long, successful life has all the drama, twists and turns of a movie script. His boxing career began with a chance encounter that would seem far-fetched if it weren't true. He wanted to be loved, but he never shied away from controversy. His conversion to Islam, his fights for civil rights, and his outspoken condemnation of and refusal to fight in the Vietnam War surrounded him with controversy for many years. Even after he retired from the ring, he stayed in the public eye through charitable work and humanitarian missions around the world. Muhammad Ali was and is simply a man no one could ignore.

"I am the greatest. I said that even before I knew I was."
Muhammad Ali

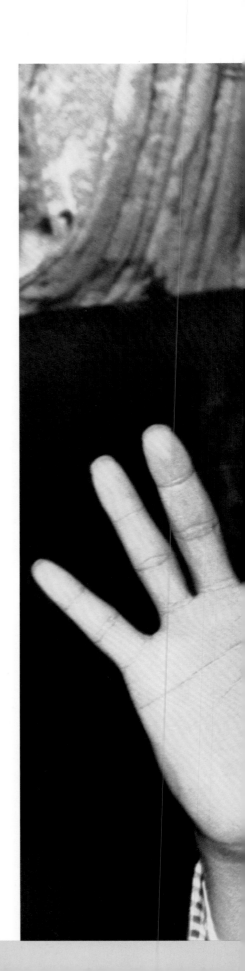

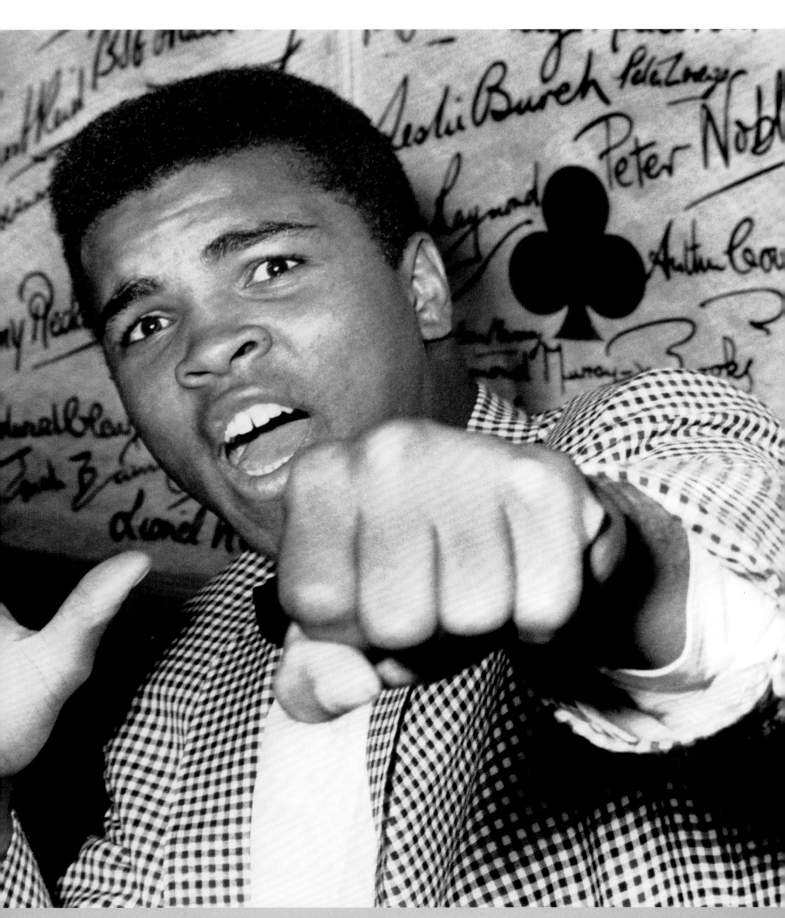

EARLY YEARS

Clay always called his mother "Mama Bird" because when he was young he said he thought she had a tiny, little bird nose. "I don't know why I thought that, because birds don't have noses, but from the moment I said it we all started calling her Mama Bird." Here he is seen fooling around with his mother in Pittsburgh, Pennsylvania, in 1963.

CASSIUS CLAY, JR

Muhammad Ali was born at 6:35 p.m. on 17 January 1942. At the first of many weigh-ins during his life, he was just 6 pounds, 7 ounces (2.92 kg). He was named Cassius Marcellus Clay, Jr., after his father, Cassius Marcellus Clay, Sr. His mother was Odessa Grady Clay. Two years after Cassius was born, his younger brother, Rudolph or Rudy (later Rahman Ali) joined the family.

All of Clay's four grandparents were free people, but his ancestors were slaves during the pre-Civil War era in the American South. Cassius Marcellus Clay, Sr. was named after Cassius Clay, the 19th century abolitionist who owned slaves but was also one of the first to set them free. Two of Cassius's paternal great-grandparents had been his slaves. His mother's paternal grandfather was Abe Grady, a white Irishman who emigrated to the United States soon after the Civil War and married a freed slave. Her maternal grandparents were a white man named Thomas Morehead and a slave.

Odessa was born in Kentucky, but moved to Louisville with her mother and siblings after her parents separated. Times were tough and she had to work to buy her own clothes so that she could go to school. She met Cassius's father when she was 16 years old. Cassius Marcellus Clay, Sr. was a muralist and painter, but earned a living painting billboards and signs. Odessa worked while the children were very young, as a house cleaner and a cook. The Clays weren't rich but they worked hard to bring up the boys in the best street they could afford. They lived at 3302 Grand Avenue, a small, four-roomed house in an all-black neighbourhood in Louisville, Kentucky. Clay remembered a mostly happy and loving home with his father always hugging and kissing him and Rudy, and his mother as a kind, gentle person.

Odessa Clay wipes down her son following a training bout in 1974. She was a calm, kind influence on him throughout her life.

CASSIUS AS A KID

As befits one of the world's great storytellers, there are many childhood tales about Clay. His mother started to call him 'GG' when he was a baby because that was the sound he made from his crib. When Clay became a Golden Gloves champion, he said of his first words, "You know what that meant? I was trying to say Golden Gloves." Odessa also used to tell people proudly that her eldest's first knockout punch was at six months old when he hit her and loosened two teeth so badly that she had to have them pulled out. Rudy remembered Clay asking his younger brother to throw rocks at him. However many rocks Rudy threw, he could never hit Clay. Even then Clay had some of the skills that would serve him so well in the ring, running left and right at speed, ducking, dodging, and weaving out of the way.

Odessa was a Baptist and Cash, as Clay Sr was known, was a Methodist but the boys always went to their mother's church. They never missed a morning of Sunday School and Clay remembered walking to church, knowing he looked handsome in his freshly ironed shirt and bow tie, and feeling proud of his pretty mother and handsome father. The Clays also instilled a sense of hard work in their boys. While Clay was at school, he worked at odd jobs to earn a few dollars a week and the boys used to accompany their father to work, where Cash taught them how to mix paint and lay out signs.

The Clays were a proud, contented family but not without problems. Cassius Clay Sr was arrested four times for reckless driving, twice for disorderly conduct and twice for assault. He had affairs and sometimes became violent when he was drunk. In fact, Odessa called the police three times when her husband turned nasty at home.

When Odessa Clay was taking her sons with her to church every Sunday, most churches, like this one, were segregated.

A DIVIDED CITY

Louisville was a quiet, peaceful city when Cassius Clay grew up in the 1950s and 1960s, but he became increasingly aware of the segregation around him. One of his first encounters with prejudice happened when he was very young, standing with his mother at a bus stop on a hot day. He was thirsty and when Odessa asked for a glass of water at a small diner nearby, the owner refused to help and closed the door in their faces.

Although he and Rudy didn't face real danger or violence in Louisville, as many people did in parts of the South, Clay was still shocked at being treated like a second-class citizen in the public realm, while being raised with pride and self-awareness at home. This was a time when laws known as Jim Crow Laws enforced segregation and made life difficult for African Americans. Louisville, like most cities, was a place where restaurants and swimming pools displayed signs that read 'Whites Only' and 'No Coloreds Allowed'. Black people had to go to separate schools, drink from separate water fountains and use separate restrooms. The boys never got into fights but white boys would call Clay and his brother 'nigger' and tell them to leave if they strayed into certain parts of town.

In spite of these challenges, Clay had a confidence and belief he was destined for great things from a young age. He remembers a time when, at about nine years old, he would wake up in the middle of the night and go outside to look at the stars and wait patiently for a message or a revelation from God. He never heard anything but never lost faith that a message would come.

In Clay's youth, segregation was a fact of life everywhere. There were separate waiting areas at bus stations (left) and separate entrances at theatres.

TURNING POINT

A message did come, but in the rather unlikely form of a local policeman named Joe Martin. In October 1954, when Cassius Clay was 12 years old, he and a friend cycled to the Louisville Home Show at Columbia Auditorium, mainly to sample the free food, popcorn and sweets on offer to visitors. When the boys had eaten their fill and were ready to leave, they discovered that Clay's bike had been stolen. Clay was furious and distraught – the bike was a new, red-and-white Schwinn that his parents had given him for Christmas. He was told to go and see a policeman, in the basement of the auditorium, who would fill out a police report for him.

Joe Martin was a Louisville cop who spent his spare time teaching boys to box for the city's recreation department in a gym, in the basement of the auditorium. When Clay burst in on Martin, the boy was crying and furious. He told Martin angrily that he was ready to search the whole state for whoever stole his bike and whip them soundly when he caught up with them. Martin asked if he knew how to fight. "No, but I'd fight them anyway," answered Clay. Martin replied, "Well, you better learn how to fight before you start challenging people that you're gonna whup," and gave Clay an application to join the gym, where boys could come and box every evening, Monday to Friday, from 6 p.m. to 8 p.m.

Call it chance or fate, this meeting was a turning point in Clay's life – everything changed when he entered the gym and started training. He began to learn the art and trade of boxing with a vengeance and would soon progress from a skinny kid with little talent into the greatest boxer that the world has ever known.

In this picture, taken at the gym in Louisville when he was just 12 years old, Clay looks young and vulnerable but his talent and training soon gave him the skills and confidence he needed to do more than strike the pose of a real boxer.

FROM AMATEUR TO OLYMPIAN

DETERMINATION AND DIET

A new boxing champion was born the first time Cassius Clay stepped into the gym. To make up for what he lacked in skill and experience, Clay had more than his share of determination and discipline. He began boxing with a vengeance. He spent all of his spare time training. He was the first one in the gym and the last to leave.

Clay trained six days a week and on school days he woke at four or five in the morning so that he could go running – what boxers call 'roadwork'. He was often seen racing city buses to school and was soon known by his peers as the kid who was obsessed with boxing. He took care about what he ate too, and over time, developed a special diet that included milk with two raw eggs in it for breakfast and a concoction of garlic and water that he drank throughout the day.

To go from skinny kid to Clay's strong boxing physique took relentless training and determination.

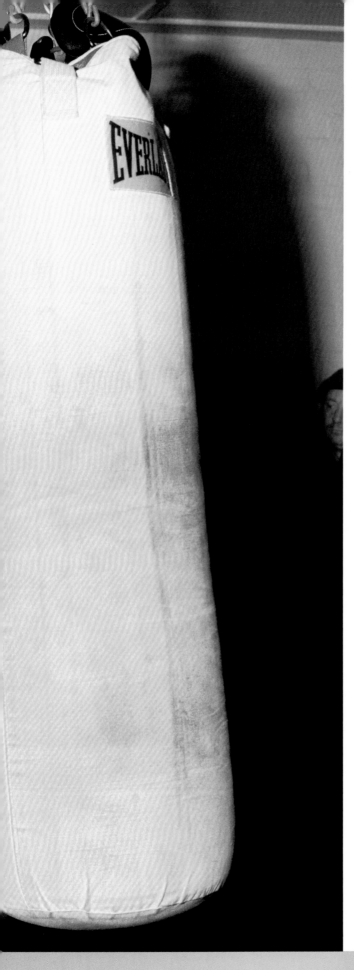

Joe Martin produced a popular local television show called 'Tomorrow's Champions' as part of the Columbia Gym's amateur programme. Boxing was important in Louisville and this Saturday afternoon show offered instant, local celebrity status to boxers. After just six weeks of training, Martin featured Clay on 'Tomorrow's Champions'. Thrilled at the prospect of being seen on television all over Kentucky, Clay trained even harder.

In his first ever televised bout, in 1954, he fought a local white boy named Ronny O'Keefe. Clay was only about 4 feet (1.2 m) tall and weighed just 89 pounds (40 kg), while O'Keefe was just a little older but bigger. The fight lasted three rounds of one minute each and Clay won by a split vote. From then on, Martin had him on the show each week. This was also the point at which Clay started bragging about being the greatest!

Clay's face shows the concentration and conviction he always had while training when he was young.

TOURNAMENTS AND TRAVEL

For the next few years, Clay continued to work and train hard, and to win the majority of the local fights. After 1958, he and other teenage boxers from the gym took part in boxing tournaments in different towns, including Indianapolis, Chicago and Toledo, staying in motels along the way. They were usually driven by Joe or his wife Christine Martin. Christine remembered young Clay as a very easy-going, polite boy who carried his Bible everywhere he went. She also recalled that in those days, the black kids were not allowed into restaurants, so she'd have to take their orders and get hamburgers for them to eat in the car.

By this time, Clay knew that he had a real talent for boxing and his dreams were going beyond earning enough to buy his parents a house and himself a fancy big car. Sometimes he would draw a picture of the back of a jacket with 'Cassius Clay, Golden Gloves Winner', or 'Cassius Clay, World Heavyweight Champ' written on it. Bob Surkein, an Amateur Athletic Union (AAU) referee and judge, recalled one tour in which Clay took all the sports sections from newspapers in a hotel shop and café so that he could cut out and keep all the pictures of himself.

Clay was also developing his own inimitable style. Instead of holding his hands up high to guard his head like most boxers, he held his gloves down low, and while most boxers stepped or ducked aside to avoid being hit, Clay leaned away from blows, risking throwing himself off balance. This unorthodox style worked for him because he had very fast reflexes and could throw a quick punch and dodge out of the way before other fighters could react. Soon, reporters, referees, and judges were talking about his presence and prodigious talent.

This is Clay in 1960 posing with Maxie Rosenbloom (left),
Light Heavyweight Champion in 1932, and Solly Krieger
(right), World Middleweight Champion in 1938.

Cassius Clay fighting against Gary Jawish during a Golden Gloves bout.

ON THE WAY TO THE OLYMPICS

Clay continued to train with Joe Martin and a more experienced coach named Fred Stoner. By the time he was 18 years old, he had fought a total of 105 amateur bouts, with 100 wins and just five losses. He won six Kentucky Golden Gloves Championships and two national Golden Gloves tournaments, in 1959 and 1960. He also won two national AAU titles.

This run of exciting wins had made Clay a local celebrity but he was yet to become really famous. This all changed when he was selected to represent the United States at the 1960 Olympic Games in Rome. Clay did well in the Olympic trials, but the trip to California for the trials was his first time on an aeroplane. It was such a rough flight that he declared he wouldn't fly again and that if he couldn't travel to Rome by train or boat, he wouldn't go at all. In the end he knew that if he wanted to be Heavyweight Champion of the world one day, he had to face his fears, so agreed to go but he bought a parachute from an army surplus store to wear on the flight!

When the Olympic team gathered in New York before the flight to Italy, Clay took the chance to try to meet one of his heroes, Sugar Ray Robinson. He waited all day outside Robinson's club but when the boxer finally appeared at ten o'clock and Clay stepped forward to talk to him, he remembers Robinson just patted him on the shoulder and said, "Later boy, I'm busy right now." Crushed, Clay vowed there and then that he would be different when he was a famous champion and that he would speak to, shake hands with or sign autographs for every fan he met.

At the Olympic Village, Clay stayed true to his vow and devoted attention not only to his training but also to meeting and greeting as many people as possible. He did as many interviews as he could and was often photographed. An unnamed team-mate said, "You would have thought he was running for mayor. He went around introducing himself and learning other people's names and swapping team lapel pins. If they'd had an election, he would have won in a walk." In fact, Clay even earned the nickname "the mayor of the Olympic Village".

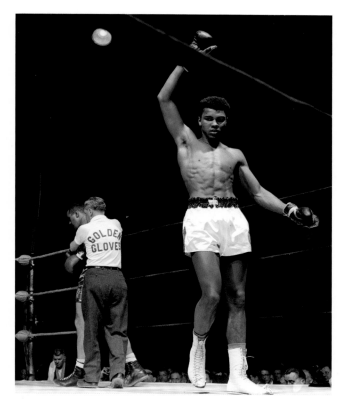

Eighteen-year-old Cassius Clay raises his arm in victory after knocking out Gary Jawish in the 1960 Inter-city championships at Madison Square Garden.

Clay stands tall and proud wearing his gold medal for light heavyweight boxing in the centre of the winners' podium at the 1960 Olympic Games in Rome. On the right is Zbigniew Pietrzykowski of Poland who took silver. On the left are Giulio Saraudi of Italy and Anthony Madigan of Australia who took joint bronze.

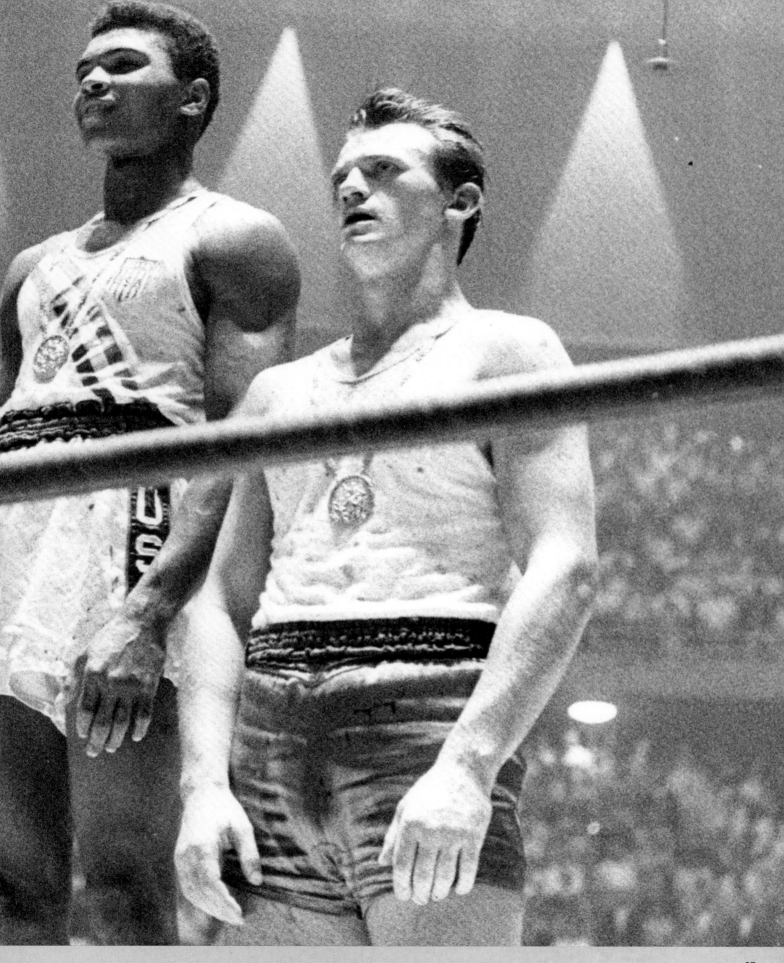

TAKING GOLD

Clay's opening fight was against the Belgian Yvon Becot. It was stopped by the referee in the second round. He then beat the Russian Gennadiy Shatkov, who had won the middleweight gold medal at the 1956 Games in Melbourne in a unanimous points decision. In the semi-final Clay won again in a unanimous decision against Australian opponent Tony Madigan. In the final battle for the light-heavyweight gold medal, Clay fought Zbigniew "Ziggy" Pietrzykowski, an older, stronger and more experienced opponent. The first round didn't go well, with Clay taking some serious punches. The second went a little better, as he managed to throw four hard rights to Pietrzykowski's head, but he was still behind on points. Clay came alive in the third and final round. He was quick, coordinated and displayed perfect timing, with a flurry of both left and right punches, almost winning by a knockout blow, but in the end taking the match on points.

A spokesperson for the US Olympic Committee told The Associated Press that Clay "is putting on an amazing performance. In the ring he murders 'em with his fists. Outside the ring he kills them with kindness and his solid Americanism."

When Clay returned to Louisville after a three-week absence he received a hero's welcome. Crowds cheered as he passed through the streets in a 30-car motorcade escorted by the police. At a celebration at his school, he was met by Mayor Bruce Hoblitzell, cheerleaders and about 200 friends and fans. The mayor, on behalf of the Louisville Chamber of Commerce, told him that his gold medal was the key to the city. Clay read aloud what would be his first published poem: 'How Cassius Took Rome'.

HOW CASSIUS TOOK ROME

To make America the greatest is my goal,
So I beat the Russians, and I beat the Pole,
and for the USA won the Medal of Gold.
Italians said, "You're Greater than the
  Cassius of Old."
We like your name, we like your game.
So make Rome your home if you will.
I said I appreciate your kind hospitality,
But the USA is my county still,
'Cause they're waiting to welcome me
  in Louisville.

Clay was so proud of his medal that he even wore it to bed. He believed that the medal could change more than his career prospects. Sadly, it didn't. Before he had left the Olympic Village, a Russian reporter had asked him how it felt to win the gold medal for his country when there were still restaurants in the United States that wouldn't serve him. He replied that there were qualified people working on that problem and to him, the United States was the best country in the world. However, when Clay returned and he and a friend were refused service at a local whites-only restaurant while he was wearing the Olympic medal round his neck, he was furious. Legend has it that his response was to angrily toss the gold medal straight into the Ohio River.

When he was young, Clay loved to read about his victories in the newspapers.

ALI'S PROFESSIONAL CAREER

THE CONTRACT

After the Olympics, Cassius Clay was possibly the hottest property in boxing. His earning potential was huge. This attracted the attention of investors in Louisville who were prepared to pay big bucks to get a piece of the action.

The first interested party was Billy Reynolds, a Louisville metals millionaire. Clay never signed the contract Reynolds offered owing to his father. Reynolds stipulated that Joe Martin should play a role in Clay's professional career but Clay Sr. disliked cops in general, and Martin in particular.

A consortium of white businessmen turned boxing enthusiasts quickly came up with a better deal. The prime mover in the Louisville Sponsoring Group (LSG) was Colonel Bill Faversham, who was Vice President, sales, of the Kentucky distillers responsible for Jack Daniels and other popular drinks. Faversham and his friends, horse breeder Pat Calhoun and tobacco magnate Bill Cutchins, reckoned on $25,000 to launch Clay professionally so they contacted some investor friends, asking, "How would you like to buy a piece of a prizefighter?" Pretty soon there were ten in the consortium, each putting in $2800.

On 26 October 1960, Clay signed the contract and became a professional boxer. His deal included a $10,000 bonus, a minimum annual salary of $4,000 for two years and $6,000 for four years. Everything Clay earned, in the ring or otherwise, was to be split 50–50 with the syndicate, who paid all expenses, from his trainer's salary to housing rent.

US boxing promoter and prime mover in the Louisville Sponsoring Group (LSG) Bill Faversham is shown here speaking with Clay in 1963.

Clay celebrated the contract with a splurge: a pink Cadillac. He was soon cruising the streets of Louisville showing it off. In the following years the LSG became very rich from Clay's fighting, but also had to pay out a lot on anything from first class flights to the legal fees that kept Clay out of jail after speeding in the Cadillac.

Clay celebrated signing his first professional contract by buying a new Cadillac.

THE FIRST PRO BOUT

The LSG's official line was, "We are behind Cassius Clay to improve the breed of boxing, to do something nice for a deserving, well-behaved Louisville boy". They said they stepped in to make sure Clay was not prey to contracts with underworld mobsters. This was the case with the Heavyweight World Champion of the day: Sonny Liston. But the truth was that they knew Clay could make them richer. This was not just through their cut of his winnings in the ring, but also from sales amongst black boxing enthusiasts of the whisky and cigarettes they made and could advertise at Clay's fights.

Just three days after signing his contract, Clay fought his first professional bout. It had been organised over the preceding weeks by the LSG. Clay was to go up against one Tunney Hunsacker. Hunsacker was the 30-year-old chief of police of the little town of Fayetteville in West Virginia. Clay arrived at the Freedom Hall fight venue at the Louisville fairgrounds in his Cadillac. Hunsacker later recalled being 'pretty impressed' by the 'brassy young boy' and his entourage of supporters.

The police chief was a seasoned fighter who had fought more than 30 bouts. He soon realised that he was, "too old to be fighting an 18-year-old fella", once he got in the ring, even though he gave Clay, "some good chops to the stomach in the second and third rounds", that allegedly almost made the youngster bring up his hamburger dinner. However, Clay was too big and fast for Hunsacker, and had a trickily varied repertoire of punches. The six-round fight ended with a unanimous points decision for Clay and Hunsacker's eyes swollen shut. Clay was far from the finished article, but still gave the LSG cause for celebration that their investment was already paying dividends.

Clay's first professional bout against Hunsacker's was just the first on his road to success. At this point Cassius Clay knew he was going places.

Trainer Angelo Dundee was Clay's (Ali's) trainer from 1960 until the boxer retired.

A NEW TRAINER

In December 1960, the LSG syndicate made a move to back up their investment in Cassius Clay. They hired him a new trainer: Angelo Dundee. Dundee, based in Miami, had a great pedigree. He had trained 1955 World Welterweight Champion Carmen Basilio, and worked with title hopeful Willie Pastrano. Clay knew of Dundee because three years earlier, the 15-year-old boxer had stalked Dundee to a Louisville hotel, blagged a brief meet, and then quizzed Dundee for hours about all aspects of the boxing art.

Dundee quickly appreciated Clay's raw talents. The boxer was unusual in combining heavyweight power with the speed typical of the lighter divisions. Clay produced stinging jabs, usually to the head, that his friend and doctor Ferdie Pacheco called 'snake-licking'. But Dundee saw the faults, too. Clay often held his guard low and back-pedalled to evade punches. This could leave him off-balance or out of range for punching back, even with his long reach.

Dundee got to work. He further developed Clay's movement and balance. This was aided by sparring with Pastrano who was widely admired for his fleeting footwork. Dundee did not try to get rid of all the rough corners on his protégé. He once said, "Training fighters is like trying to catch fish," meaning that you have to go with what is already there.

The pair formed a close bond. Dundee was to remain as Clay's trainer through the coming years. His extraordinary abilities at training champions were sought by many other fighters, too. These included George Foreman, who in 1994, became the oldest Heavyweight Champion in history at the age of 45, and Sugar Ray Leonard who became World Champion in five different weight divisions.

Angelo Dundee was a brilliant motivator and was with Clay for virtually his entire career.

BOXER FOCUS: WILLIE PASTRANO

Wilfred Raleigh Pastrano was a pudgy child known as 'fatmeat' from the French Quarter in New Orleans. He took on a bully who was smacking him after his father, Frank, gave him the ultimatum: fight back or get a licking from me. Willie decided to take up boxing to lose weight at the suggestion of his friend Ralph Dupas. He went to the gym at night when there were fewer people around.

Pastrano lied about his age to fight his first professional bout when he was 15 years old and still at school. He was fined and had to remain amateur until he was 18. He started to spend summers in Miami at the training gym of Angelo Dundee, along with Dupas, who was a junior boxing champion. After high school, Pastrano moved to Miami where he further developed his fast hands and feet, and technical skills. In the early 1960s, Pastrano started to work with Dundee's new recruit, Cassius Clay.

Pastrano fought at heavyweight in the early professional years but with Sonny Liston rising to prominence, dropped down a division. In 1963, Pastrano's career had its high point. He won the Light Heavyweight World Championship, on a narrow points decision, against the overwhelming favourite Harold Johnson in Las Vegas. He only got the fight because other boxers had backed out. Pastrano defended the title twice, with unexpectedly hard hitting, before losing to José Torres in New York in 1965. This was when he retired. Pastrano by then was using drugs and had little money left. After working as nightclub bouncer and casino greeter, he eventually escaped the mean streets of Miami. He ran a municipal gym back in New Orleans where he trained many young fighters.

US heavyweight boxer Willie Pastrano training in 1958.

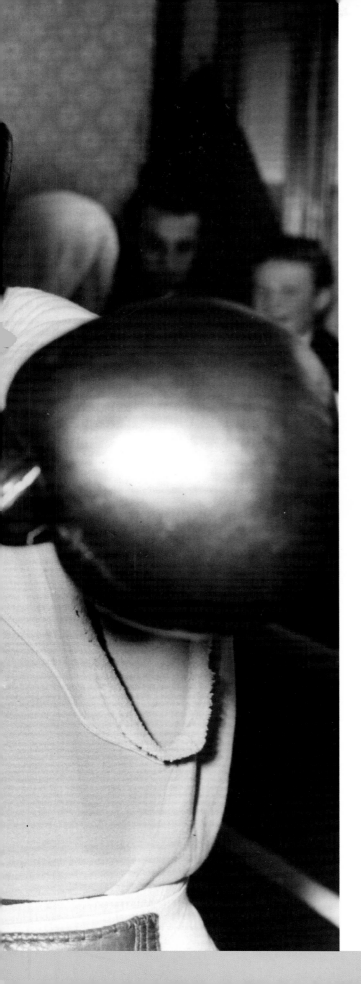

Pastrano held the World Light Heavyweight crown from 1963 until 1965.

STATISTICS

BORN	New Orleans (LA), November 1935
DIED	New Orleans (LA), December 1997
TURNED PROFESSIONAL	1950
NUMBER OF PRO BOUTS	84
WINS-LOSSES-DRAWS	63-13-8
NUMBER OF KNOCKOUTS	14
RETIRED	1965

Clay showing why he earned the nickname 'The Louisville Lip' at a press conference after he signed to fight Sonny Liston in 1963.

THE LOUISVILLE LIP

In the early 1960s, Cassius Clay was morphing into the boxing personality that the world came to know. At this time across the United States, the Civil Rights Movement was hitting its stride. There was pressure from black people to remain quiet and modest, aware that the opposite traits might offend some whites and derail the movement for race equality. Clay was a proud, loud, arrogant black man, happy to tell anyone who was listening about his boxing gifts. He also knew what he said – the boasts and the taunts – could impact his opponents, which is why Angelo Dundee called him 'The Louisville Lip'. The next step was to hone his public persona.

A seminal figure in this was the professional wrestler, George Wagner, who in his late 20s was transformed from a jobbing wrestler into the personality Gorgeous George. He became one of the first wrestling stars of the early days of colour television. Gorgeous George looked dramatic with long, curled blonde hair and sparkly robes. He entered the ring with special entrance music and valets threw roses and sprayed perfume into the crowd. He bad-mouthed his opponents and boasted at his triumphs. Crowds cheered or booed him.

Clay went to see Gorgeous George in Las Vegas in 1961 and was star-struck with his persona. And so he mimicked the wrestler's swagger, without the costumes and perfume. He proclaimed phrases such as, "To beat me, you have to be greater than great," and, "I will be the youngest champion in history". Some older boxers, such as Joe Louis, cautioned Clay; some people hated his self-praise, but as his fights and victories notched up, it was becoming clear that Clay did have something to shout about.

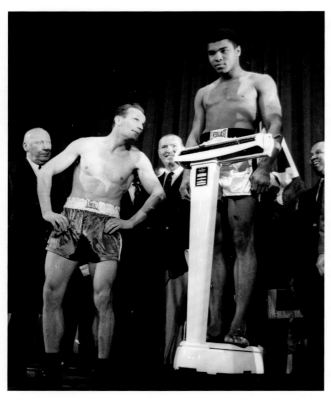

Henry Cooper jokingly looks at Clay's scales during the weigh-in before their fight at the Arsenal Stadium, London, in 1966.

SPREADING REPUTATION

Between his professional debut in 1960 until early 1963, Cassius Clay fought 18 different opponents and he won each fight: 14 by knock-out or technical knock-out. He fought across the United States, from Miami and New York to Las Vegas and Los Angeles. His reputation was growing fast and boxing was more popular than ever before, buoyed by increasing television audiences and the clamour for tickets to live boxing bouts.

Clay occasionally faced adversity in the boxing ring. In February 1962, he faced Sonny Banks in his 11th professional bout. This was the first time that Clay was ever knocked over. Near the start of the bout, Banks threw a left hook to the jaw that sent Clay flying but he got straight up. Angelo Dundee saw then that Clay could not only take punches, but also come back stronger. "That's when I knew I had a guy with greatness. It was remarkable how he survived that one punch. God he was exciting." Clay went on to win inside four rounds.

Clay devised a game with Dundee around this time. He started to predict the outcome of fights – how many rounds it would last. A good example of this is his fight against Archie Moore later in 1962. Moore was an old professional champion who had briefly trained Clay after the Olympics, but Clay did not like his authoritarian style. He correctly predicted a fourth-round knock-out, chanting, '"Archie Moore... Must fall in four."

Cassius Clay reached an even wider audience by travelling to London in 1963 for his 19th fight and first overseas professional bout. He took on British Heavyweight Champion Henry Cooper in front of 55,000 people and, again, correctly predicted a win in five. But Clay was lucky – he was floored by a phenomenal left from Cooper. Clay struggled to get up, but was saved by the bell marking the end of the round.

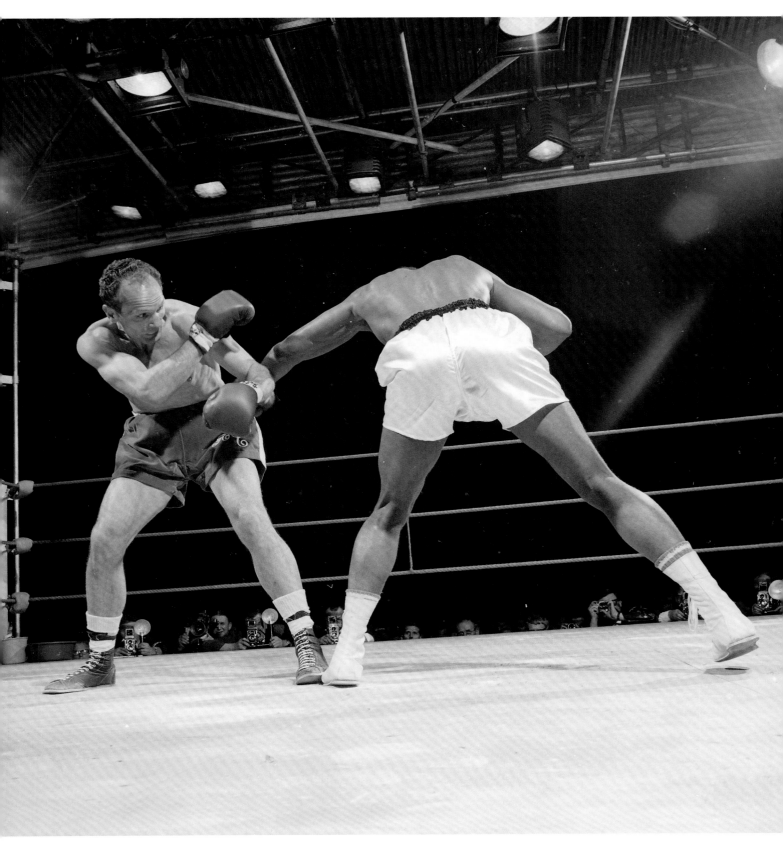

Henry Cooper and Clay in action in 1966.

BOXER FOCUS: SIR HENRY COOPER

Henry Cooper and his twin George were born in London and grew up during the Blitz years of the Second World War when the city was under attack. The boys came from a boxing lineage. Their father was a good amateur boxer in the Royal Artillery, and their horse trader grandfather was a bare-knuckle fighter who could fight 20 rounds. Henry and George joined Eltham Boxing Club and moved through the amateur ranks in England. Cooper won 73 of 84 contests, including the Amateur Light Heavyweight Championship in 1952.

Cooper became a dominant force in British professional boxing. In 1959, he won both the British and Commonwealth heavyweight titles. Back then he was still living at home, sharing a bedroom with George. He moved out only in 1960 when he got married. In the mid-60s Cooper was becoming internationally known for his crushing left hook – his left fist was popularly known as 'enery's hammer'. Buoyed by his close loss to Clay in 1963, Cooper challenged for the world title in a rematch against Muhammad Ali in 1966. History repeated itself as Cooper lost again after swelling and persistent bleeding above the left eye where the skin was thin – his jagged brow did him no boxing favours.

Cooper remained British champion until his narrow defeat to Joe Bugner in 1971. He became a national celebrity following release of a popular autobiography, appearances on BBC's *A Question of Sport*, television advertising for Brut aftershave and flu jabs, and his dedication to charitable work. His fundraising bought 100 coaches enabling sick or disabled children to go on holiday. Henry Cooper was knighted in 2000.

British boxer Henry Cooper at a function with his old rival Muhammad Ali in 1984.

Henry Cooper and his brother George during a training session in 1958. Henry was preparing for a Commonwealth heavyweight title fight against Brian London.

STATISTICS

BORN	London, May 1934
DIED	London, May 2011
TURNED PROFESSIONAL	1954
NUMBER OF PRO BOUTS	55
WINS-LOSSES-DRAWS	40-14-1
NUMBER OF KNOCKOUTS	27
RETIRED	1971

WORLD CHAMPION

Cassius Clay talks up his chances of beating Sonny Liston at a press call before the fight in 1964.

GETTING A SHOT

In early 1964, boxing in the United States was massive. It had far more press coverage than basketball, tennis and athletics were still amateur-only sports and it was the quiet season for baseball and American football. Heavyweight was the most talked about boxing division. The two biggest stars in this division were the champion, Sonny Liston, and the young pretender, Cassius Clay.

The contrast between the two men fascinated the nation and the boxing world. Clay was handsome, eloquent and brilliant but his near defeat to Henry Cooper suggested he was an unfinished article. Liston, however, was a sullen and quiet, unstoppable force of nature.

Clay had had Liston in his sights for years and in 1964, thought he was ready. The boxers' handlers fixed a match for 25 February at Miami Convention Hall. In the run-up to the match, Clay trained hard in Miami, with the occasional break for press events including meeting the phenomenally popular Beatles, who were on tour. He also took time to plague Liston with taunts and boasts. At 3 a.m. outside Liston's rented Miami house, Clay parked a vehicle sign-written with 'Cassius Clay Enterprises' and shouted out that he was 'bear hunting' until the furious Liston ran out with a poker in his hand. At a press conference Clay read out a poem in which he imagined he'd punch Liston out of the ring:

*"Who would have thought when they came to
   the fight,
That they'd witness a launching of a human satellite.
Yes the crowd did not dream when they put down
   their money
That they would see a total eclipse of the Sonny."*

Clay noisily predicted he would knock out Liston in eight rounds. When reporters asked Liston how long Clay would last, he simply raised two fingers. The public antipathy between the men only pumped up expectations for the fight.

BOXER FOCUS: SONNY LISTON

Charles 'Sonny' Liston was the youngest of 25 children. His abusive and alcoholic father, Tobe, worked in cotton fields near Little Rock, Arkansas, and forced Sonny and his other children into hard labour, too. Sonny and his mother Helen escaped Tobe's domination when she started a new life working in St. Louis.

Sonny was 6 feet (1.82 m), 200 pounds (90 kg), incredibly strong and illiterate. Out of place amongst city kids, he fell into gang fighting and armed robbery. In 1950, he was jailed for five years at Missouri State Penitentiary Life. In jail a priest encouraged him to take up boxing and Liston soon rose to jail heavyweight champion.

Liston was paroled in 1952 by boxing handlers with alleged links to organised crime. He shot through the amateur ranks and turned professional in 1953. He became known as 'The Bear' owing to his frightening power, 15-inch (38-cm) circumference fists, and record of short bouts with knockouts. After a stretch in the St. Louis Workhouse for assault in 1956, Liston relocated to Philadelphia, where his professional contract was bought out by Mafia bosses. Liston defeated the popular fighter Floyd Patterson to take the World Heavyweight Championship in 1962. After two defeats to Clay in 1964/5, he carried on boxing for a further five years.

Sonny Liston was found dead at his Las Vegas home on 5 January 1971. Many suspected a mob execution, probably by enforced overdose, as there were traces of heroine in Liston's blood and needle marks on his arm and Liston had always been afraid of needles. It is alleged that he signed his own death warrant by refusing to throw a fight.

Sonny Liston in 1958.

Sonny Liston and Floyd Patterson (left), during a championship fight won by Liston in just one and a half minutes.

STATISTICS

BORN	St. Francis County, May 1932 (uncertain)
DIED	Las Vegas (NV), December 1970
TURNED PROFESSIONAL	1953
NUMBER OF PRO BOUTS	54
WINS-LOSSES-DRAWS	50-4-0
NUMBER OF KNOCKOUTS	39
RETIRED	1970

8-1 CHANCE

It was not looking good for Cassius Clay. The bookmakers were giving odds of 8-1 for a Liston whitewash. In the days before the fight just 3 out of 46 boxing writers predicted a Clay victory. At the weigh-in on fight day Clay was pumped up more than anyone could remember. He screamed at Liston, "Someone's going to die at ringside tonight!"

The Convention Hall was only half full owing to limited hopes for a long fight, but many ex-world champions, including Sugar Ray Robinson, Willie Pastrano, Rocky Marciano and Joe Louis, were there to see how Clay would fare, and maybe even witness an upset.

Onlookers saw how Clay was taller than Liston and refused to be stared down by 'The Bear'. The fighters started warily with Cassius evading jabs and wild punches from Liston, but then Clay threw a rapid combination of punches. Liston staggered, outboxed. The champion fought back in the second round, but in the third he was hurting as Clay ramped up the head blows. Liston was cut on the cheekbone and reeling.

In the fourth round, Liston landed his best punch and Clay started blinking, rubbing his face, ducking and backpedalling. At the bell, he told Angelo Dundee he couldn't see properly, and Dundee demanded he continue but stay out of the way of Liston. Later it was alleged that Liston had put stinging liniment on his gloves to slow his opponent. Clay's eyes were wide open by the start round six and he laid into Liston's face, punch after punch. Liston appeared dazed as he slumped in his chair at the bell. He didn't come out for round seven.

There was pandemonium in the ring. Clay bounded around, arms raised, shouting, "eat your words" at the assembled press. Cassius Clay was the new Heavyweight World Champion.

Cassius Clay's expression says it all in the moments after he beat Sonny Liston and became Heavyweight Champion of the World.

Cassius Clay shows off his World Champion belt.

THE GREATEST

"I don't have a mark on my face. I upset Sonny Liston. I just turned 22. I must be the greatest. I shook up the world! I shook up the world! I shook up the world! I shook up the world!" Cassius Clay

Cassius Clay ponders his stratospheric rise in US and world sport, and boxing opportunities to come. What would happen to top his achievements in the early 1960s?

Cassius Clay's victory was one of the biggest upsets in boxing history. He had talked the talk and walked the walk. But he had had severe doubts he could win. Clay's doctor, Ferdie Pacheco, later said, "This was the only time I saw him nervous... he had no idea if he could do what he had been saying he could do."

Clay put his victory down to being too fast for Liston. But there were other factors. One was complacency on Liston's part. In the three-and-a-half years preceding their bout, Liston had been in the ring for just more than 13 minutes! That was because he kept beating opponents quickly. Another was an alleged injury. Straight after he quit on the night, he told a reporter that his left shoulder "feels like it's broke". He later claimed he could not punch properly after the flurry in the initial round owing to a strained muscle, possibly resulting from extravagant punching in round one, or a training injury. Many thought the claims were just sour grapes. After all, Liston could fight through pain – his only defeat as a professional before the Cassius Clay fight had been against Marty Marshall, when he had suffered a broken jaw and carried on fighting until the end.

Suddenly Clay's claims in interviews, at the ringside or even on later records and in books, to being 'The Greatest', were no longer sounding like hollow boasts. Everyone witnessing his performance now knew that he was the real deal. His boasts still irritated many, but their substance was undeniable.

BECOMING MUHAMMAD ALI

I'M FREE TO BE ME

Two days after his victory in the Liston fight, which had made Cassius Clay the youngest Heavyweight Champion in history, he made an important announcement. He told a press conference that he was a follower of the religion of Islam, and that among the reasons for his conversion from Christianity was the discrimination against black people in the United States and his refusal to support integration. By making this stand, Clay was telling the United States, "I don't have to be what you want me to be. I'm free to be me."

Clay had first stepped into a mosque in 1961 and later said it was the first time he felt truly spiritual. He liked what he heard and started to read the Islamic newspaper *Muhammad Speaks* and attend regular meetings. He was soon seriously considering becoming a Muslim. He was linked to an organisation known as the Nation of Islam and the teachings of one of their leaders called Elijah Muhammad, a man who preached powerful messages of emancipation and believed Islam was the only religion for black people and that Christianity was the religion of white people. This argument proved a powerful one to Clay, who had seen injustices all his life and faced discrimination every day.

Clay attended meetings in the temple and read and learned from the Quran – the only difference between him and other Muslims was that he didn't have the same duties to carry out because of his profession. Clay also introduced his brother Rudy to his mosque and to Islam, and although he had discovered Islam later than Clay, it was Rudy who converted first, changing his name to Rahaman Ali. Clay waited to make a public declaration of his faith because he feared he would not have been allowed to fight in the championship if people knew that he had converted to Islam.

Clay's victory against Liston gave him the confidence to pursue his beliefs.

Cassius Clay with Malcolm X (left).

FROM CLAY TO ALI

Clay was also influenced by his friendship with Malcolm X, who he met in 1961 at a Nation of Islam meeting. Malcolm X supported Clay and stayed at the Miami training camp before the Liston fight. In March 1964, Malcolm X met Clay in New York and took him on a tour of the United Nations where they were photographed with African delegates. While at the UN, Clay signed his name Cassius X Clay and later that day, he rejected what he'd come to see as his slave name and accepted a new name, as given to him by Elijah Muhammad, Muhammad Ali. Muhammad meaning 'worthy of praise' and Ali the name of a great general and cousin of the Prophet Muhammad.

Many in the boxing establishment and the press did not respond well to Ali's change of religion and name. Some treated it as a fad he'd soon get over; many believed he was being used as an instrument of hate and refused to call him anything other than Cassius Clay. When Ali went to watch a fight at Madison Square Garden in March, the President refused to use the name Muhammad Ali when introducing well-known boxers in the audience. When Ali walked out by way of protest, the audience booed.

In May 1964, to get some respite from these tensions and the glare of the press, Ali began a month-long tour of Africa, visiting Ghana, Nigeria and Egypt. He met Egyptian President Gamal Abdel Nasser and Ghanaian President Kwame Nkrumah and was greeted by cheering crowds wherever he went, repeatedly calling out, "Who's the Greatest?" for the response, "You are!" In a speech during his trip, he announced, "In America everything is white. I am glad to be here among my own people."

Residents of Ghana cheer for Muhammad Ali during his visit there in 1964.

Muhammad Ali sits attentively listening to Elijah Muhammad giving
a speech at a Nation of Islam meeting in 1964.

TIME OF TENSIONS

Muhammad Ali returned from Africa to rising tensions in the Nation of Islam. A rift between Elijah Muhammad and Malcolm X had become publicly apparent when Malcolm X said President Kennedy's assassination in 1963 had been, "chickens coming home to roost", which went against the Nation's stance of no comment on the popular leader's death.

In early 1964, Malcolm X had made a pilgrimage to Mecca where he witnessed people of different colours worshipping together, making him question the Nation's core belief of Islam being a black religion. In spite of Malcolm's attempts to persuade him otherwise, Ali chose to side with Elijah.

In Africa, Ali snubbed Malcolm, and after Malcolm X was assassinated in early 1965, Ali was not there at the funeral. In later life Ali expressed his regret at his treatment of his former close friend.

Ali also faced tension from his parents. His mother was convinced her son would not have converted if the LSG had not sent him far from home to Miami. His father was concerned that the Nation was just after Ali's money. Elijah had asked his son, Herbert, to help with Ali's business dealings with LSG and other white sponsors. Herbert became Ali's personal manager and also spiritual advisor, and was a constant presence in the Ali entourage. Ali's parents were concerned that Herbert would ruin Ali's professional life. They were also aware of their diminishing influence over Ali. A prime motive in Ali's life was now that of pleasing Elijah and, in many ways, the Nation had become his close family.

Ali also faced the threat of physical danger in the world outside the ring as a result of being in the Nation of Islam. In the days following Malcolm X's funeral, there was a mysterious fire in Ali's apartment, which was unoccupied at the time, and the Nation's headquarters were firebombed.

People queued to pay their respects at the funeral of Malcolm X. Malcolm X was a divisive figure in the United States and in the Nation of Islam. Although he had uncompromising beliefs, his powerful speeches attracted large crowds of people. He played an important role in Ali's life by introducing him to Islam.

Ali, wearing a white towelling robe, wades through members of the press to reach the ring for his rematch with Sonny Liston in St. Dominic's Arena, Lewiston, Maine, on 25 May 1965.

LISTON REMATCH

In early 1965, Ali was focussing all his energy on his rematch with Sonny Liston. The fight had been postponed from November 1964 in Boston when, three days before the fight, Ali was rushed to hospital for surgery on a swelling hernia. Liston, who after training was in better condition than the first match, had little sympathy for Ali, saying the hernia had been caused by, "all that hollering".

The fight was rescheduled for 25 May 1965, this time in Lewiston, Maine, rather than Boston, owing to concern about attacks by anti-Nation of Islam factions. The crowd in Lewiston was just a few thousand strong, but the fight was shown in movie theatres and on television nationwide. Liston was 9-5 favourite and people expected a closer, longer encounter. Ali predicted victory in the ninth.

Ali won in round one with his third punch, which became known as 'the phantom punch'. Ali had set his feet before throwing a fast, powerful right into Liston's jaw. Liston was up-ended onto the canvas. Ali stood over Liston shouting: "Get up and fight, sucker!" He was livid to be denied the chance to demonstrate he was champion by rights – Ali felt that Liston's claims of a bad shoulder had devalued his earlier victory. Liston did get up before the count had finished, but the referee called the fight a few seconds later.

There were allegations that the fight was fixed and that Liston took a fall so his mafia connections could make good betting money. It was rumoured that Liston was in poor shape having been taking heroin in the run-up to the rescheduled bout. Liston said that Ali standing over him at the count prevented him getting up. Just after the fight, Liston said of the phantom punch that he, 'saw it too late'.

Ali reacted angrily to Liston's first round defeat in 1965. He had won again but had also been denied the chance to prove his mastery in the ring.

A relaxed Floyd Patterson (left) sniggers at one of Ali's jibes at a press conference announcing their title bout in 1965.

BATTLE OF IDEALS

On 22 November 1965, Floyd Patterson challenged Ali for a championship fight. Patterson and Ali were old friends. Patterson as a past (1952) Olympic champion had mentored Ali at the 1960 Olympics. The pair had been in contact ever since. Patterson had been World Champion in 1956 and again in 1960, before losing badly to Liston in 1962, and was now aiming to regain the crown for the third time.

Ali typically decided that adding an edge of jibing before the bout would generate interest. Although friends, there was a fundamental difference in ideals of how to empower African Americans. Patterson was vocal in the Civil Rights Movement and wanted to end all segregation. The Nation of Islam supported segregation. For some, the bout pitted the two sides against each other. Frank Sinatra implored Patterson, his friend via civil rights rallies, to, "win the title back for America".

So, at press conferences, Ali called Patterson 'Uncle Tom' meaning he was subordinate to white people and 'rabbit' suggesting he was running scared of standing up for himself in society. He even showed up with a bag of carrots at Patterson's training camp. Patterson called Ali 'Cassius' to taunt him, although later he said he did it because a speech difficulty made it hard for him to say Muhammad.

The fight itself was a mockery. It was clear from the start to all, including Ali, that Patterson had an injured back – a slipped disc during training – and could not defend himself properly. Both fighters thought the bout would be stopped but the referee kept it going. The press viewed the match as an attempt by Ali to humiliate Patterson by keeping on punching and not delivering a knockout until round 12. But Ali did not want to hurt his friend unnecessarily. Patterson later said he had never felt such soft blows.

BOXER FOCUS: FLOYD PATTERSON

Floyd Patterson was the third of his parents' 11 children. He grew up in poor tenements in Brooklyn, New York. Floyd was a regular truant from school, stealing to try to help the family make ends meet. After several court appearances at age 11, he was sent to live in an upstate New York school for emotionally disturbed boys, for 18 months, where he learnt to read and write, and also took up boxing. Floyd turned amateur in 1951, and professional after winning Olympic heavyweight gold in 1952. For his first professional match, Floyd earned just $300.

Floyd was a leading professional when Rocky Marciano retired in 1956. He fought Archie Moore for the title in Chicago, in November that year. Floyd was sufficiently relaxed that he had a nap before the match, which he won on a technical knockout in the fifth, becoming the youngest heavyweight champion in history at that time. He defended his title twice before being beaten by the right hand – called the Hammer of Thor – of Swedish fighter Ingemar Johansson in 1959. Floyd regained his belt the next year but in 1962, was knocked out in round one by Sonny Liston. Floyd was so embarrassed that he left the venue afterwards wearing a false beard, moustache and dark glasses.

He failed to beat Liston again and Ali twice before retiring in 1972, after 20 years professional fighting. Patterson was a quiet, thoughtful man who became chairman of the New York State Athletic Commission and promoted boxing as a way out for children living in inner city ghettos. He suffered from Alzheimer's in later life to the point that he could not remember who he had fought for the title in 1956.

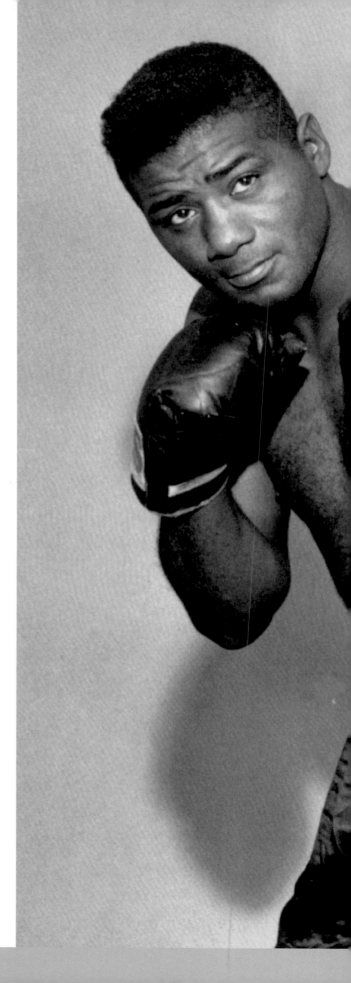

Boxer Floyd Patterson
strikes a pose.

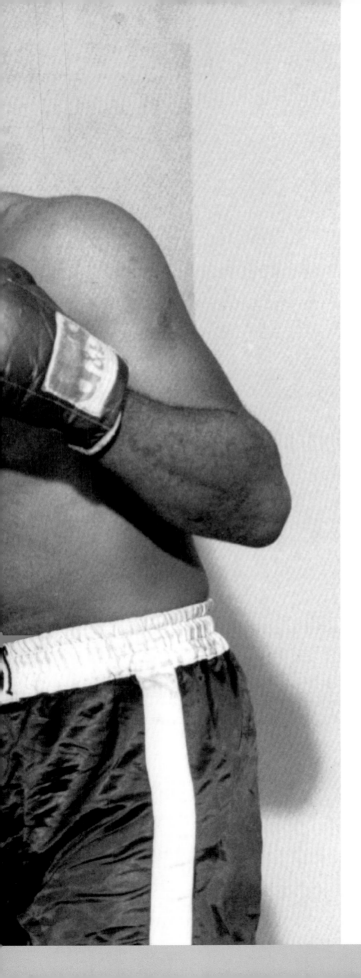

Patterson is declared victor. He retained his World Heavyweight title after a technical knockout in round 12 against Tommy Jackson in New York on 30 July 1957.

STATISTICS

BORN	Waco (TX), January 1935
DIED	New Paltz (NY), May 2006
TURNED PROFESSIONAL	1952
NUMBER OF PRO BOUTS	64
WINS-LOSSES-DRAWS	55-8-1
NUMBER OF KNOCKOUTS	40
RETIRED	1972

CALLED TO SERVE

In 1964, Ali had failed a mental aptitude test that would have qualified him to fight in the Vietnam War, a fact that caused him some embarrassment, especially when his less-than-impressive school records were publicised, too. By 1966, the Vietnam War was escalating and Ali was declared eligible and received his draft notice to join the US Army. He objected on the grounds of his religious beliefs and his response to the press: "Man, I ain't got no quarrel with them Vietcong," soon made front-page news. Many in the media and many ordinary US citizens, who at this time still supported the war, were vitriolic in their condemnation of his stand.

In Chicago, feelings ran so high that Ali's much-publicised fight with Ernie Terrell, scheduled for March, was cancelled and although promoters tried for venues in other cities, soon Terrell himself wanted no part in it either. An alternative opponent was found, Canadian heavyweight champion George Chuvalo, for a fight in Toronto, but there were calls for people to boycott this bout, too. The fight went ahead, and although Chuvalo was a tough nut to crack, Ali had more talent, and won 14 out of the 15 rounds.

After Chuvalo, Ali's promoters decided the best way to make money was to have him fight abroad. Three European bouts were scheduled. In May 1966, Ali fought and won a rematch against Henry Cooper. In August Ali was in England again and knocked out Brian London in three rounds. Then as undefeated Heavyweight Champion, he fought Karl Mildenberger in Frankfurt, Germany. Mildenberger put up a good fight, but Ali ended it in round 12 with a right hand that sent his already-bloodied opponent staggering against the ropes, prompting the referee to stop the fight.

New conscripts group after being conscripted to fight in the Vietnam War. By the mid-1960s there was a major drive to draft men over the age of 18 in the United States and other countries, including Australia, to bolster ground troop numbers in the escalating conflict. Part of this was making changes to eligibility so fewer fit people were exempt from the draft.

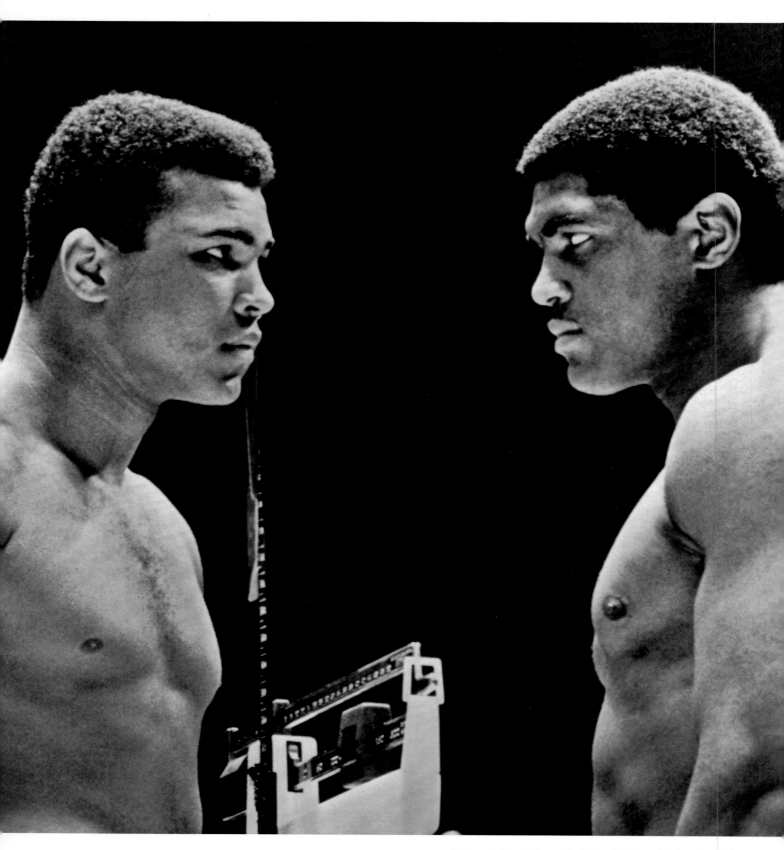

Ali eyeballs his challenger Ernie Terrell at the weigh-in before their championship bout in Houston, Texas, in 1967.

GRUDGE MATCH

There was no love lost between Ernie Terrell and Ali in the run-up to their bout in the Houston Astrodome on 6 February 1967. In a television interview the previous December, Ali read a poem, probably written by his friend and cornerman, Drew 'Bundini' Brown, about how Terrell, "will catch hell at the sound of the bell".

Terrell responded, repeatedly calling Ali 'Cassius' to which Ali angrily asked why he could not call him by his chosen name. The two scuffled on camera. Two days before the fight, Ali announced that he wanted to 'torture' Terrell. Terrell later claimed: "I had no animosity. I understood it's a fight. What he say, all that don't count."

The fight was brutal. Terrell's defence of holding his hands high with his elbows together worked in the opening round. Ali could not hit Terrell's head and had to keep his distance from Terrell's arms. In round two, Terrell was cut under his eye. He later said it was the result of Ali intentionally poking his thumb in his eye. Round four was Terrell's best, with a right that sent Ali staggering against the ropes.

Round five, Ali had gauged Terrell's hitting radius and had started to move closer, close enough to make his rapid, hard punches count. Terrell grew gradually groggier with multiple head shots. In round seven Ali almost knocked him out with a violent right-left combination. In round eight Ali started to repeatedly taunt Terrell saying: "What's my name? What's my name," before hitting his head. By the 12th round, Dundee was telling Ali to "finish him" as his fighter was tiring, but the bout did not finish until the end of round 15.

Terrell's defence proved increasingly inadequate against Ali's speed and power as their fight progressed.

ARREST AND TRIAL

By March 1967, the issue of Ali's stand against the Vietnam War was coming to a head. He received an order to report for induction into the army on 11 April, which his lawyers had changed to 28 April so that he could fight Zora Folley on 22 March at Madison Square Garden. Ali knocked out Folley in the seventh round.

As 28 March approached, Ali became more vocal about his protest, saying: "Why should they ask me to put on a uniform and go 10,000 miles from home and drop bombs and bullets on brown people in Vietnam while so-called Negro people in Louisville are treated like dogs?" His stand made him a figure of hate for many people and even his supporters received death threats and had their car windows smashed. When the day finally came, Ali went through the morning's formalities and health checks, but when the time came for him to step forward, he refused. He was taken back into the room and given a second chance to take the oath, but he again refused. He then signed a statement to that effect.

Within an hour of Ali refusing the induction, the New York State Athletic Commission suspended his boxing licence. The rest of the boxing world soon followed suit, and Ali was stripped of his heavyweight title. His trial began on 19 June 1967. Ali argued he was entitled to exemption as an appointed minister of the Nation of Islam. However, exemptions from military service on religious grounds were allowed only for conscientious objectors who opposed war in any form, whereas when questioned, Ali acknowledged that he would take part in an Islamic holy war. He was convicted of refusing induction into the US Army and given the maximum sentence allowable – five years in jail and a fine of $10,000.

Ali holds up the cover of Nation of Islam newspaper. Muhammad Speaks referring to his trial to the watching media in 1967.

Ali appealed against his conviction and he was allowed to remain free, out on bail, while the appeal was processed. As he was banned from fighting in the United States and his passport was confiscated, he could not travel abroad to fight so he could not box to earn a living. It seemed that Ali was going to take his hardest hits outside, not inside, the ring. "He did not believe he would ever fight again," Ali's wife at the time, Belinda Ali, whom he married on 17 August 1967, said: "He wanted to, but he truly believed that he would never fight again."

Ali spent much of the next three-and-a-half years, while the courtroom fight ensued, going to Nation of Islam meetings and travelling the country giving talks at university campuses. He talked about the war in Vietnam, about integration and segregation, black pride, his views on being stripped of his title and denied the right to fight, and even on the financial hardships that brought him to make those lecture tours! He often got a mixed reception. In some places he was heckled and abused but even many of those who supported his anti-war and civil rights views, were shocked by some of his anti-gay, sexist and conservative statements.

These were tough times. Earnings from the lecture circuit didn't cover attorney fees for the ongoing appeal and Ali was still under constant government surveillance. In December 1968, he served ten days in jail for driving without a valid licence. Another blow came in April 1969. Elijah Muhammad had never agreed with boxing and after a statement Ali made to the press about wanting to go back into boxing if the money were right, Elijah suspended Ali from the Nation of Islam for a year.

Ali greets students while visiting St. John's University, New York, in May 1968. Ali's presence and messages of racial equality – by separation – transfixed student audiences across the United States during the years when he was banned from boxing.

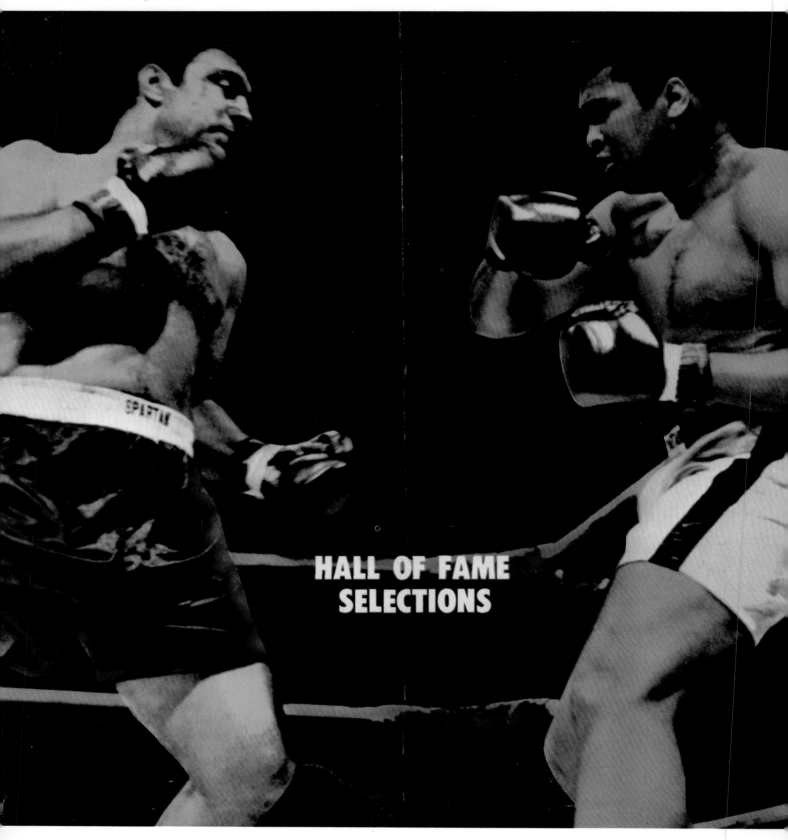

HALL OF FAME
SELECTIONS

Clay and Marciano battle it out in the ring.

FANTASY FIGHTING

Ali was running out of money and was desperate to find ways to earn outside the ring. In early 1969, he took a part in a documentary called *a.k.a. Cassius Clay* for $1000 a day to shoot interviews and recollections of his fights, which would be interspersed with archive footage.

Ali's next payday was more bizarre – a fantasy fight. A Miami advertising man named Murry Woroner had created a fantasy boxing tournament between the best heavyweights of all time in 1967. He input data about each fighter into a computer – such as speed, killer instinct, how prone to cuts – and then pitted each set of data against another in a "bout". Woroner presented this information as a blow-by-blow tournament radio show, which he successfully sold to many stations and gathered millions of listeners by 1968. Ali was outraged to hear that he had lost in the tournament to Jim Jeffries who he considered 'history's clumsiest' heavyweight, and sued Woroner for $1 million.

Woroner cleverly turned the situation around, offering to pay Ali $10,000 to film a fantasy fight supposedly controlled by computers against Rocky Marciano. The two champions met in a blacked-out gym in Miami and got on famously. Both were overweight and in poor fighting shape. Their job was to film 70 one-minute rounds of fake but realistic fighting, avoiding any hard or head punches – although Ali did accidentally knock off Rocky's toupee! They simulated cuts using ketchup as blood and filmed different knockout endings. No one knew who won until the film was presented in 1,000 movie theatres across the United States in 1970 – Rocky beat Ali. People in the audience booed, cried and yelled, not believing their eyes. Ali's supporters said he had humiliated himself: "They want your ass whipped in public... and not just by anybody, but by a real Great White Hope."

BOXER FOCUS: ROCKY MARCIANO

Rocco Francis Marchegiano's parents left Italy, during the depression era, for the United States in the hope of starting a new life. They settled in Brockton, MA, an area favoured by other Italian immigrants. Although his father found work in the city's shoe industry, the Marchegiano family lived in poverty. Rocco, who came to be known as Rocky Marciano, was one of six children and between casual jobs, was a keen amateur baseball player.

He was drafted to the US Army in 1943 and took up boxing to avoid duties such as washing dishes and cleaning latrines. He turned professional after leaving the military in 1947. Within two years he had knocked out 16 opponents and established his nickname: the Brockton Blockbuster. He was considered tough and rough but too short at under 6 foot (1.82 cm), too light at just 13 stone (82.5 kg), old (at 25) and lacking great technique. But he continued to improve and by 1951, faced up to his boxing hero, Joe Louis. Rocky knocked him out in round eight and then cried in Louis's dressing room afterwards in guilt.

In 1952, he took the World Heavyweight Championship in style by knocking Jersey Joe Walcott unconscious in round 13. Days afterwards, a triumphant Rocky rode in a convertible amongst crowds 10,000 strong – one of their own had become a sporting hero. Rocky defended his belt six times, coming close to defeat after a nose cut against Ezzard Charles. He retired in 1956, having never been beaten as a professional. For the following decade or so, Rocky made many personal appearances capitalising on his fame. He died in a private plane crash aged 46.

Rocky Marciano holds a victory pose after knocking out Jersey Joe Walcott to take the World Heavyweight Championship on 23 September 1952. Until that punch, Rocky had been trailing badly on points and an upset looked highly unlikely.

Rocky lands the right-hand piledriver that took out his childhood idol, Joe Louis, in their 1951 bout.

STATISTICS

BORN	Brockton (MA), September 1923
DIED	Des Moines (IA), August 1969
TURNED PROFESSIONAL	1947
NUMBER OF PRO BOUTS	49
WINS-LOSSES-DRAWS	49-0-0
NUMBER OF KNOCKOUTS	43
RETIRED	1956

Track and field athletes Tommie Smith (centre) and John Carlos (right), first and third place winners for the United States in the 200 metres, protest with the Black Power salute at Mexico City Olympics in 1968.

BLACK POWER

In 1969, Black Power was a mainstream issue in the United States. In in the previous year, millions of television spectators had witnessed two US athletes giving the Black Power salute from the Olympic medal podium in Mexico City. It symbolised that many African Americans believed white politicians were failing them and that they needed Black Power to help themselves.

The Black Panther Party was an extreme faction of the Black Power Movement. In this political party the members carried guns and believed that violence was justified in bringing about black justice. Many in the movement disagreed with their aggressive tactics and rhetoric, while endorsing their work in helping poor black communities.

In 1969, the musician, social activist and playwright Oscar Brown Jr opened and starred in his musical comedy about Black Power, *Buck White*. It was about the confusion and conflict in a black social organisation when a militant black leader, Buck White, addresses its members. The play did so well in California that producers decided to run it at the George Abbott Theatre on Broadway. The producers surprisingly cast Ali as Buck White in hope of drawing in crowds. Ali was 'dignified and impressive', singing songs such as 'We Came in Chains' with 'pleasant' voice. Unfortunately New York audiences were not taken and the musical ran for just seven performances. Theatre critic Kushauri Kupa said Ali had made a mockery of genuine protests by presenting a militant leader as a buffoon.

While on Broadway, Ali made a point of seeing the play *Great White Hope* about brilliant black heavyweight champion of the early 20th century, Jack Johnson. Johnson was a rebel in the Jim Crow era, dating white women, racing cars, openly displaying his wealth and bragging about his abilities. Ali said: "That's Me. You take out the white women, and that play is about me."

Ali poses outside the Broadway theatre showing a play about Jack Johnson, the revolutionary black boxer of the early 20th century. Ali saw deep parallels between his own outspoken stance and Johnson's views.

RETURN TO THE RING

Ali had to put in hard hours in the gym to get himself mentally and physically ready to fight at an elite level once more after his ban.

THE COMEBACK

In 1970, Ali's struggle to get back in the ring and win back the title of Heavyweight Champion of the World, now in the hands of the talented fighter Joe Frazier, heated up. Ali's lawyers and promoters worked hard to get permission for him to fight in different states but were denied time and again. Finally, a mayor in Atlanta, Georgia, was persuaded to allow Ali to fight against Jerry Quarry there, in spite of attempts by several members of Congress to stop it.

And so it was that on 26 October 1970, Ali fought again. It was a big moment for Ali and a stressful one: Quarry was strong and younger, a world-class opponent. The arena was filled with the rich and famous from the black community including Sidney Poitier, Bill Cosby and Jesse Jackson, and the crowd roared a delighted welcome to Ali as he entered the ring. Although Ali started well, he was slowing noticeably in rounds two and three, when he suddenly dealt Quarry a right punch that opened a huge, deep cut over the boxer's eye. This injury ended the fight and Ali was declared the winner but unsurprisingly, after three and a half years out of the ring, Ali's fitness was clearly not what it had once been.

While Ali's absence from the ring might not have been good for his training, the publicity that came from it certainly increased his fame and earning power. Ali was paid more for the Quarry fight than he had ever been paid before. While Ali's refusal to go to war and his exile had made him unpopular to begin with, by 1970, protests against the Vietnam War were growing and more people were thinking that perhaps Ali should not have been punished for his beliefs.

A deflated Jerry Quarry (left) looks past a triumphant Ali at the referee Tony Perez as he signals the end of Ali's comeback fight on 26 October 1970. Ali had won but he was not yet convincing championship material.

BOXER FOCUS: JOE FRAZIER

Joe Frazier was the seventh of 13 children of a sharecropper in South Carolina. He was a hard worker and strong – at age 12 Joe was making money filling sandbags – but to become fitter, he joined a gym. At the gym he discovered boxing and sailed through the amateur divisions until he faced Buster Mathis in the 1964 Olympic trials. Mathis beat him on points but then had to pull out of the event with a hand injury. Joe took his place, and the opportunity, winning heavyweight gold.

Joe turned professional in 1965 and sealed his reputation as a scrapper who could take heavy punches and still come through, with the help of a fearsome left hook, earning him the nickname 'Smokin' Joe'. In 1968, after Ali was banned, Joe fought Mathis again, this time for one of the several world championship titles being contested at that time. He took the New York State title on a technical knockout in round 11. He defended this title several times before beating Ali, who had returned after his ban and held one of the other heavyweight titles. With a famous left hook and unanimous points decision, Smokin' Joe became the undisputed Heavyweight Champion in 1970.

Smokin' Joe defended his title over the next two years but was then beaten by George Foreman – Olympic champion from 1968 – in Jamaica in 1973, Ali (twice) in 1974, and Foreman again in 1976. He then announced his retirement but five years later, returned to fight and draw a professional bout just once more. Joe went on to train fighters in his gym, but died after a long battle against cancer.

Joe Frazier in his mid-20s poses in a fighting stance in the ring with his trainer, Eddie Futch, looking on.

Frazier stands jubilant on 16 February 1970 after taking the World Heavyweight title against Jimmy Ellis on a technical knockout in New York.

STATISTICS

BORN	Beaufort (SC), January 1944
DIED	Philadelphia (PA), November 2011
TURNED PROFESSIONAL	1965
NUMBER OF PRO BOUTS	37
WINS-LOSSES-DRAWS	32-4-1
NUMBER OF KNOCKOUTS	27
RETIRED	1981

THE FIGHT OF THE CENTURY

After the Quarry fight, Ali won permission to fight in New York and on 7 December 1970, he took on Oscar Bonavena, winning in round 15 with a crowd-pleasing left hook. Now it was Ali's chance to win back his title by fighting Joe Frazier, who knew that he needed to defeat Ali before he would truly be accepted as the best in the world. Their meeting on 8 March 1971 at Madison Square Garden was billed as 'The Fight of the Century'. It was watched by 300 million people in 35 countries around the world. It made $1.3 million on the gate and guaranteed each fighter a fee of $2.5 million.

The promotional build-up was as tense as the fight itself. Ali infuriated Frazier by calling him 'Uncle Tom' and saying that anyone black who supported Frazier was an Uncle Tom, too. He even called Frazier ugly and dumb. Ali was clear afterwards that this was all pre-match hype, but Frazier never forgave him and this dislike formed a backdrop to this and their subsequent fights.

Ali was famous for nifty footwork and fast hands. Frazier's style was to stand firm and keep delivering hits. The two fought with skill and style and traded punches for an electrifying 15 rounds. In round six, Frazier pinned Ali to the ropes and battered him relentlessly, while in round nine it was Ali who dominated, hammering Frazier with right-left combinations. In round 11, Ali was nearly knocked to the floor by a Frazier hook but in rounds 12 and 13, Ali took the fight to Frazier. In round 15, Frazier knocked Ali to the floor and although Ali got up again, the fight was awarded to Frazier. Ali had lost his first professional fight since returning to the ring and he had officially lost the heavyweight title.

The moment when Ali's dream of becoming Heavyweight Champion once more was dashed by the power of Smokin' Joe Frazier at the end of the Fight of the Century.

Ali shows off the spangled robe given to him by Elvis Presley, before his fight against the Briton Joe Bugner in February 1973.

FREE TO FIGHT AGAIN

The loss in March 1971 was a huge blow to Ali and his supporters but after a rest, he resumed training. On 28 June, he received good news when the Supreme Court reversed his conviction. At last, Ali was free to fight anywhere again and his conscientious objection had been accepted.

While Ali waited for his next meeting with Frazier, he toured the world defeating opponents in Switzerland, Japan and Ireland as well as in the United States. In February 1973, he beat Joe Bugner in Las Vegas in an uninspiring bout that is mainly remembered for his jewel studded robe emblazoned with the words 'People's Choice' – a gift from Elvis Presley. Then in March 1973, a little known opponent, Ken Norton, surprised everybody by breaking Ali's jaw in the second round of a fight. Ali continued to fight on but finally lost in round 12. It took six months for Ali's jaw to heal. When the two fought again, it took 12 rounds for Ali to get even, winning a close but unanimous victory.

At last, Frazier agreed to a rematch with Ali and the date was set for 28 January 1974. By this time Frazier had lost the title to George Foreman, but Ali had a point to prove and Frazier hated Ali. In the build-up to the bout, the two traded bitter insults and were even involved in a brawl in a television studio. The event was another sell-out. On the night, the boxers kept up the brutal pace that had characterised their first meeting but this time, after 12 rounds, Ali was awarded a unanimous decision over Frazier. The two rivals had taunted each other throughout the bout and although Frazier had made Ali wait almost three years for a rematch, he was demanding another as soon as this one was over.

Ali was the People's Choice because he was a magnetic performer but many boxing experts were concerned that his best fighting days were over.

PROMOTING A LEGEND

Don King was a new boxing promoter on the block in 1972. King wanted to use Ali's legendary status to help him find fortune. After organising a hospital fundraiser featuring Ali in 1972, his ambitions stretched to putting on a heavyweight title bout between Ali and the incumbent champion, George Foreman. He promised the two fighters $5 million each but hit a brick wall in finding funding. Magically, a funder emerged: President Mobutu Sese Seko of recently independent Zaire would pay but only if the fight happened in his capital, Kinshasa. King met with Mobuto's advisers in Paris to forge a deal.

Don King and his friend Lloyd Price came up with King's up-combed hairstyle to give the promoter a distinctive look to accompany his distinctively flamboyant approach to boxing promotion.

Ali poses for the press with fight
posters advertising his Zaire
Foreman fight in 1974.

Mobuto wanted to bring a major sporting event
to Africa for the first time and thus demonstrate
that he was a major player on the continent.
African Americans including Ali and Foreman
liked the symbolism of returning to their
ancestral 'home' – Africa – for such a big fight.

Mobuto also had strong links with the United
States. He had seized power in a military coup
after killing the previous democratically elected
leader, Patrice Lumumba, who Ali had met on
his earlier African trip, with the clandestine aid
of the CIA. The US government was concerned
that Lumumba was giving too much power to
'communist' influences. Mobuto stabilised the
country after years of turmoil, which earned
him the friendship of several US presidents, but
at a high cost. He amassed a massive personal
fortune based on Zaire's mineral wealth while
the vast majority of the population was living in
poverty and brutally repressed by his state police
and army. Tales abounded of Mobuto feeding
opponents to crocodiles, and executing known
criminals to maintain law and order in the months
before the fight.

In late September 1974, Ali was in intense training so he remained fighting fit while Foreman's eye injury healed.

ALI BOMAYE

When fight organisers arrived in Kinshasa in March 1974, they were shocked by what they found. The tiny runways at Kinshasa's airport were unsuitable for jumbo jets, there was a dirt track rather than road to the fight stadium and there was a lack of satellite technology so the fight could not be broadcast worldwide. However, when Ali and Foreman arrived in September, Mobuto had transformed the capital's infrastructure. Billboards along the airport road pronounced, "Black power is sought everywhere in the world. But it is realised in Zaire".

From meeting the locals to audiences with Mobuto, Ali felt at home in Zaire. Foreman was a more closed-off figure at this time, who stuck mostly with his entourage. Ali was 32 years old to Foreman's 25 years and the 3-1 underdog following Foreman's defeat of Frazier. Yet he talked up his chances of regaining his crown using speed and skill, repeating a famous phrase first coined by Bundini Brown:

'Float like a butterfly, sting like a bee His hands can't hit what his eyes can't see'

Ali learnt a phrase, "Ako bomaye," meaning, "I will kill him", in Lingalla dialect. From that point on the crowds that came to see him chanted, "Ali bomaye", meaning, "Ali, kill him".

Eight days before the fight, Foreman's eye was badly cut by an accidental elbowing from a sparring partner. The fight was delayed for five weeks so it could heal, which was worrying for organisers as the impending rainy season risked making the open stadium event a washout. In the wait for the fight, Ali enjoyed spending time with musicians such as James Brown and Hugh Masakela at the Zaire '74 music festival, organised by Lloyd Price, a friend of King's, to take advantage of the fight's media attention.

Ali enjoys the noise from the adoring crowd lining his route, held in check by Mobuto's army, as he travelled around Kinshasa in late summer 1974.

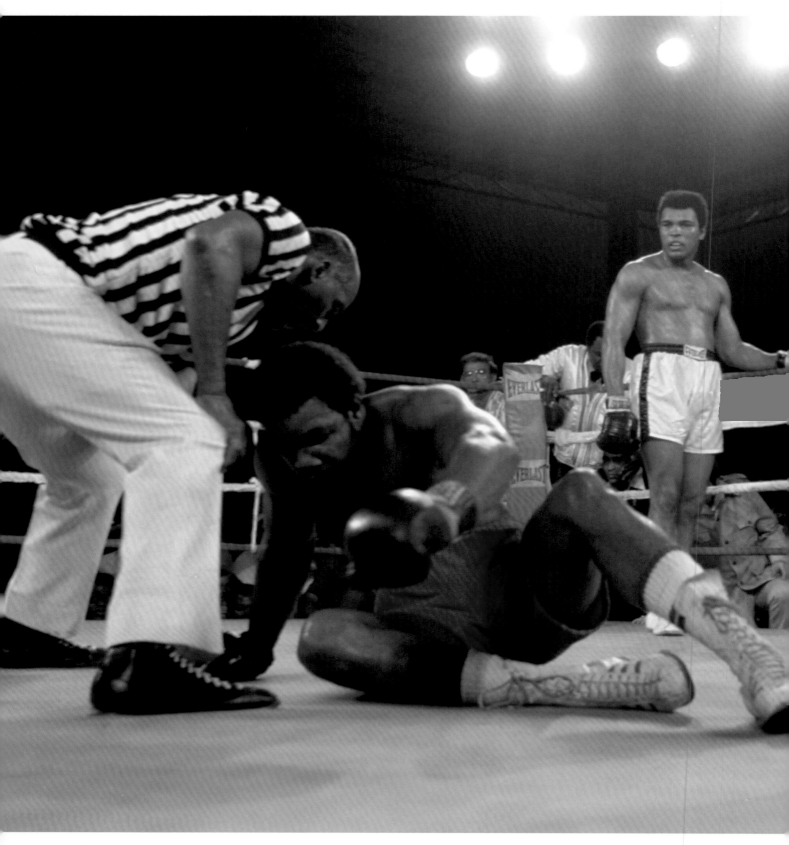

Foreman tries in vain to scramble to his feet in round eight, still reeling from Ali's championship-winning punch combination. For all his power, Foreman had been outsmarted by Ali's tactics.

RUMBLE IN THE JUNGLE

In the early hours of 30 October, Ali and Foreman arrived at the Zaire national football stadium, the Stade du 20 Mai, in darkness. Ali, wearing a white satin robe trimmed with an African blanket, and his vast entourage arrived to the sounds of, "Ali bomaye" from the 60,000-strong crowd. In contrast, Foreman arrived in a simple red velvet robe. Mobuto was not even there. He watched the fight on television as he feared being assassinated in the open stadium.

Two national anthems, the Star Spangled Banner and Le Zarois, were played while the United States' and Zaire's flags were shown off in the ring. Ali said to Foreman: "You have heard of me since you were young... Now you must meet me, your Master." And then the fight began.

Ali landed two powerful head shots to signal his intent and then started to defend. He took whatever Foreman could throw at him. By the middle of round eight, Foreman started to tire after all that punching. Ali taunted him: "George, is that all you got?" then leapt at the opportunity when Foreman's guard was down. He summoned a fast, sledgehammer left-right combination that floored Foreman. Ali had predicted that Foreman would fall on his face from exhaustion in the tenth round, but his punches proved to be knockout blows. Foreman was counted out before he could stand up.

After a seven year gap, Ali was World Champion once more, only the second heavyweight after Floyd Patterson to regain a title. It was Foreman's first defeat in 41 bouts. Ali crowed: "I did it. I told you he was nothing but did you listen? ... I told you I was going to take all his shots. I told you he had no skill. I told you he didn't like to be punched."

Ali started fast against Foreman to remind his imposing opponent of his speed and power. But much of the bout was about a war of attrition.

ROPE-A-DOPE

The Rumble in the Jungle was a stark demonstration of Ali's changed tactics following his return to the ring. Ali remained confident of his phenomenal speed of hand. A 1969 photographic analysis in *Sports Illustrated* magazine showed he could deliver a six-punch combination of jabs, hooks, body and head shots in just more than 2 seconds. Ali knew, though, he was slower on his feet and could no longer dance around younger opponents.

He and Angelo Dundee devised a risky tactic for the Foreman fight. Instead of trading blows toe-to-toe, Ali stayed on the ropes and let Foreman hit him! This was astounding to onlookers because Foreman was known as the all-time hardest-hitting heavyweight. Ali would then lean forward inviting a knockout head punch and rapidly lean back out of the way. Ali was well prepared to take rib and belly shots because he had spent months before leaving for Zaire in the gym practising being beaten up by sparring partners such as Larry Holmes, a future Heavyweight Champion. Also he relied on give in the ropes to limit the damage. Dundee later confessed his part in the tactic: adjusting the rope tension to help Ali use the ring edge to his advantage.

Ali called the technique rope-a-dope, but it was not new. Ironically, Archie Moore, who was in Foreman's training camp, had called the tactic of absorbing heavy punches until the time was right to counter-attack, 'the turtle'. Rope-a dope almost failed for Ali in round two when he was pinned to the ropes and appeared to wobble and grabbed Foreman's shoulder. Before round six, a Zairean official accidentally loosened the ropes – if Dundee had not noticed and told Ali, he may have leant back and fallen from the ring!

Ali is shown here on the ropes using his rope-a-dope tactic while defending against Foreman's onslaught.

BOXER FOCUS: GEORGE FOREMAN

George Foreman grew up in Texas in a poor family, and as a teenager was a mugger and brawler on the streets of Houston. He fell into boxing by chance when he was put on a job corps programme to teach vocational skills to the disadvantaged. One of the corps counsellor's was also a boxing coach and saw the punching potential in George's 6 foot 3 inch (1. 9 m), muscular frame.

George proved to be so good that he became 1968 Olympic Heavyweight Champion in his 25th amateur fight. Within three years of turning professional, he had knocked out opponents 35 times in 37 matches. By 1973, he was crowned World Champion when he floored the mighty Joe Frazier. A year later, he was defeated by Ali in Zaire, and in 1977, announced his retirement after a claimed religious experience in the dressing room following his last fight. George was ordained a minister the next year.

By the early 1980s, he was a boxing commentator for the HBO network and had set up a youth centre. However, he was short on funds so returned to professional boxing ten years after retiring.

George resumed where he left off, knocking out opponents. However, there were allegations that his promoter bribed officials to up his ranking to get a title shot, first against Evander Holyfield, which he lost on points, and then Michael Moorer in 1994. At age 45 Foreman became the oldest ever World Heavyweight Champion when he knocked out Moorer. When Foreman retired for good in 1997 he had already started promoting a range of electric cookers branded Lean Mean Grilling Machines. By 2014, an estimated 100 million Grilling Machines had been sold. Foreman continues to juggle evangelism, developing and marketing products, and running a ranch in Texas.

George Foreman at ease out of the ring.

Foreman poses as he trains in 1972 in New York.

STATISTICS

BORN	Marshall (TX), January 1949
TURNED PROFESSIONAL	1969
NUMBER OF PRO BOUTS	81
WINS-LOSSES-DRAWS	76-5-0
NUMBER OF KNOCKOUTS	68
RETIRED	1997

Ali in his pomp, mocking Joe Frazier's p
conference in 1975.

RESURRECTION

Ali was now king of the boxing world and suddenly a national treasure on his return to the United States. In December 1974, he was invited to visit President Gerald Ford in the White House. Ford wanted to meet Ali as a boxing enthusiast but also out of national reconciliation now that the US troops were out of Vietnam and racial divisions were declining. He said prophetically: "Because of his principles... Muhammad Ali will be remembered for more than just excellence in athletics."

Ali became a darling of the media, featuring in many photoshoots and pictured attending numerous events. Of course, Ali fed the hero worship, reading from epic poems about his achievements such as:

"This is the legend of Muhammad Ali, the greatest fighter that ever will be."

In 1975, Elijah Muhammad died and the Nation of Islam changed course. Led by Wallace Muhammad, it stated that the Quran taught that colour does not matter and that Muslims hate any injustice and evil. Ali said: "We're in a new phase, a resurrection." This change in tack created deep divisions in the Nation and was the beginning of its end.

By now Don King was looking for the next payday after Zaire for himself and for Ali. Allegedly using mob money, King matched Ali against Chuck Wepner, 'the Bayonne Bleeder' as he often got cut. It wasn't much of a contest, but King negotiated a $1.5 million payout for Ali. Soon King had made Ali's wish come true: a return bout with Joe Frazier. Again the big match was to be held overseas, this time in Manila, Philippines, on 1 October. The country was under martial law and its autocratic leader President Ferdinand Marcos thought a sporting event would take attention away from his mistreatment of his own people.

Ali wearing a Manila Gorilla T-shirt mock punches Frazier at a press conference in Quezon City, Philippines, in front of invited television crews, reporters and boxing enthusiasts.

THRILLA IN MANILA

**'It will be a killer
And a chiller
And a thrilla
When I get the gorilla
In Manila'**

Ali was ruthless in his pre-match taunting of Joe Frazier. At a press conference with Frazier he mocked Frazier for saying, "gonna" not "going to" and "inta" not "into". He christened Frazier "the gorilla" and repeatedly thumped a black rubber gorilla, saying: "All night long, this is what you'll see."

Before the fight, Frazier's trainer, Eddie Futch, made plans for victory. He negotiated replacing the planned US referee with a Filipino, as the former had officiated Ali versus Frazier II and he felt had insufficiently penalised neck holding by Ali. Futch also trained his man to avoid rope-a-dope by hitting Ali's arms to weaken him. It later emerged that Frazier had a cataract in his left eye, and an arthritic left shoulder. Ali was 2-1 favourite for this battle.

The fight was an intense war of attrition in sapping tropical humidity. Ali outboxed Frazier in the first third of the bout, delivering many big punches that made Frazier wobble. In the middle third, Frazier took the upper hand. In round six he whacked Ali so hard that Ali's head turned away. In the final third, Ali took control and doled out the punishment. Frazier's left eye was closed and his right closing. In the heat, there was insufficient ice to reduce the swelling. In the 14th Frazier was a sitting duck for Ali's punches but the round finished with both men slumped in their corners.

Before the bell for the 15th, Futch threw in the towel, and Ali begged Dundee to cut his gloves off as he was done. Ali had won again – netting in the region of $6 million – but this victory had taken its toll.

In the sapping heat of the Philippines the bout ebbed and flowed between both fighters,
Frazier taking the upper hand mid-fight, but Ali finishing stronger.

In this classic duel, Ali only won because he was not first to quit. Both men were completely spent at the end of the fight.

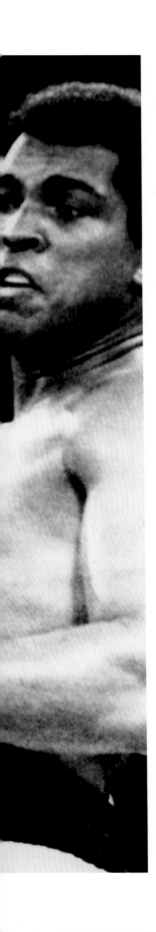

THE CLASSIC DUEL

For many people Ali v Frazier III was one of the best boxing matches in history. It was between two boxing legends who threw everything they had at each other. Ali said it was the closest to dying he had ever been. The fight had the ebb and flow of many classic fights and a gladiatorial fight-to-the-death spirit. In 1997, *The Ring* magazine awarded it, 'Fight of the Century' and in 1999, ESPN's Sports Century Series pronounced it the fifth greatest sporting event ever.

Some boxing aficionados believe the match has been overhyped, partly because Ali finally convincingly beat his nemesis, whereas in reality it was rather uninteresting. In 2012, boxing historian Mike Silvers described his sadness at seeing, "two former giants of the ring struggle and suffer."

Many people thought that Ali crossed a line in his verbal attacks on Joe Frazier out of the ring. They said that he had called Frazier ignorant, slow in speech and ugly for the sole purpose of entertaining a predominantly white audience and thus reinforced some unfortunate and persistent stereotypes about black people.

Frazier said of Ali the fighter: "In Manila, ... those punches, they'd have knocked a building down. And he took 'em... and he came back, and I got to respect that part of the man." He could never forgive how Ali tainted his image. In 1991, when Ali was first having difficulty speaking, Frazier said: "He can't talk no more because he was saying the wrong things. ... Tell me now. Him or me; which one talks worse now?" Ali himself saw the taunts as merely part of the game and retained immense respect for Frazier the warrior: "If God ever calls me to a holy war, I want Joe Frazier fighting beside me."

THE
LAST
FIGHTS

THE ALI ROAD SHOW

After beating Frazier in Manila, Muhammad Ali was probably the best-known and one of the most popular celebrities in the world. Those around him say this was not just because of his fame, but also because of his personality.

He was warm and friendly to those he met and generous to those in real need, for example handing over $100,000 dollars to save a Jewish community centre for old people, after he saw a feature about it closing due to lack of funds on the news.

Ali skipping before his World Championship bout with Jimmy Young. At this point, Ali was his heaviest weight ever and taking a lot of less-than-taxing fights against also-rans.

People loved to watch Ali fight, but they loved to watch him win more. In the years after Manila, Ali fought several opponents that did not stand a chance of beating him but were happy to fight the champion and, like him, entertain audiences while reaping great financial rewards.

On 20 February 1976, Ali fought Jean-Pierre Coopman, the heavyweight champion of Belgium. Ali justified the fight against this lesser opponent saying he needed a rest after the major workout in Manila. Coopman was so delighted to meet Ali that he kept trying to kiss him at press conferences, making it hard to build up too much drama or excitement about the event, which Ali won all too easily.

Two months later, Ali fought Jimmy Young in Maryland. Ali was slow and at 230 pounds (104 kg), he was the heaviest he had ever been. He took 15 rounds to win a fight that was universally panned as boring. Less than a month after that, Ali was on primetime television fighting England's Richard Dunn in Munich, Germany. Tickets sold badly and Ali was open to the press about his regret at having let the public down so he put on a better performance in the fight, knocking Dunn down four times before knocking him out in round five. The Ali Road Show seemed to be back in town but in reality, this was to be the champ's last ever knockout win.

The Coopman fight in Puerto Rico in 1976 was a simple workout for a boxer of Ali's skill.

POWER STRUGGLE

In the background at this time, there was a power struggle going on for the control of Ali's career. Herbert Muhammad, who was Ali's manager, was pulling away from Don King, because he believed King wanted to take over. King's efforts were to no avail however, because Herbert's friendship with Ali was so strong and long-standing, and because he distanced Ali from King, choosing promoters like Bob Arum to promote Ali's future bouts, such as his next, a controversial fight against pro-wrestler Antonio Inoki in Tokyo on 25 May 1976.

The fight was billed as a battle between the two toughest men on the planet but many viewed it as a staged circus show. When asked his reasons for taking part in a fight that many felt demeaned the boxing title, Ali was honest: "$6 million, that's why,' he replied. Nevertheless, the fighters tried to build-up some tension at press events, with Ali calling Inoki 'The Pelican' because of his big chin and Inoki presenting Ali with a crutch for after the match.

There are still disputes about whether the fight was genuine but it is known that Ali's camp renegotiated the rules of the meeting just before it took place, stating that Inoki was not allowed to do things like leg-dive or tackle. Whatever the truth, the result was 15 rounds of dull, almost farcical fighting, with Inoki bending the rules by spending much of the bout lying on the floor kicking at Ali's legs. At one point Ali tried to grab Inoki's ankle but got flipped on to the canvas with Inoki sitting on his chest and squatting over his head. The fight was scored as a draw but no one really saved face: it had been a humiliating spectacle for everyone involved. There was a cost to Ali, too: blood clots and muscle damage in his legs from all those kicks.

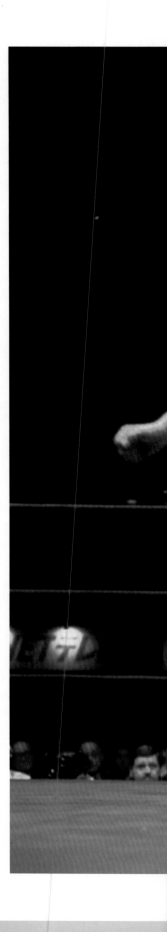

Inoki shown mid-air for a double foot drop kick – the big-money exhibition fight had a high cost for Ali: his famously powerful legs took such a beating, that Ali's movement was probably permanently slowed.

The powerhouse Ken Norton defends himself against an Ali blow during their 1976 encounter. Ali took revenge for the jaw-busting points defeat of 1973 but was a less-than-convincing victor.

ALI V NORTON

Bob Arum and Ferdie Pacheco were worried by infections to Ali's leg injuries, yet Ali spent a minimal period in hospital before starting to train for a bout against Ken Norton at Yankee Stadium, on 28 September 1976. Norton dominated the early rounds, but after round eight the tables turned as Ali, with superhuman effort, started to claw his way back. Ali, spurred on by Dundee, won the next three rounds, lost round 12, and won the next two, making the fight even by round 15. He won on a close and disputed points decision. It was clear to all that the leg problems had taken their toll on Ali's mobility.

Ali did not step into the ring again until spring 1977, for what proved to be a tedious win against Spanish newcomer Alfredo Evangelista. Even Ali was more interested in what was going on outside the ring, where his marriage to Belinda was breaking up, he had a nine-month-old child with his soon-to-be new wife Veronica, and an autobiography and a movie of his life, *The Greatest*, about to be released. It seemed that Ali's focus was on his personal ventures, not his boxing.

Just as people were speculating that Ali might retire, he booked a fight against Earnie Shavers on 29 September 1977, at Madison Square Garden. Shavers was tough and Ali was out of shape, but Ali fought 15 hard rounds to scrape another win. However, he had been hammered in the head by Shaver's brain-jarring punches so many times he suffered severe head trauma and other injuries. Several prominent people called for Ali to retire before permanent damage was done, including Pacheco, for whom the Shavers fight was the final straw. When Ali refused to stop fighting after this, his doctor of 15 years quit.

Ali makes a breakthrough against Norton.

BOXER FOCUS: KEN NORTON

Ken Norton was born and brought up in Jacksonville, Illinois, the son of a fire service engineer and a hospital therapist. After school, Norton won a football scholarship to Northeast Missouri State College. He didn't start boxing until after he joined the Marine Corps in 1963. He was a formidable athlete who took to the sport quickly.

Norton turned professional after taking the All-Marine Heavyweight Champion title three times during his four-year stint in the forces. He fought many great fighters in his time, including George Foreman, for the title in 1974. He also put his 6 foot 3 inch (1.92 m), 220 pound (99.7 kg) physique to good financial use by starring in Hollywood films such as *Mandingo* (1975), with Susan George, and *Drum* (1976), with Pam Grier, as well as television shows including *The A-Team* and *Knight Rider*.

Norton was bitterly disappointed when he lost to Ali in 1976, but he went on to take three wins in 1977 against the likes of Duane Bobick and Jimmy Young, and became the mandatory challenger for WBC Heavyweight Champion Leon Spinks, who claimed the title in 1978. The World Boxing Council stripped Spinks of the title and awarded it to Norton instead after the former agreed to a rematch with the ageing Ali instead of Norton. Norton lost the title to Larry Holmes in June the same year, after an intense 15-round fight ending in a split decision. Norton was never the same fighter again.

In 1986, Norton almost died in a car accident in which he suffered multiple injuries, including a fractured skull and a brain injury that left his speech slurred. He died after a long period of declining health, after a succession of strokes and a heart attack, since which he'd lived in a care home.

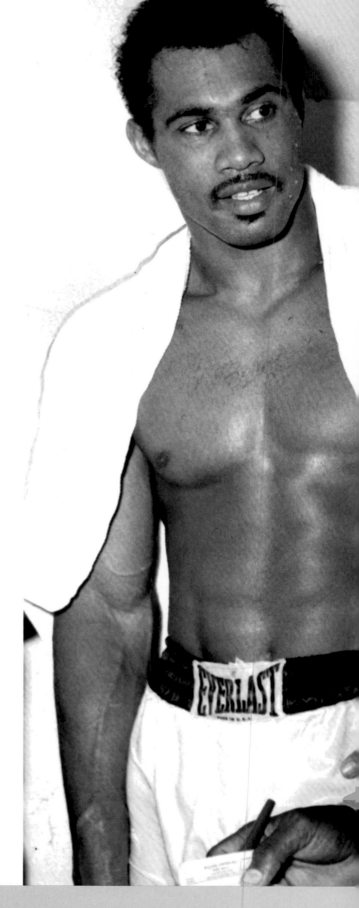

A young Ken Norton (centre) with Joe Frazier (right) in 1950.

Norton chalks up a win against Ron Stander in early 1976, before his Ali rematch.

STATISTICS

BORN	Jacksonville (IL), 9 August 1943
DIED	18 September 2013
TURNED PROFESSIONAL	1967
NUMBER OF PRO BOUTS	50
WINS-LOSSES-DRAWS	42-7-1
NUMBER OF KNOCKOUTS	33
RETIRED	1981

ALI V SPINKS

Ali's next match was in February 1978 in Las Vegas against Leon Spinks, an Olympic gold medal winner who only had seven professional bouts to his name. Ali seized the chance to take down another gold medal winner and declare himself the greatest again, but he did not bother training much, assuming it would be an easy win. It wasn't. Spinks was young and strong and went on punching Ali for the entire 15 rounds, never tiring as Ali expected. Ali tried to make a comeback in the final round but it was too late. The judges awarded the win and Ali's World Heavyweight title to Spinks. The loss hurt Ali badly and as soon as the fight was over, Ali was calling for another, to win back his title.

The rematch was arranged for 15 September that year in New Orleans. Ali began training harder than he had ever trained in his life, including sparring more than 200 rounds in the ring. On the day, Ali soon settled into his rhythm, moving and punching solidly and using improvised moves that could only come from a fighter of his experience. Over the course of the match, he jabbed and hooked with ever increasing confidence and accuracy. He even displayed the odd speedy and devastating mix of hooks and uppercuts, and landed overhand rights, which left his opponent frustrated and helpless. Ali won by unanimous decision and at 36 years old, became the first three-time Heavyweight Champion in history.

After the match, Ali said: "I've always planned to be the first black man to retire undefeated, and to do it now after being champion three times would be something no one could ever equal. I have made suckers out of all of you." He announced his retirement the following June.

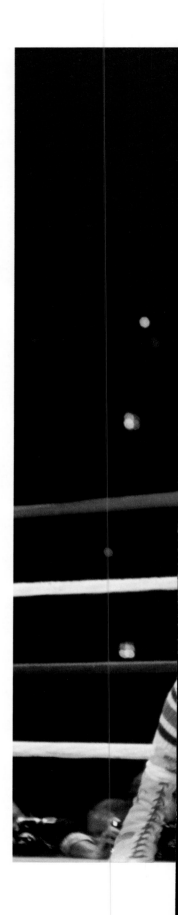

Ali backs away from a punch thrown by Leon Spinks during their 15 September 1978 bout in the Superdome, New Orleans. Ali trained incredibly hard to make sure he did not make the same mistakes as before against Spinks.

BOXER FOCUS: LEON SPINKS

Leon Spinks was born in a rough area of St. Louis, Missouri, and brought up by his mother on welfare assistance. He left school after the tenth grade and went into the US Marine Corps where he joined the All-Marine boxing team. He won light heavyweight bronze at the World Games in Cuba in 1974, silver at the Pan-American Games in 1975, and gold at the 1976 Summer Olympics in Montreal. His brother Michael won gold in the middleweight, making them the first brothers in history to be champions in the same sport at the same Olympics.

In 1977, Spinks turned professional and moved up to the heavyweight division. He took the World Heavyweight title from Muhammad Ali in 1978, in one of the greatest upsets in boxing history, but was stripped of the title after agreeing to fight Ali rather than the number-one contender: Norton. In 1981, Spinks challenged Larry Holmes for the title but lost in three rounds. His last championship chance was in 1986 when he fought Dwight Qawi at cruiserweight level but he lost in six rounds. Financial problems forced Spinks to continue fighting autograph shows and boxer-versus-wrestler matches long past his prime until he retired in 1995.

Although he and Michael were the first brothers in boxing history to win World Heavyweight titles (Michael defeated Larry Holmes in the IBF Heavyweight Championship in 1985), their later lives took divergent paths. Michael Spinks left boxing with his health and his money. Leon Spinks allegedly squandered his winnings on alcohol and gambling, and for a while was homeless and living in a shelter. Since then he has worked in restaurants, at a YMCA and has done other odd jobs. He has also helped to start a gym in Detroit, and in Nebraska, he volunteers at an after-school programme for youth.

Spinks in training before his first Ali fight, which catapulted him to boxing stardom.

Spinks had his front teeth loosened by boxing and then removed in 1971 while in the marines. He often wore false front teeth, but they were sometimes stolen as trophies!

STATISTICS

BORN	St. Louis (MO), 11 July 1953
TURNED PROFESSIONAL	1977
NUMBER OF PRO BOUTS	46
WINS-LOSSES-DRAWS	26-17-3
NUMBER OF KNOCKOUTS	14
RETIRED	1995

Larry Holmes stands
victorious over Ali,
who sits hurt and
beaten in his corner.

THE LAST FIGHT

After the Spinks victory, Ali concentrated on other projects for a while. He played an ex-slave in a four-hour television mini-series called *Freedom Road*, with Kris Kristofferson, he moved into a huge, luxurious mansion in Las Vegas, and he travelled the world, for example to India to raise money for Indian charities. In 1979, after Russia invaded Afghanistan, President Carter asked him to visit countries in Africa to represent the United States' reasons for boycotting the Moscow Olympics.

Ali was soon planning to get back in the ring. He did it partly for the money, because although he'd earned millions over his career, he had spent a lot, given away a lot of it, and had been conned out of some, but also because he loved the roar of the crowd, loved to fight and to show people he could still win.

On 2 October 1980, and in spite of public statements issued by his mother and former doctor, Pacheco, saying he should not return to boxing, Ali stepped out of retirement and into the ring at Caesars Palace, Las Vegas, to face Larry Holmes, a former sparring partner and current heavyweight champion.

It was a disaster. Ali never had a dominant moment in the fight, but he would not stop or drop. He just absorbed the severe beatings that Holmes dished out. In round nine, an uppercut from Holmes threw Ali against the ropes and as Ali turned away and covered his face with his gloves, Holmes delivered a right hand to his kidney that made Ali scream with pain. After round ten, Ali's trainer, Angelo Dundee, finally stopped the sad spectacle. This time there was no denying that Ali was in terminal decline.

Ali eyeballed Trevor Berbick in vain at the weigh-in in Nassau, the Bahamas, but many knew his boxing days were near the end and he did not have the moves to back up his pre-match talk. Berbick would prove to be his last ever boxing opponent.

Ali was hurt in more ways than one after the Holmes disaster. He refused to accept the decision and wanted to prove his worth in the ring. At the age of 39 he was fixated with the idea of becoming champ for a fourth time: "Why do people go to the moon? Why did Martin Luther King say he had a dream? People need challenges."

In September 1981, a ten-round fight against the Jamaican-Canadian, Trevor Berbick, was announced. Berbick had recently lost closely to Holmes, too. But US boxing commissions were officially concerned about the state of Ali's health and would not sanction the fight on US soil. US networks were not interested in televising the bout, planned for Nassau, the Bahamas, and promoted by a Bahamian company, Sports Internationale. They tagged it 'The Drama in Bahama'. Pre-fight things were shoddy – ringside tickets were on sale in a supermarket and there were concerns Sports Internationale would go bust. In early December, to soothe anxieties about the fight, Ali publicly released a medical report from UCLA Medical Center stating: "There is no evidence from a health standpoint that he should be limited whatsoever in his activities."

On the evening of 11 December Ali and Berbick stepped into the ring. Shambolic organisation meant the referees had to ask around for a stopwatch and bell. Ali looked fresh at the start, dancing round and flicking jabs, but it was immediately apparent that he could not move out of the way of Berbick's solid head shots. By round three he was tiring. Ali traded blows but they had little effect on the 27-year-old. Ali's reactions and speed had gone and he could not dodge Berbick's blows. He put off the inevitable until the final bell: a Berbick victory. This sad fight was the last in Ali's auspicious career in the ring.

A SECOND LIFE

RETIREMENT

"Father Time caught up with me. I'm finished. I've got to face the facts. For the first time I could feel that I'm 40 years old."

In the press conference in Nassau the morning after Berbick fight, Berbick described beating Ali as his, "great honour and also a sad one". However, journalists were far more interested in the main story: the end of Ali's boxing career. At the conference Ali teased Berbick for beating up an old man and proclaimed Berbick, "as good as any man I ever fought". But out of Berbick's earshot he said: "If I was 27, Trevor would have been my sparring partner."

Ali said he would have retired even if he had won because he felt conclusively that during the rounds he could not, "make certain attacks". At the end of the conference, to everyone's surprise, he suddenly pronounced: "I shall return!" But then added: "To Los Angeles", where he lived.

For Ali the early 1980s were difficult times. He had the trappings of success such as an enormous mansion, he had a glorious boxing record, international renown, and had met a pantheon of famous people. But he was bereft to be out of the boxing cycle of talking up his chances against opponents, training, competing and so on. Angelo Dundee said: "He met every big name in the world but what really energised him was being around fight guys." He knew he had left the ring with a whimper rather than a roar and that the boxing world believed he had brought the sport into some disrepute by fighting on when he was not really able. Ali retained close advisors who organised public appearances, but he was no longer surrounded by a large entourage. For the first time in years, Ali felt all alone.

Muhammad Ali with actor Tony Curtis in 1982.

When Ali visited China in 1985, he was already suffering from the effects of Parkinson's disease.

ILLNESS

Ali knew he was struggling with neurological symptoms before his last fights. At the time of the 1980 UCLA report, he blamed the symptoms on the thyroid pills that he took to help lose weight before the Holmes fight. He kept quiet the findings of a report from the Denver Mayo Clinic, which found he could not accurately touch his finger to his nose tip, he had trouble coordinating speech and could not hop well on one foot. Publicly he kept up pretences that all was OK: "You listen to me talk. Do I sound like I've got brain damage to you?"

After retirement Ali's health was under great scrutiny. It was apparent that his speech was more slurred than in the past, he moved more slowly and had tremors. He had many more tests at leading neurological institutions in the United States over the following years, and finally a PET scan in 1984 revealed that Ali had damage to his brain stem. This, along with response to medication and other tests, confirmed that he had Parkinson's Disease. Parkinson's symptoms, from tremor, slowness and rigidity to fatigue, pain and sleeplessness, result from the brain not producing a neurotransmitter called dopamine.

Parkinson's resulting from head trauma has been the prevailing theory since Ali's diagnosis, especially given that other boxers, including Sugar Ray Leonard, have also suffered neurological damage post-career. Many people blame the punishing later fights including those with Frazier and Holmes. Henry Cooper blamed it on Ali's fighting style: "We were always taught as kids that you never turned your head on a punch... But [Ali] used to turn, and he took [too] many punches to the back of the head." However, Parkinson's has many causes, from family history to viruses and exposure to toxins. Some doctors think Ali may have got the disease even without stepping into the ring.

PUBLIC APPEARANCES

After the world finally knew for sure that Ali was suffering from Parkinson's, the ex-champion reassured people that he was far from finished and that he would get on with life. He said that on Parkinson's medication to lessen the symptoms, he felt fine and that he was in no pain, even though he admitted that he was, "older and fatter, but we all change." Ali remained firmly in the public eye.

In 1985, Ali got back in the ring but this time, a wrestling ring. The event was called WrestleMania, which was held at Madison Square Garden – the scene of some of Ali's most famous fights. The main event in this pay-per-view match was a tag-team bout between the professional wrestler Hulk Hogan and the television actor Mr T against 'Rowdy' Roddy Piper and 'Mr. Wonderful' Paul Orndorff. The 19,000 crowd saw Ali dressed as referee, along with Liberace as timekeeper, introduce the wrestlers. Ali did not actually stay in the ring to referee, fearful of being bowled over by the wrestlers but he remained ringside to mock-punch people thrown from the ring. He held Hogan's hand aloft in victory at the end.

Ali retained a strong interest in heavyweight boxing and in particular, the emergence of Mike Tyson. In 1985, Mike Tyson had just turned professional at age 18 and was setting the heavyweight world on fire. In about 1977, Ali had inspired Tyson to focus on boxing when he visited the detention centre in the Bronx where Tyson was staying. Tyson was also promoted by Don King. In 1986, he became the youngest world champion in history when he knocked out Trevor Berbick, who was by then trained by Ali's close friend Dundee.

Ali is shown getting ready to participate as a guest referee in the inaugural
Wrestlemania at Madison Square Garden, New York, in 1985.

Ali poses with released hostage Royce Smart, on 4 December 1990 after the latter's arrival at Kennedy International Airport.

MEETING SADDAM

In August 1990, Iraqi military forces invaded Kuwait and annexed it as part of Iraq. Saddam Hussein, the Iraqi leader, said it was retaliation against Kuwait drilling into their oil reserves. NATO condemned the invasion and the United States threatened Saddam with war if he did not withdraw Iraqi forces. Saddam took Western hostages to act as a 'human shield' to prevent military strikes on Iraq. The United States used sanctions and also took part in diplomatic moves to try to release US hostages. One venture, organised by a former US Attorney General, was sending 'celebrity diplomats' to Baghdad to meet with Saddam to try to make him release captives. Ali was asked to be one of those diplomats.

Ali arrived in Baghdad in November 1990. He was well-known in the Middle East owing to his very public Muslim faith and his past history of standing up to his own government. He was considered a reasonable person to with whom to negotiate. Ali met people on Baghdad's streets and in schools, and visited important holy shrines. He waited a week before Saddam would meet him, in which time he ran out of his Parkinson's medication, making it difficult to talk.

Back in the United States some questioned his presence in Baghdad: was he there for self-promotion? Did he break sanctions by negotiating with Saddam? According to Ali, Saddam was a 'man of conviction' and accepted the logic that hostage release would be, "good for maintaining peace in the area". Ali managed to negotiate the release of 15 hostages, whom he accompanied back to the United States in December 1990. He said of Iraq that it was, "the Garden of Eden" and should not be bombed. He was unaware that Saddam was releasing hostages anyway because he had now built up sufficient Iraqi forces to fight a war. He was unaware, too that President George Bush was intent on fighting that war regardless of hostage release. In February 1991, US forces invaded Iraq in Operation Desert Storm.

NATION'S HONOURS

"I've always wanted to be more than just a boxer. More than just the three-time Heavyweight Champion. I wanted to use my fame, and this face that everyone knows so well, to help uplift and inspire people around the world."

In the wilderness of the late 1970s and through the later boxing years, few people in the US government or US organisations wanted to have much to do with Muhammad Ali. How things had changed then when Ali, sporting a white tracksuit, slowly jogged carrying a torch. He used it to send a flaming arrow that lit the Olympic flame in Atlanta, Georgia, in the opening ceremony of the summer games in 1996. This was symbolic of his return from the cold, especially as he was given a gold medal. This was to replace the one he supposedly threw away after his Rome victory in 1960. Ali's part in an Olympic ceremony was to be repeated in 2012 at the London Games, but this time he helped to carry the Olympic flag from a wheelchair, aided by his wife Lonnie.

Ali had been officially recognised earlier than 1996 by his nation, for non-sporting reasons. In 1987, he was selected by the California Bicentennial Foundation for the U.S. Constitution as someone who personified the vitality of the Bill of Rights in striving for the equality of each person before God, and the responsibility of government to secure the rights of all. In 2005, Ali was awarded the Presidential Medal of Freedom in 2005, which is the highest civil award in the United States, in recognition of, "his lifetime of achievement and for his principled service to mankind." In 2012, Ali won the Liberty Medal for embracing the ideals of the US constitution. President Bill Clinton said: "Ali embodies the spirit of the Liberty Medal by embracing the ideals of the Constitution – freedom, self-governance, equality and empowerment – and helping to spread them across the globe."

Ali holds the torch before lighting the Olympic flame during the Opening
Ceremony of the 1996 Centennial Olympic Games in Atlanta, Georgia.

INTERNATIONAL WORK

In 1998, at a brief ceremony in New York, UN Secretary General Kofi Annan pinned a dove of peace badge to Ali's lapel and named him a Messenger of Peace. This high honour was recognition of his global pursuit of peace outside the boxing ring.

Ali had spoken against inequalities in South Africa at the UN nearly 20 years earlier at a Special Committee against apartheid. In 1993, he went to South Africa on a benevolent mission and met Nelson Mandela who had been recently released from jail. In 2013, he paid tribute to Mandela, who he said had reached for the impossible in uniting South Africa and "taught us forgiveness on a grand scale".

Ali has widely preached and acted to help those in need. As UN messenger of Peace, he took part in missions to raise awareness of the needs of people in the internationally vilified countries of Afghanistan and North Korea. In Afghanistan, Ali visited a UNICEF-backed girls' school, a rare institution as pupils and teachers were in danger from Taliban forces that banned the education of women. He also gave support to a women's bakery that employed widows of war, and a Kabul boxing club where photographs of his fighting days decorated the walls.

Ali, in his role as UN Messenger of Peace, arrives at Kabul Airport, Afghanistan, for a three-day goodwill mission in 2002.

Ali has helped to distribute food and medical supplies to Cuba during the years of US embargo, to street children in Morocco, and to a refugee orphanage in Ivory Coast. More generally he has worked with the World Food Programme and helped to facilitate more than 200 million meals for the world's hungry. In the United States he has visited and fundraised numerous ventures, from soup kitchens and hospitals to summer camps for disadvantaged children and adoption agencies. Ali may have raised more for US charities than any other single person. Little wonder that for the breadth of his humanitarian work, Ali was granted an Amnesty lifetime achievement award.

Actress Julia Roberts shares a joke with Ali at the Amnesty International Media Spotlight Awards. There, Ali received a lifetime achievement award.

Ali and fellow Parkinson's sufferer Michael J. Fox are seen here in Washington where they asked the Senate for more funds for Parkinson's research.

MUHAMMAD ALI PARKINSON CENTER

Jimmy Walker is a philanthropist who made his money through financial planning and investments in sports teams such as the Phoenix Giants baseball team in the 1980s. As a trustee on the Barrow Neurological Foundation, he came up with the idea of using his contacts in sports and other media to help raise funds for and awareness about a new unit specialising in treatment of Parkinson's disease. The unit was being set up by Dr. Abraham Lieberman. Lieberman has been Ali's physician since his diagnosis with Parkinson's Disease in the mid-1980s, seeing him every other week since then, and is an authority on the disease. Lieberman said: "Jimmy had the idea that if Muhammad had his name in the event, it would be a bigger deal... He's the greatest sports figure of the 20th century and I think the fact that he has Parkinson's disease makes people much more aware."

Lieberman realised that there was a pressing need for a more holistic approach to treating the disease. Rather than having patients diagnosed in one place, treated in another and having disconnected access to strategies for living with Parkinson's, the Center brought together clinical and research expertise on Parkinson's with its treatment, from using surgery such as stimulation of brain movement centres to therapies, including drugs, and teaching tactics for living with the progressive disease.

Ali was a rich man when he was diagnosed with Parkinson's and could afford to see the best medical experts, wherever they were located. He was also prey to suspicious medical advice at times, such as blood filtering to remove pesticides that some experts thought were causing his Parkinson's syndromes. So he endorsed having everything in one place, run by respected experts, and the Center's emphasis on promoting community integration and outreach, through recreational therapy programs and excellence in education about Parkinson's, for people at the thin end of the wedge – patients and caregivers.

CELEBRITY FIGHT NIGHT

In 1994, a celebrity charity fundraising event was organised in Phoenix, again by Jimmy Walker, the philanthropist. Invited wealthy guests and charity workers in tuxedoes and glamorous dresses witnessed a humorous fight in a boxing ring between two stars of local Phoenix Suns basketball team, Charles Barkley and Dan Majerle, wearing outsize boxing gloves. Auctions of objects and experiences, ticket and drinks takings raised $100,000. It was a smash hit and the next year, a long set by singer Kenny Rogers helped the event morph into an evening of entertainment. In 1996, Muhammad Ali was invited as the featured guest.

Ali's involvement upped the stakes for Celebrity Fight Night. His global name in boxing and in other fields proved a real draw for celebrities. Ali used the spotlight in 1996 to tell the world about the Muhammad Ali Parkinson Center. Since then the Center has become the focal charity for the event and has received some $45 million in donations from Celebrity Fight Night. Each year, The Muhammad Ali Celebrity Fight Night Awards, are presented to leaders in the sports, entertainment and business communities who best represent the qualities associated with Ali and his fight to find a cure for Parkinson's disease. Recipients have included Halle Berry, Arnold Schwarzenegger, fellow Parkinson's suffererer Michael J. Fox and boxer Evander Holyfield. Entertainment is kept at a high standard by multi-Grammy winner David Foster, featuring such global stars as Celine Dion, Lionel Richie, Gloria Estefan and Jennifer Lopez.

By 2013, Celebrity Fight Night had become one of the highest grossing charity events in the United States. No wonder, with tickets selling at up to $5,000 and auctions for unique experiences, such as a night with Jennifer Lopez on the red carpet in Hollywood, dinner with Billy Crystal and Robert De Niro in New York, or lunch and golf with golfer Phil Mickelson.

Ali and wife Lonnie attend Muhammad Ali's Celebrity Fight Night in Phoenix, Arizona in 2013.

THE BIOPIC

In 1994, the idea of a biopic about Ali was kicking around Hollywood. The original screenplay by Gregory Allen Howard focused on the troubled relationship between Ali and his father Cassius Sr. Directors including Oliver Stone and Steven Spielberg had contemplated making it. The charismatic young film star Will Smith was identified to play Ali but he refused as the screenplay was controversial and Ali was so universally scrutinised, saying "I didn't want to be the dude that messed up the Muhammad Ali story."

That changed in the late 1990s when a new script emerged by *Forrest Gump* screenwriter, Eric Roth, and director Michael Mann came on board. Smith confessed: "If there's a role I was born to play, this is it," and Ali said at their first meeting: "Man, you're almost pretty enough to play me." Smith immersed himself in the role by watching endless interviews with Ali to perfect the voice and getting fighting fit. He entered a professional training camp with Sugar Ray Leonard's trainer, Darrell Foster, running 3 miles (4.8 km) and boxing for 2 hours each morning, watching fight films and then lifting weights to bulk up. At the end of the camp, Foster said Smith "could fight for real. His hand speed's real good."

Mann filmed scenes as authentically as possible. For example, he recreated the Rumble in the Jungle in a football stadium in Mozambique, with a crowd of 20,000 volunteers and 2,000 paid extras plus, some cardboard cutouts! Sony Pictures was so worried about the budget that they temporarily pulled out until Mann and Smith took partial financial risk in the project. Ali opened in 2001. It had cost $100 million to make but recouped a tenth of this on opening weekend. Ali said at the Louisville premiere: "It's a great movie. Will Smith did a great job."

Actor Will Smith portraying Ali in a fight scene from *Ali*.

Ali jokes with US actor Will Smith, who plays him in the film *Ali* at the film's premiere in Hollywood in 2001, watched by Smith's son.

Ali holds a flame with former Heavyweight Champion Evander Holyfield during the Grand Opening Gala for the Muhammad Ali Center in Louisville in 2005.

MUHAMMAD ALI CENTER

"A visitor of the Muhammad Ali Center experiences the hows of Ali's life: how he found the courage, the dedication, and the discipline to become who he is today; how he found the conviction to stand up for what he believed; and how he turned his passion for excellence in the ring to a passion for peace on the world stage."

The other big charitable cause in Ali's life is his eponymous center in his home city of Louisville, Kentucky. Ali had always retained strong links with the place where he grew up, which had celebrated him in different ways, from naming a street after him in 1978 to naming him the greatest athlete of all time in 2000. Ali co-founded the Center in 2005 with his wife Lonnie. At its heart is an interactive museum about Ali but its mission is to promote respect, hope and understanding, and inspire greatness, in the spirit of Ali's life.

The Center is linked to the Muhammad Ali Institute for Peace and Justice at the University of Louisville. This advances the study and practice of social justice, peace building and violence prevention. It does this through initiatives such as SeeRedNow, an educational media campaign designed to encourage better understanding of root causes of violence, and The Ali Scholars Program for undergraduates to travel internationally to explore, witness and collaborate in peace and social justice work.

Funding for the Center came from the city from an anonymous donor and Ford Motor Company. City leaders invested in the project as part of urban re-development of downtown Louisville. However, the project is not without controversy. Critics have questioned the building of the Center downtown, rather than in the predominantly black, run-down West End part of the city, where Ali grew up and where re-development would have arguably had a greater impact, and the Center's goals would have had greater relevance.

The Muhammad Ali Center, in Louisville, Kentucky.

In 2004, sports company Adidas created this 1,544 square mile (4,000 m2)
advert using a portrait of Ali, which covered the façade of the Berlin Park Inn.

BRAND ALI

Muhammad Ali is an icon. Ali knew his brand had a value from selling signed goods. For years the going rate was $25 and annually he might sign around 15,000 for profit, on tickets, posters, boxing gloves (that would sell for $200), statues and the like. He marketed sports collectibles through a company called Sports Placement Services, but he and his family had limited control of, and therefore limited earning power from, his wider brand, such as use of his face, of his names Cassius Clay and Muhammad Ali, and even phrases such as "Float like a butterfly, sting like a bee".

In 2006 Ali signed a $50 million deal with the Entertainment and licensing firm CKX. This was to form a new company G.O.A.T. LLC, which stands for "Greatest of All Time," in which Ali received 20 per cent and CKX 80 per cent from selling his name and likeness. CKX had many other 'partners with iconic content', including Elvis Presley's name and likeness, found on objects such as velvet paintings and commemorative shot glasses, Graceland, and the American Idol television series. Some of the first Ali-inspired goods were snack foods with names such as 'Rumble' and flavours including 'Thrill-A-Dill-A' and a limited edition luxury book. It was called *GOAT: A Tribute to Muhammad Ali*. Weighing 75 pounds (34 kg) with nearly 800 pages and more than 3,000 images of Ali and his life, it was covered in silk and Louis Vuitton leather and sold for $7,500.

In 2011, the brand giant IMG Licensing bought out G.O.A.T. and acquired the newly formed Muhammad Ali Enterprises and the Ali brand, which represents, "rebelliousness, excellence and inspiration in equal parts". Brand Ali is now in a stable that includes Ferrari, Dole bananas, World Series of Poker, and Goodyear tyres. In 2014, the first line of Adidas Muhammad Ali boxing apparel appeared in stores.

A copy of the book *Greatest Of All Time: A Tribute to Muhammad Ali* published by Taschen.

BIRTHDAY CELEBRATIONS

There were at least five parties to celebrate Muhammad Ali's 70th birthday but one of the biggest and most star-studded, was the "Power of Love Gala" on 18 February 2012, at the Grand Garden Arena, Las Vegas, the site of most of boxing's major fights in the last 20 years. Famous faces, including David Beckham, Anthony Hopkins and Samuel L Jackson, paid ticket prices starting at $1,500. The gala raised awareness about conditions such as Alzheimer's and Parkinson's Disease, and funds for the Cleveland Clinic Lou Ruvo Center for Brain Health and the Muhammad Ali Centre in Louisville. The event also raised funds through an auction, in which the pair of Ali's boxing gloves that he used to defeat Floyd Patterson in 1965, were sold for $1.1 million to Lorenzo Fertitta, a casino owner. A four-night stay at private islands in the Bahamas owned by magician David Copperfield raised $300,000.

During the 5-hour long birthday bash, the former heavyweight boxing champion was honoured by singers, athletes and actors who spoke and performed in tribute to Ali. Stevie Wonder sang Happy Birthday and there were also performances by Cee-Lo Green, Lenny Kravitz, Snoop Dogg, and LL Cool J, who rapped, "Mama Said Knock You Out". Footballer David Beckham paid tribute to Ali saying he was an inspiration and President Obama made an appearance via a heartfelt video message. The event was televised on 25 February and Samuel L Jackson told the audience: "He's done it with guts and grace, with his fists, and with his wits. He's one of the groundbreaking figures of the generation that helped make the world a more open place when it comes to who we can love, where we can go and what we can do."

Lonnie, Ali and recording artist Sean "Diddy" Combs onstage during the Keep Memory Alive foundation's Power of Love Gala celebrating Ali's 70th birthday.

ALI TODAY

By 2014, there had been numerous stories about the possible demise of Muhammad Ali. In 2011, he was taken to hospital after falling unconscious soon after attending the funeral of Joe Frazier, where although frail, Ali had stood to energetically applaud his old adversary. In 2013, there were rumours he could no longer speak and was on the verge of death, but in response, Ali's family posted a picture of him watching the Superbowl on television and striking a defiant pose with boxing fists. A year later, in April 2014, Ali was pictured with boxer Andre Berto at his home in Arizona, where Berto reported that Ali had dished out pearls of wisdom such as "Stay focused on the task" and "Don't worry about the outside noise". As at many other times in his life, the Greatest appeared to be defying expectations and fighting on when he seemed to be down and out.

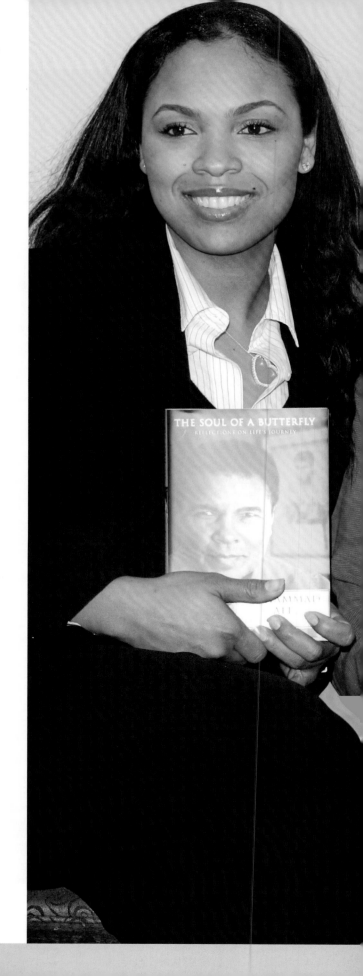

Ali and his daughter, Hana
Yasmeen Ali, promoting his
book, *The Soul of a Butterfly*
in 2004 in New York.

Ali is rarely seen at public events and spends much of his time at home nowadays, enjoying the family times he missed out on when he was boxing. Laila Ali, his daughter, said: "...he lights up when he sees the kids, especially my son who looks exactly like him. He loves that."

One of his latest, rare public appearances was in October 2013, at the inaugural Muhammad Ali Humanitarian Awards in Louisville, proving that he may be frail but his commitment to social justice has not diminished. While Parkinson's disease has taken a severe toll on Ali, his wife Lonnie said: "Every day he gets up with a smile in his face and looks forward to whatever the day brings. He doesn't let things stop him and he does as much as he can every day and he still finds meaning in life."

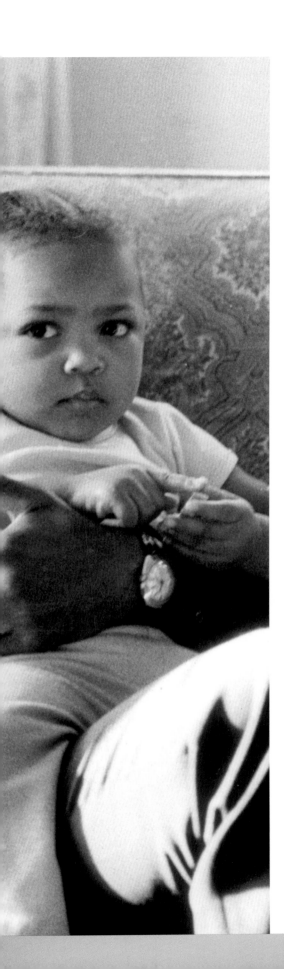

PERSONAL LIFE

Ali training for a fight in Munich while spending time with his twin daughters, Jamillah and Rasheda in 1971.

FAMILY LIFE

Being one of the most famous men on the planet and travelling as much as he did away from home must have made it difficult for Ali to maintain a home life. He has been married four times and has nine children: seven daughters and two sons. Two of his daughters, Miya (born 1971) and Khalilah (born 1974), were from affairs he had while married to his second wife, Belinda.

When Ali met 23-year-old Sonji Roi, she was working as a cocktail waitress. She was very beautiful and Ali was so taken with her that he proposed the night they met. They married in August 1964, first under Islamic law and then with a Justice of the Peace to make it legal under US law, but by June 1965 Ali filed for divorce. One reason stated was that Sonji refused to follow the religion of Islam as she had promised to, for example never wearing a headdress or veil. When the divorce was finalised on 10 January 1966, Ali sent her a note saying: "You traded Heaven for Hell, baby."

Ali met Belinda Boyd because her mother worked as a sort of companion for Elijah Muhammad's wife. They had a quiet private marriage ceremony in Chicago, after which Belinda changed her name to Khalilah Ali, although old friends and family continued to call her Belinda. She stayed in the background as she believed a Muslim wife should do and she and Ali had four children: Maryum (born 1968), twins Rasheeda and Jamillah (born 1970), and Muhammad Junior (1972). She recalled some of their happiest times were when the government stripped Ali of his title, and they travelled together to his lectures at colleges around the country and she managed their depleted finances.

Ali holds up his 4-month-old son Muhammad Ali, Jr., in 1972, outside his Deer Lake, PA, training camp.

BELINDA AND ALI BREAK UP

Ali and Belinda were married for almost ten years before their marriage broke up because of Ali's affair with Veronica Porsche. Veronica was one of four poster girls who helped to promote the 1974 Rumble in the Jungle fight. At first, Belinda turned a blind eye to the affair, believing Veronica was just, "one of the bunch", even allowing Veronica to join them on family trips, billed as the babysitter.

However, when Veronica accompanied Ali to Manila and met Ferdinand and Imelda Marcos before the big fight, she was introduced as his wife and Ali did not correct the error. Once the story broke, Ali tried to justify his need to have a girlfriend at a press conference and it became big news. Belinda flew straight to Manila and Ali's heated fight with her at his hotel became almost as big a story as the upcoming boxing match! Belinda finally admitted defeat and filed for divorce in 1976. She got a generous divorce settlement and Ali put $1 million in a trust fund for their four children.

Ali with his second wife, Belinda, and three of their four children at Deer Lake, Pennsylvania, in August 1973.

When Ali and Veronica got married on 19 June 1977 their first daughter, Hana (born 1976), was about ten months old and Veronica was pregnant with their second daughter, Laila Ali (born 1977). Veronica and Ali lived in luxury in a huge mansion in LA but the strain soon started to show on their relationship. Ali missed his busy life as a boxer and Veronica felt confined because while she wanted to continue her career, Ali wanted her to stay at home. By now Ali was also feeling tired all the time and his speech was slurred. On a visit home to Louisville in 1982 he met his fourth wife-to-be, Yolanda Williams, and by 1985, he and Veronica had filed for divorce.

Ali poses with his third wife Veronica outside his home at Freemont Place, Los Angeles in March 1982.

Ali with Lonnie Williams in Michigan, in July 1999.

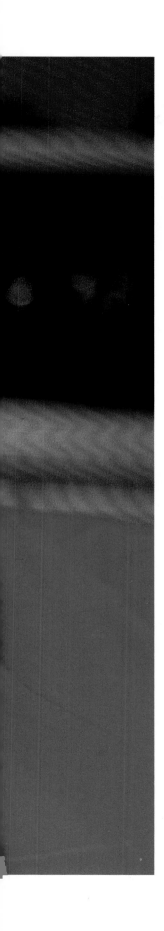

YOLANDA WILLIAMS

Ali married his fourth wife, Yolanda Williams, known as Lonnie, in 1986 but they first met back in 1962, when her family moved into a house opposite his, when she was five and he was 20. Her mother recalls Yolanda, like all the local kids, being in awe of him and Ali looking after her like an older brother. She recalled Ali playing driving around town before his fight with Sonny Liston in a bus with "Cassius Clay" written on the sides, with as many kids as would fit on it, him shouting: "Who's the Greatest!" and the kids calling back: "You are!"

When Lonnie and Ali met for lunch in 1982 she was studying for an MBA at Louisville University but was upset by the noticeable decline in his health, and, with Veronica's permission, moved to a house near his in LA to help to care for him and continue her studies there. She converted to Islam and when he divorced Veronica in 1986, she and Ali were married at a quiet ceremony in Louisville. His mother-in-law said this was an example of Ali not forgetting his roots: "A lot of people, when they get famous, they forget old friends, or at least they expect you to come to them. But not Muhammad." Ali and Lonnie are still together and have one son, Asaad Amin, whom they adopted when he was five months old.

Many people who know Ali and Lonnie say she is very good for Ali and that his physical and financial state stabilised after they got married. However, there is still some controversy. In 2014, Ali's eldest son, Muhammad Jr., accused Lonnie of making it difficult for him to see his father while he and his family live on the breadline in Chicago. A similar accusation was also made by Ali's brother, Rahman.

BOXER FOCUS: LAILA ALI

Laila Amaria Ali was born on 30 December 1977 in Miami Beach, Florida. She grew up in California with her parents Muhammad Ali and Veronica Porsche-Ali, and her older sister, Hana. During troubled teenage years, she spent time in a juvenile detention centre but afterwards, earned a degree in business management and owned a nail salon. She was inspired to become a boxer after seeing a televised fight between female boxers Christy Martin and Deirdre Gogarty in 1996.

Laila had first her professional fight on 8 October 1999, knocking out opponent April Fowler 31 seconds into round one. Over her career, she fought many leading names in women's boxing, including Jacqui Frazier-Lyde, daughter of boxer Joe Frazier, who she defeated in 2001 after a fight that was widely promoted as "Ali vs. Frazier IV". In 2002, she won the IBA title with a two-round knockout of Suzette Taylor and in November the same year, she retained that title and added the WIBA and IWBF belts, after an eight-round knockout win over world champion Valerie Mahfood. Laila retired from boxing in 2007 as undefeated Super Middleweight Boxing Champion of the World. Her ring nickname was "She Bee Stingin", a nod to her father's famous phrase, "Float like a butterfly, sting like a bee."

After retiring from boxing, Laila Ali has become a television host and personality, featuring in shows such *Dancing with the Stars* (2007), *American Gladiators* (2008) and *Stars Earn Stripes* (2012), *All in with Laila Ali* (2013) as well as exercise videos. She wrote a book, *Reach!* in 2002, and launched a range of beauty products. She is married to former NFL star Curtis Conway and they have two children, son Curtis Jr and daughter Sydney.

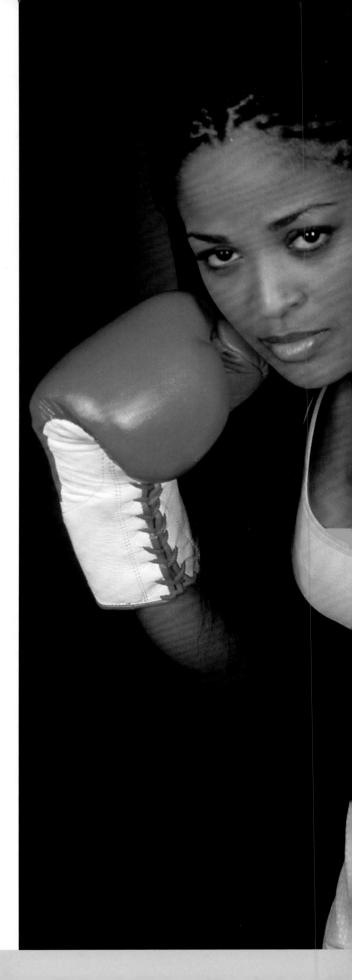

Laila Ali poses for a portrait in August 2001 in New York.

Laila Ali with her father, Muhammad Ali, after a WBC/WIBA Super Middleweight title bout in Washington, DC.

STATISTICS

BORN	Miami (FL), 30 December 1977
TURNED PROFESSIONAL	1999
NUMBER OF PRO BOUTS	24
WINS-LOSSES-DRAWS	24-0-0
NUMBER OF KNOCKOUTS	21
RETIRED	2007

Ali prays at the Alabaster Mosque in Cairo, Egypt in October 1986.

RELIGIOUS LIFE

A belief in one God, who created everything in the universe, has been the driving force in Muhammad Ali's long life, although his religious views have developed over time. After he began to study the Quran in the mid-1970s, he converted from his mother's Baptist religion to become a follower of Islam. He joined the Nation of Islam, an organisation that combined elements of traditional Islam with black nationalist ideas, and followed the teachings of Elijah Muhammad, who proclaimed all white people were 'devils' who hated black people and that it was time for black people to unite and assert themselves. Ali was vilified by the press and the white establishment for his change of religion and the change of name that came with it.

In 1972, Ali began to turn from the Nation of Islam to a mainstream Sunni Islam faith. In this year, he also made his first hajj, or pilgrimage, to Mecca, wearing the correct orthodox ihram attire. He began to pray five times a day and to fast during Ramadan. Ali himself expressed a broader tolerance and acceptance that other religions contain truth too: "Rivers, ponds, lakes and streams – they all have different names, but they all contain water. Just as religions do – they all contain truths." He also said that no matter what religion you believe in, if you live a good life you'll receive God's blessing and go to heaven.

In 1975, Elijah Muhammad died and when his son Wallace D Mohammed became leader of the Nation of Islam, he, like Malcolm X before him, also converted to orthodox Islam and most Nation of Islam members followed him. The Nation of Islam was eventually known as the American Society of Muslims and welcomed people of all races, too.

In 2005, according to Ali's daughter, Hana, Ali embraced spiritual practices of Sufism, a mystical branch or sect of Islam, after reading Sufi teachings in a collection of books by a man named Hazrat Inayat Khan. Sufism is a belief and practice in which Muslims seek to find the truth of divine love and knowledge through direct personal experience of God.

In his later years, Ali has seen himself primarily as a holy man. He published a memoir entitled *The Soul of a Butterfly: Reflections on Life's Journey*, which he wrote over the course of two years with his daughter Hana. It is an unconventional autobiography that combines reminiscences with stories, poems, and spiritual lessons, and in which he discusses the meaning of religion. He is also the co-author of *Healing: A Journal of Tolerance and Understanding* and *The Greatest: My Own Story*.

His religious beliefs gave him the values that shaped and sustained him and continued to guide him throughout his life. In his later years, it has become much harder for Ali to follow strictly the daily pattern of the call to prayer, but he still prays or reads when he can, saying that although his physical abilities were taken from him, he was given something greater: a chance to focus completely on his journey to forgiveness and peace.

Ali sums up his belief in spirituality best in his own words: "The only true satisfaction comes from honouring and worshipping God. Being a true Muslim is the most important thing in the world to me. It means more to me than being black or being American. I can't save other people's souls: only God can do that. But I can try to save my own."

MUHAMMAD ALI

Ali watches a
basketball game
between the Phoenix
Suns and Miami Heat
at US Airways Center,
Phoenix, in 2010.

THE ALI LEGACY

Float Like A BUTTER FLY Sting Like A BEE

Ali and fellow boxing legend Lennox Lewis pose with television presenter Harry
Carpenter at the BBC Sports Personality of the Year Awards in London in 1999.

INSPIRING ATHLETES

Muhammad Ali was an outstanding athlete, who inspired generations of sportsmen and women around the world to follow their dreams. Of course, many of the athletes inspired by his determination and success, are from the world of boxing, such as Lennox Lewis, who said: "Muhammad Ali inspired me – from when I was a young boy growing up – he motivated me to chase my dreams inside and out of the ring."

Ali is also an inspiration for athletes from other sports disciplines and to both men and women. Footballer David Beckham has said of Ali: "Muhammad Ali has shown us one man can make a difference. His example of love, character, dignity, makes us want to be better." US tennis star Serena Williams said that she was inspired by Ali's fighting spirit not to give up after she struggled to get back on form after recovering from a blood clot on her lungs in 2011.

In December 1999, as the 20th century drew to a close, Ali was awarded no fewer than three Sportsman of the Century awards. He won the Sports Illustrated Athlete of the Century Award, the World Sports Award's World Sportsman of the Century and the BBC Sports personality of the century, in which he had garnered more votes than all of the other four candidates put together. Other legendary sportspeople were shortlisted for all awards, including Brazilian football star Pele and US tennis player Pete Sampras, whose sporting successes had no doubt equalled Ali's. Once again it was Ali's compelling skill, style, personality and his campaigning for causes he believed in, which made him stand out above the others. Ali collected the Sports Illustrated award at New York's Madison Square Garden, in front of many of the world's greatest athletes who gave him a standing ovation.

US tennis star Serena Williams is just one of many athletes who have been inspired by Ali's sporting skills and determination in some way.

INSPIRING ACTION

Muhammad Ali is more than an inspiring athlete. He is also a role model who encouraged people to stand up for what they believe in and to use their positions of privilege for positive action. After Australian Aboriginal sprinter Nova Peris-Kneebone presented Ali with the Olympic torch at Sydney in 2000, she explained that meeting him was important to her because, like Ali standing up for civil rights in the US, she used her celebrity to promote Aboriginal health and other issues in Australia. Standing with Ali at a press event, she said: "If you believe in something strong enough and you go out and stand for it, people start to take notice," at which point Ali said: "She's telling the truth."

Jack Newfield in *The Nation* magazine said Ali believed that if he fought he could persuade others to do so, too: "Ali believed that if he could beat Liston or Foreman or Frazier, that would inspire a junkie to get off drugs, a child to survive a terminal illness, a welfare recipient to get a job, a drunk to go to rehab. He believed his life could change other lives…"

Ali has also inspired leaders of nations. In 2005, President George Bush awarded Ali the United States' highest civilian honour, the Presidential Medal of Freedom. One year earlier and four years before being elected the first ever black US president, Barack Obama wrote about how Ali inspired him in an essay for a special edition of *USA Today:* "This is the Muhammad Ali who inspires us today – the man who believes real success comes when we rise after we fall; who has shown us that through undying faith and steadfast love, each of us can make this world a better place. He is, and always will be, the champ." Ali's picture is a reminder of this inspiration hanging in pride of place on the White House wall.

Ali never stops playing to the crowds! Here he is making a humorous gesture to George W. Bush after receiving the Presidential Medal of Freedom in 2005.

Picture Credits

4–5 Phil Greitzer/NY Daily News Archive via Getty Images; 6–7 Keystone-France/Gamma-Keystone via Getty Images; 8–9 Express/Archive Photos/Getty Images; 10 Charles 'Teenie' Harris/Carnegie Museum of Art/Getty Images; 11 AFP/Getty Images; 12–13 Jack Delano/Getty Images; 14 Buyenlarge/Getty Images; 15 New York Times Co./Getty Images; 16–17 Popperfoto/Getty Images; 18–19 FPG/Getty Images; 20 AFP/Getty Images; 20–21 Keystone-France/Gamma-Keystone via Getty Images; 22–23 The Ring Magazine/Getty Images; 24 NY Daily News Archive via Getty Images; 25 Frank Hurley/NY Daily News Archive via Getty Images; 26–27 Central Press/Getty Images; 28–29 Focus on Sport/Getty Images; 30 Tony Triolo/Sports Illustrated/Getty Images; 32–33 James Drake/Time & Life Pictures/Getty Images; 33 James Drake/Time & Life Pictures/Getty Images; 35 James Drake/Time & Life Pictures/Getty Images; 36 Ray Fisher/Time Life Pictures/Getty Images; 37 Focus on Sport/Getty Images; 38–39 Ron Case/Keystone/Getty Images; 39 Keystone/Getty Images; 40 Lee Balterman/Sports Illustrated/Getty Images; 42 Tony Triolo/Sports Illustrated/Getty Images; 43 Tony Triolo/Sports Illustrated/Getty Images; 44¬–45 Doug McKenzie/Hulton Archive/Getty Images; 45 John Pratt/Keystone Features/Hulton Archive/Getty Images; 46–47 Keystone-France/Gamma-Keystone via Getty Images; 48–49 OLDPIX/ANSA/UIG/Getty Images; 50–51 The Ring Magazine/Getty Images; 51 George Silk/Time Life Pictures/Getty Images; 52–53 Herb Scharfman/Time Life Pictures/Getty Images; 54 Popperfoto/Getty Images; 55 James Drake /Time & Life Pictures/Getty Images; 56–57 Popperfoto/Getty Images; 58–59 NY Daily News Archive via Getty Images; 60 John Peodincuk/NY Daily News Archive via Getty Images; 61 Gerry Cranham/Sports Illustrated/Getty Images; 62 Universal History Archive/UIG via Getty images; 63 Buyenlarge/Getty Images; 64 John Dominis/Time & Life Pictures/Getty Images; 65 The Ring Magazine/Getty Images; 66–67 Frank Castoral/NY Daily News Archive via Getty Images; 68–69 Central Press/Getty Images; 69 Popperfoto/Getty Images; 70–71 The Sydney Morning Herald/Fairfax Media via Getty Images; 72 Underwood Archives/Getty Images; 73 James Drake/Sports Illustrated/Getty Images; 74–75 David R. Lutman/Getty Images; 76–77 Joe Farrington/NY Daily News Archive via Getty Images; 78 The Ring Magazine/Getty Images; 80–81 Walter Kelleher/NY Daily News Archive via Getty Images; 81 Charles Hoff/NY Daily News Archive via Getty Images; 82 John Dominis/Time & Life Pictures/Getty Images; 83 Bob Gomel/Time Life Pictures/Getty Images; 84–85 Popperfoto/Getty Images; 86 Anwar Hussein/Getty Images; 87 Underwood Archives/Getty Images; 88–89 American Stock/Getty Images; 89 The Ring Magazine/Getty Images; 90–91 AFP/Getty Images; 92 Anthony Casale/NY Daily News Archive via Getty Images; 93 The Ring Magazine/Getty Images; 94 Evening Standard/Getty Images; 94–95 AFP/Getty Images; 96 AFP/Getty Images; 97 AFP/Getty Images; 98–99 Tony Triolo/Sports Illustrated/Getty Images; 100 Rolls Press/Popperfoto/Getty Images; 101 AFP/Getty Images; 102–103 Popperfoto/Getty Images; 103 The Ring Magazine/Getty Images; 104 Dieter LUDWIG/Gamma-Rapho via Getty Images; 105 Neil Leifer/Sports Illustrated/Getty Images; 106 Rolls Press/Popperfoto/Getty Images; 107 Rolls Press/Popperfoto/Getty Images; 108–109 Neil Leifer/Sports Illustrated/Getty Images; 110–111 Focus on Sport/Getty Images; 112 AFP/Getty Images; 112–113 Herb Scharfman/Sports Imagery/Getty Images; 114–115 Takeo Tanuma/Sports Illustrated/Getty Images; 116 Popperfoto/Getty Images; 117 John Iacono/Sports Illustrated/Getty Images; 118–119 The Ring Magazine/Getty Images; 119 The Ring Magazine/Getty Images; 120–121 Focus on Sport/Getty Images; 122–123 The Ring Magazine/Getty Images; 123 Tim Chapman; 124–125 Manny Millan/Sports Illustrated/Getty Images; 126–127 John Iacono/Sports Illustrated/Getty Images; 128–129 Robert Riger/Getty Images; 130–131 Time & Life Pictures/Getty Images; 132–133 Peter Charlesworth/LightRocket via Getty Images; 135 The Ring Magazine/Getty Images; 136–137 MARIA BASTONE/AFP/Getty Images; 139 Michael Cooper/Getty Images; 140–141 Paula Bronstein/UNICEF/Getty Images; 141 Richard Corkery/NY Daily News Archive via Getty Images; 142–143 STEPHEN JAFFE/AFP/Getty Images; 144–145 Mike Moore/Getty Images for Fight Night; 146–147 LUCY NICHOLSON/AFP/Getty Images; 147 Peter Brandt/Getty Images; 148 JEFF HAYNES/AFP/Getty Images; 149 Dennis Macdonald/Photolibrary/Getty Images; 150 FABIAN MATZERATH/AFP/Getty Images; 151 Michael Buckner/Getty Images for Baby2Baby; 152–153 Ethan Miller/Getty Images for Keep Memory Alive; 154–155 Kramer/Getty Images; 156–157 Frank Tewkesbury/Evening Standard/Getty Images; 158 Central Press/Getty Images; 159 Popperfoto/Getty Images; 160–161 Popperfoto/Getty Images; 161 AFP/Getty Images; 162–163 Steve Liss/Time Life Pictures/Getty Images; 164–165 The Ring Magazine/Getty Images; 165 Ed Mulholland/WireImage/Getty Images; 166 MIKE NELSON/AFP/Getty Images; 168–169 John W. McDonough/Sports Illustrated/Getty Images; 170–171 Anwar Hussein/Getty Images; 172 Craig Prentis/Allsport; 173 Mike Hewitt/Getty Images; 174–175 MANDEL NGAN/AFP/Getty Images

Endpapers: front left NY Daily News/Getty Images; front right Popperfoto/Getty Images; back left Popperfoto/Getty Images; back right NY Daily News/Getty Images
Cover: front R.McPhedran/Stringer/Getty Images; back Thinkstock/Getty Images

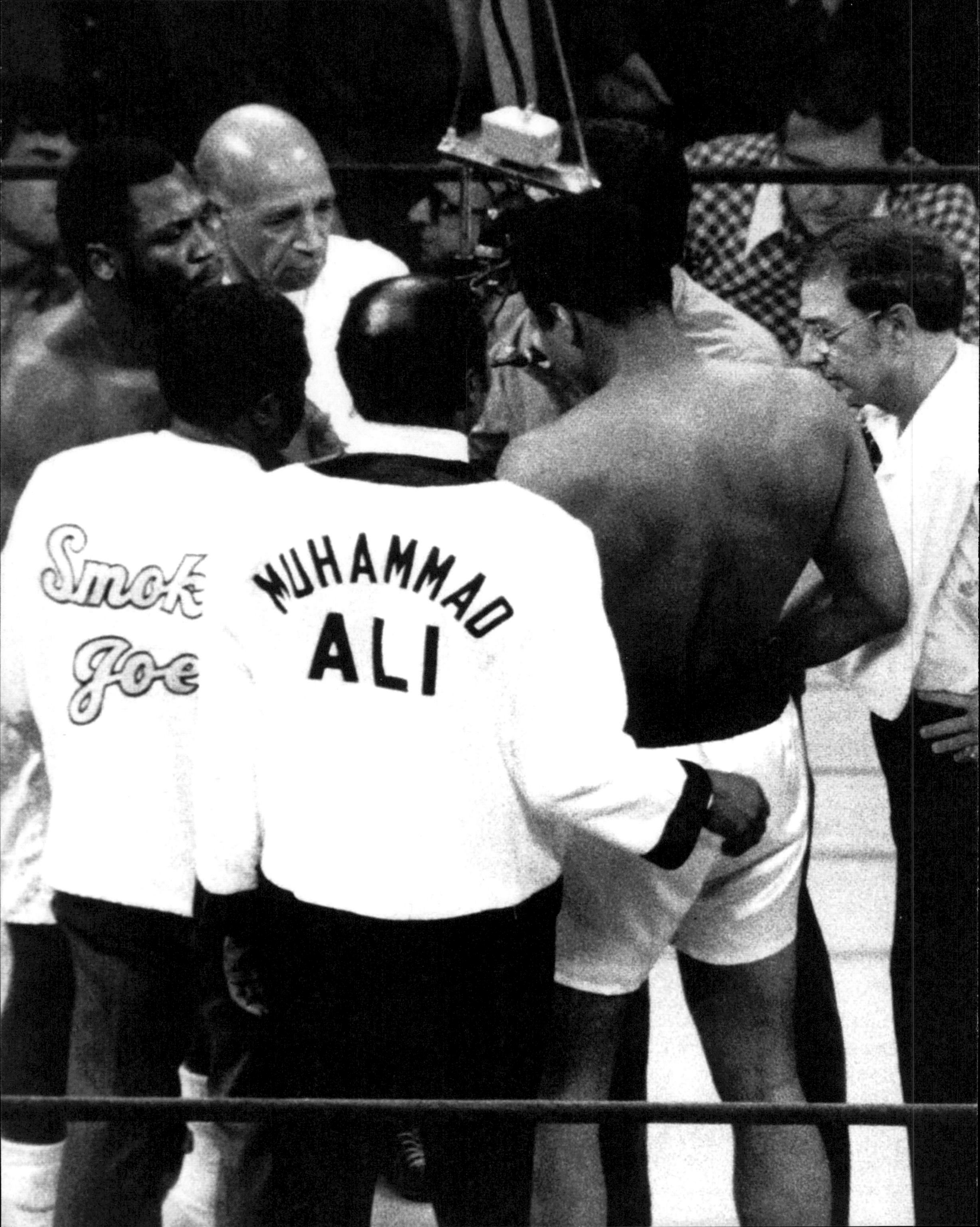
Smok
Joe
MUHAMMAD
ALI